THE SOURCEBOOK

● INTERMEDIATE ● STUDENTS' BOOK

SOAS
University of London
Intermediate
Certificate Course

JOHN SHEPHERD ● ANDY HOPKINS ● JOC POTTER

An alternative English course Longman

Longman Group UK Limited,
Longman House, Burnt Mill, Harlow,
Essex CM20 2JE, England
and Associated Companies throughout the world.

© Longman Group UK Limited 1992

All rights reserved; no part of this publication may be reproduced, stored in a retrieval system, or transmitted in any form or by any means, electronic, mechanical, photocopying, recording, or otherwise, without the prior written permission of the publishers.

First published in 1992
Reprinted 1994

Set in 9½/11 pt. Aster and 10/11 Frutiger

Printed and bound in Spain
by Mateu Cromo, S.A. Pinto (Madrid)

ISBN: 0582 00952 9

Acknowledgements

The authors are indebted to Frances Cox for her part in the overall design of the series, as well as for the specific help she gave in this book.

The authors would like to thank all those who kindly allowed themselves to be interviewed: Mel Calman, Marisol Gower, Thomas Hopkins, Anne Melville, Angela Phillips, Marieanne Spacey, Clare Walsh, and Barbara Weatherill. We also appreciate the help given by the following people, who agreed to participate in informal discussions despite the intrusive presence of a microphone: Jeannette Croft, Penny Faux, Steven Faux, Rita Krishna, Victoria Martin, Martin Parrott, and Tessa Shepherd.

The authors also wish to express their appreciation for the work of the Longman team and Jenny Lee and Giles Davies.

The authors and publishers would like to thank the following for their invaluable comments on the manuscript: Donald Adamson, David Brown, Martyn Ellis, John Flower, Roy Kingsbury, Janet Leifer, and Brenda Townsend.

All dictionary extracts are from the *Longman Active Study Dictionary* (New Edition) or the *Longman Dictionary of Contemporary English*.

We are grateful to the following for permission to reproduce photographs; Ace Photo Agency, pages 24 centre right (photo Paul Steel), 27 above (photo Paul Steel), 54 above left (photo John Glover), 60A (photo Lesley Howling), 82 left, 83 left (photo Lesley Howling), 88 left (photo Gabe Palmer), 94 (photo Pat Shirreff-Thomas), 97 left, 113 (photo Mauritius), 150 left (photo Paul Steel) and 150 right (photo Auschromes); Action Plus Photographic, pages 58 right (photo Mike Hewitt) and 86 right (photo David Davies); Adams Picture Library, page 89; Allsport UK, pages 36 (photo David Cannon), 37B (photo Bob Martin), 37C (photo Pascal Rondeau), 37F, 37G (photo David Cannon), 37J (photo Steve Cauthen), 58 below centre (photo Simon Bruty) and 86 left (photo Christine Calla); Alpha, page 178 left and right (photos R. Pelham); Art Directors Photo Library, page 63 right (photo Randy E. Taylor); Associated Sports Photography, pages 37D, E, I and 58 left; Aviation Picture Library, page 52D; Bubbles Photo Library, pages 24 centre left (photo J. Woodcock) and 46B (photo Ian West); Camera Press, page 24 above right; J. Allan Cash, pages 52C and 117 below left; Collections, page 60D (photo Brian Shuel); Colorsport, pages 37A (photo Jarret), 37H, 58 above centre and 87; Lupe Cunha, page 54 below left; Giles Davies, pages 52B and 77; Greg Evans Photo Library, pages 52E, 60C and 117 below right; Julie Evans/Longman ELT Promotion, page 95 left; Mary Evans Picture Library, page 38; Malvin van Gelderen, pages 55 and 60E; Ronald Grant Archive, page 30 below right; Hutchison Library, page 85 right; Image Bank, pages 27 below (photo Schmid/Langsfeld) and 54 centre (photo Murray Alloser); Camilla Jessel, page 82 right; Kobal Collection, pages 30 above left and above right; Life File, pages 130 (photo Mike Evans) and 143 (photo Keith Curtis); Link, pages 41 (photo Paul Velasco) and 46C (photo Greg English); Magnum Photos, page 51 (photo Ian Berry); Network Photographers, pages 24 below (photo Lewis), 46A and D (photos Katalin Arkell), 48, and 85 left (photo Paul Reas); Pearson Group Pension Plan, page 95 right; Pictures Colour Library, page 84 left; Quadrant Picture Library, page 52A; Rex Features/Today, page 98 centre; Select Photo Agency, page 50 (photo Julio Etchart); Still Pictures, page 90–91 (photo Mark Edwards); Tony Stone Worldwide, pages 24 centre, 26 (photo Peter Lorrez), 30 below left (photo Chris Craymer), 83 right (photo Chris Craymer), 90 left (photo Ernst Hohne), 115 right (photo Thomas Zimmermann), 117 above right (photo Fiona Alison) and 133 (photo Tim Brown); *Sunday Times* London, page 73 (photo Red Saunders); Telegraph Colour Library, pages 54 above right (photo C. Ridley), 54 below right (photo Bavaria Verlag), 97 right and 136 (photo V.C.L.); Thames Television, page 88 right; Topham, page 60B; Universal Pictorial Press, page 98 left; Simon Warner, page 31; Zefa Picture Library (UK), pages 22, 24 above left, 49, 63 left, 76 and 84 right (photo R. Morsch).

The photographs on pages 68A, C, D, E, F, 93 and 117 above left were taken by Peter Lake; pages 68B, 80–81 and 117 centre right were taken by Longman Photographic Unit. All other photographs were taken by Con Putbrace, with art direction by Sandie Huskinson-Rolfe (Photoseekers).

We are grateful to everyone who helped with the location photography, especially Bishops Tearooms, Clement Joscelyne Ltd, Photosound Vantage Ltd and Wiskin Antiques.

We are also grateful to the following for permission to reproduce other copyright material;
Arrow Books/The Diagram Group, *The Complete Book of Exercises*, 1982, pages 58 above and 59; Association of County Councils, *Gypsy Sites 1986*, page 49; David Austin, *The Book of Nasty Legends*, International Thompson Publishing Services, page 74E; Basic Books Inc, a division of Harper Collins Publishers, excerpt from *The Secrets of Sleep*, Alexander Borbely, translated by Deborah Schneider, copyright © 1984 by Deutsche Verlag-Anstalt GmbH, Stuttgart, English translation copyright © 1986, page 56; John Brown Publishing Ltd/House of Viz, *The Viz Book of Crap Jokes*, 1989, page 74F; Collett, Dickenson, Pearce and Partners/Gallaher Tobacco, page 99 right; Dateline International, page 25; Express Newspapers/Paul Crosbie, page 52 below; Futura MacDonald, *The Book of Mistakes*, Giles Brandreth, page 74A and B; Liz Gill/*The Times*, page 33; Grafton Books, *The Dangerfield Diaries*, Anne Melville (cover design by Gwyneth Jones), page 18; Hago Products, page 70 above left; Jennifer Hargreaves/The Sports Council, page 38; Max Factor, page 70 right; Methuen, page 160, *What Else Do You Do?*, Mel Calman, page 72; Nissan UK, page 70 below left; *The Observer*, London, page 40; Reader's Digest Association, page 160; Royal Mail International, page 71; Severn House, *Snapshots*, Anne Melville, 1990, page 34; Simon and Schuster, *How to Live With a Calculating Cat*, E. Gurney, page 74D; Solo Syndication/*Daily Mail*, Amy Tempest, page 74C; Thorsons, *The Kid's Workout Guide for Parents*, John Pearce, 1987, page 44; World Press Network/*New Scientist*, page 55.

Illustrated by: Andrew Aloof, Julie Anderson, Philip Bannister, John Batten, Chris Burke, Tony Coles, Jerry Collins, Hardlines, Ian Kellas, Frances Lloyd, Andrea Norton, David Simonds, Trevor Stanesby, Sue Williams

Cover illustration: Giles Davies

CONTENTS

Introduction 6

STARTING OUT

Getting to know each other 8
Exchanging information – discussion and description

What will you be doing? 9
Getting to know the materials – exploration and discussion

Know yourself 10
Getting to know your learning style – doing a questionnaire, reading and discussion

Talking about words and grammar 12
Getting to know language – analysis, matching and discussion

The right language for the right situation! ... 14
Saying what you mean with the right level of formality – reading, analysis and discussion

Keeping records 15
Recording your work and your feelings – reading and writing

SKILLS

1 WRITING

Books and writers 18
Describing pictures; predicting story content
Reading book covers
Listening to an interview

Choosing something to read 20
Asking questions; making suggestions and recommendations
Reading short book reviews
Listening to a conversation

Descriptions 22
Reading and writing descriptions

2 PRIVATE LIVES

Romance and friendship 24
Describing people and discussing personal qualities
Listening to an interview
Reading personal advertisements

Parents and children 26
Expressing opinions; discussing personal relationships; persuading someone
Listening to a conversation
Reading magazine articles

Family matters 28
Reading and writing a paragraph from a personal letter

3 FEAR

Is fear good for you? 30
Describing pictures; describing feelings
Listening to an interview

Overcoming fears 32
Discussing ways of dealing with fears; giving advice; supporting and calming someone
Reading a newspaper article

Describing fear 34
Reading an extract from a short story
Describing a terrifying situation
Writing a short narrative – adding descriptive detail

4 SPORT

Women and sport 36
Stating information; speculating, describing sports; giving opinions
Listening to an interview
Reading a magazine article
Making notes from an interview

Sport and violence 39
Listening to a discussion
Discussing problems and finding a compromise

Sport and politics 40
Reading a letter to a newspaper
Writing a letter to a newspaper

5 DISCIPLINE

Children and discipline 42
Describing pictures; discussing opinions; persuading someone; making threats
Listening to an interview
Reading an extract from a book
Listening to short dialogues

Discipline in society 46
Describing different types of discipline; giving opinions
Reading an information sheet
Writing a short essay

6 PEOPLE ON THE MOVE

A way of life 48
Describing photographs; talking about advantages and disadvantages; speculating
Developing awareness of text type, audience and purpose in written text
Listening to a song

Living away from home 50
Discussing the problems of refugees; speculating
Reading a magazine article
Listening to an interview and making notes

Journeys 52
Listening to travel announcements
Apologising; making excuses
Reading a short newspaper article
Writing a letter of apology

7 HEALTH

Staying healthy 54
Discussing illness, treatments and experiences with doctors
Listening to two short interviews containing contrasting viewpoints
Reading an extract from a magazine article

Getting enough sleep? 56
Describing and responding to pictures; making suggestions; giving explanations; asking questions; persuading someone
Reading a case study
Listening to a conversation
Reading a chart
Making general statements and comparisons

A healthy body 58
Listening to instructions
Giving instructions; discussing instructions
Reading instructions
Writing instructions

8 BUSINESS

The right job? 60
Describing jobs and job skills; allocating types of people to suitable jobs
Listening to an interview and classifying information
Reading a list of personality types

Applying for a job 62
Reading job advertisements, application forms and job details
Listening to a job interview
Asking and answering questions at a job interview

Dealing with companies 64
Using the telephone – being polite, getting through, making an appointment
Writing a letter of complaint

9 POWER

Power in conversation 66
Listening to a group discussion
Discussing power in conversation; interrupting politely; attracting attention; asking for repetition, clarification, exemplification, more information
Listening to a short story

The power of the way you look 68
Describing and interpreting pictures
Listening to a group discussion
Reading a newspaper article

The power of advertisements 70
Describing and interpreting advertisements
Reading about advertising techniques
Writing text for an advertisement

10 HUMOUR

The cartoonist 72
Describing and interpreting cartoons
Reading an introduction to a biography
Listening to an interview

Jokes 74
Describing, interpreting and telling jokes; discussing humour
Listening to jokes and anecdotes

Telling stories 76
Reading an amusing story
Writing a story based on a cartoon sequence

VOCABULARY

WORD GROUPS
Writing	80
Private lives	82
Fear	84
Sport	86
Discipline	88
People on the move	90
Health	92
Business	94
Power	96
Humour	98

KEY WORDS

- see look at watch hear listen to 100
- become (an architect) go (deaf)
  get (cold) turn (brown) 101
- have take give 102
- make let force allow 103
- rob steal burgle swindle thief
  pickpocket burglar crook theft
  burglary fraud 104
- expect look forward to hope (for)
  wait (for) 105
- on off in out 106
- up down away back 107
- travel flight drive tour journey
  voyage expedition 108
- road street track path way route . 109
- pay income salary wages fee 110
- work job career vocation profession 111
- customer client patient guest
  tenant 112
- talk speech lecture meeting
  conference 113
- cloth clothes material garment dress
  clothing 114
- next previous last the last latest 115
- very fairly quite really extremely
  terribly awfully pretty reasonably
  absolutely totally completely 116

The dictionary – extending its use 118

GRAMMAR

NOUNS
Review 122

Articles 1: *the* Ø 123
Articles 2: *a* *some* *any* 124
Quantities 1: *a few* *a little* *not many*
  not much 125
Quantities 2: *all* *most* *some* *no* *none*
  both *neither* *(of the)* 126
Quantities 3: countables and uncountables 128
Quantities 4: *a box of* *a jar of* *a tube of*
  a tin of *a packet of* *a bunch of* *a pair of*
  a couple of 129
Comparative adjectives: *easier (than)*
  the easiest *more useful (than)*
  the most useful 130
Joining nouns: *'s* *of* Ø 131
Modifying the noun: *a woman (who) I like*
  a man in a suit 132
Reference: a summary of grammatical forms ... 134

VERBS
Review 135

Tenses 1: present simple present progressive 136
Tenses 2: dynamic and stative verbs:
  see/look *hear/sound* *feel* *smell* *taste* 137
Tenses 3: past simple past progressive
  and *used to* 138
Tenses 4: present perfect past perfect 140
Tenses 5: future time 141
Modals 1: probability: *will* *should*
  could/may/might (well) *won't* 142
Modals 2: ability: *could* *managed to*
  can *be able to* 144
Modals 3: deduction: *must be* *can't have* ... 146
The passive 147
Multi-part verbs 148
Reporting statements/questions/
  instructions 150
Modifying the verb 1: adverbs of manner 152
Modifying the verb 2: comparative adverbs .. 153
Verbs followed by: *to* + infinitive/noun *to* +
  infinitive/clause (*that*) 154

Reference: a summary of grammatical forms ... 156

PREPOSITIONS
Review 158

Prepositions of place 1: *away from* *towards*
  over *under* 159
Prepositions of place 2: *not far (from)*
  (quite) a long way (from) *beside* *behind*
  beyond *along* *past* 160
Other prepositions: *by* *for* 162
Fixed expressions 163

Reference: a summary of grammatical forms ... 166

SENTENCES
Review 167

Conditionals: *if I were...* *if I had been...*
  unless *even if* *no matter*
  whether... or not 168
Linkers: *if* *because* *although* *so that* 170
Questions and answers 1: tag questions 171
Questions and answers 2: short answers 172
Infinitives and gerunds: *it...to run* *-ing* 173

Reference: a summary of grammatical forms ... 174

PARAGRAPHS
Introduction 175

Linking ideas with phrases 176
Linking ideas by reference 178
Linking ideas with general words 180

Self-check key 182

Tapescripts 187

INTRODUCTION

These notes about *The Sourcebook* are for students and teachers.

The Principles of *The Sourcebook*

Teachers and learners all have different needs, and like to work in different ways. Teachers need to be able to adapt a book to the students and the course; students need a book for self-access and reference as well as for use in class.

Most course books dictate not only the content of a course, but also the methodology and sequence of learning. *The Sourcebook* is different. It has been designed to supply flexible classroom materials and self-access work for both teachers and students.

The Sourcebook allows you to learn and teach English in your own way.

How this book is organised

STARTING OUT
This is an introductory unit which helps learners to get to know each other and the book, and to talk about language and using language well.

SKILLS
This part has 10 units, which offer integrated listening, speaking, reading and writing activities; the emphasis is on English in use. The **Skills** part is designed to be used in class, and can be used in the order presented in the book.

VOCABULARY
Word groups Each unit is thematically linked to the corresponding unit in the **Skills** part. The groups of words and phrases can also be used as a reference source for the student to consult.

Key words This section presents words and phrases that cause special problems for students at this level. The units can be used in the order which suits the course, either in class or for self-study.

GRAMMAR
Teachers and students can use this part when and how it suits the course, and for revision and self-study. The five sections present and practise the main items needed at intermediate level under these headings:

Nouns   Verbs   Prepositions
Sentences   Paragraphs

How to use *The Sourcebook*

A FIRST ROUTE

The easiest and most obvious route is as follows:

- Begin with **Starting Out**.
- Work through the **Skills** units. You can work through this part in order. The units are cross-referenced to **Vocabulary** and **Grammar**.
- Turn to the **Vocabulary** part as appropriate. You can use each section before or after the corresponding **Skills** unit, or you can use the sections alone.
- Turn to the **Grammar** part as appropriate. Here you have considerable freedom. You can study items as your students need them or as the syllabus requires. For further free practice of an item turn to the Communicative activities listed under the items in the Teacher's Book.

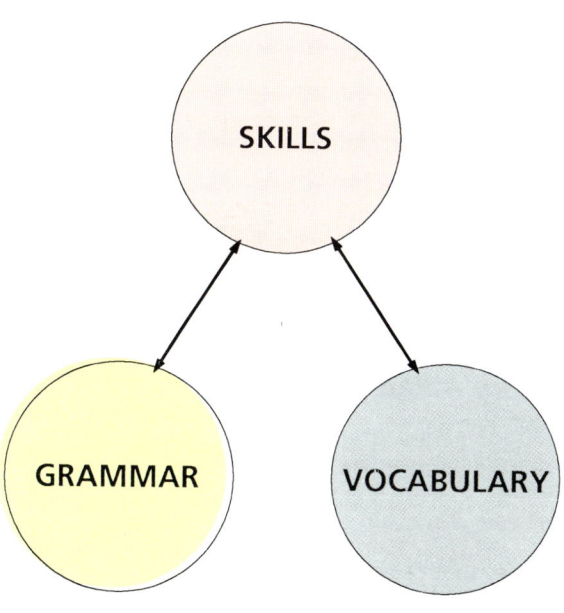

ALTERNATIVE ROUTES

Once you are familiar with the materials, you can organise them in the way that suits you and your students best. As well as following a skills-driven syllabus, you can also construct vocabulary-driven or grammar-driven programmes.

CLASS WORK AND SELF-ACCESS

- The **Skills** part is more appropriate for use in class. It is organised progressively, and can be worked through in order.
- The **Word groups** (in the **Vocabulary** part) can be used in class or for self-access; teachers may wish to link each unit to the corresponding **Skills** unit.
- **Grammar** and **Key words** (**Vocabulary**) can be used in class or for self-access. The units should be used in the order that suits the class, since they are not progressive, and are not in teaching order.

An answer key is provided for all closed exercises in the three parts of the book, so that students working on their own can check their work and monitor their progress.

Activities for discussion and interaction are included in all three parts. These can be used in class, or for consideration by students working on their own.

CROSS-REFERENCING

The 'See also' boxes on the Students' Book pages link the units to other parts of the Students' Book, to the Workbook, and to the Teacher's Book. The Teacher's Book contains detailed notes and additional ideas for every unit.

OTHER COMPONENTS

- **Two cassette tapes** accompany the listening tasks.
- **The Workbook** provides revision and consolidation exercises for individual use in class or for self-access.
- **The Teacher's Book** provides general and detailed notes to help course planning, and also provides extra extension activities.

STARTING OUT

Getting to know each other

If you don't know each other . . .

1 Turn to a partner, and ask questions to find out:
- your partner's name
- where they come from
- where they live
- what they do.

2 Think for one minute about why you are in this group, and make notes.

In turn, give your reasons to the group.

Make notes of other people's reasons, and together discuss whether your reasons are similar or different.

Example:
I'm here because I have to read business letters written in English.

If you know each other . . .

Working in pairs, practise describing familiar items:

3 Student A: Close your eyes, and describe the room you are in. Use as many adjectives as you can.
Example: *There are three large windows and two comfortable chairs.*

Student B: Make notes of what student A says.

Together, see if what student A said was right, and what else could have been included.

4 Student A: Describe what *you* are wearing today. Can you remember? Close your eyes, give details, and use as many adjectives as you can.
Example: *I'm wearing a pair of new, brown leather shoes with low heels.*

Student B: Make notes of what student A says.

Together, see if what student A said was right, and what else could have been included.

5 Student A: Tell your partner everything you did yesterday evening. How much detail can you remember?

Student B: Make notes of what student A says.

Tell a story about yourself!

6 Think of something interesting or amusing that has happened to you or someone you know in the last month or so. Working in pairs, tell your partner about it, in no more than two minutes.

When you have both spoken, change partners and tell your new partner the story you have just heard from your first partner.

What will you be doing?

1 Find these items in *The Sourcebook* (or the Workbook), and match them with the activities A–E listed below:

1 Skills, Children and discipline, exercise 6
2 Grammar, Nouns, Quantities 2
3 Vocabulary, Word groups, Power
4 Vocabulary, Key words, cloth, clothes, etc.
5 Workbook, The passive

A study a grammar point
B study how a group of nouns are related in meaning
C do additional exercises on a grammar point
D use the vocabulary related to a topic
E read and make notes

2 You are ready to use the book and you want to work on the Skills unit called 'Fear':

1 On which page does the unit begin?
2 On which pages can you find vocabulary work related to the topic?
3 Which Workbook exercises build on this vocabulary?
4 Which Grammar pages are referred to?

3 You want to find out about the passive. Match the following questions with the answers below:

1 Where will you find a grammatical explanation?
2 Where will you find a summary of information about the passive?
3 Where will you find some examples?
4 Where will you find a simple checking exercise?

A in LOOK, page 147
B in CHECK, page 147
C in the GRAMMAR box, page 147
D in REFERENCE, page 156

4 In pairs, discuss what you think you are going to do on this course. Think about the activities listed in the table on the right, and decide how much time (as a percentage of all the time you spend learning English) you need to spend on each one, with your group and alone:

Activity	Percentage of time	
	in group	alone
Listening to tapes		
Reading		
Studying grammar		
Talking to partners		
Doing vocabulary exercises		
Writing		
	100%	100%

5 What other activities can you do on your own? Discuss the ones listed below. Can you do them? Do you want to?

Listen to the radio in English
Watch English language films
Try to meet people who speak English
Record your work in a notebook
Read magazines and journals
Write down lists of new words and phrases

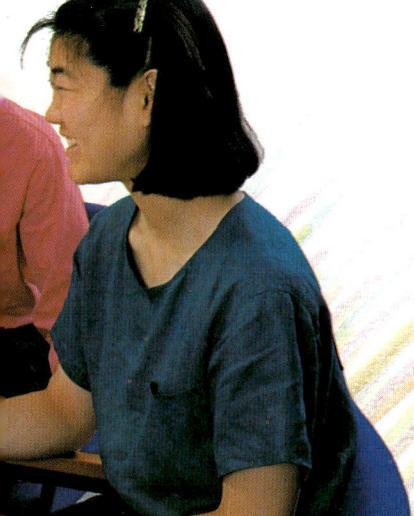

Know yourself

What kind of learner are you?

There is no such thing as an 'ideal learner'. Different people learn in different ways.

1 Here are two sets of statements about the English language and how you can learn it. To each statement you may say:

1 No, for me it's not true.
2 Well, it's partly true.
3 Yes, I think this is absolutely true.

Make a note of the number, 1, 2 or 3, which best describes your opinion:

SET 1

		No	↔	Yes
1	You need to learn grammatical terms.	1	2	3
2	When you read, you should look everything up in a dictionary.	1	2	3
3	Writing from dictation is a very good exercise.	1	2	3
4	A good teacher is essential.	1	2	3
5	You need to learn lists of irregular verbs, etc.	1	2	3
6	When you make mistakes you want them corrected at once.	1	2	3
7	It's important to keep a well-ordered notebook when you study anything.	1	2	3
8	Grammar exercises are a major part of learning English.	1	2	3

Now add up the numbers you have noted down.

SET 2

		No	↔	Yes
1	You should take every opportunity to speak English.	1	2	3
2	Languages have grammar rules, but native speakers don't know them, so you don't need to learn them.	1	2	3
3	A very good way to learn English is by listening to the radio and cassettes.	1	2	3
4	The best way to learn English is to pretend to be an English speaker, and then act out a situation.	1	2	3
5	When you read, you can guess what you don't know.	1	2	3
6	It doesn't matter if you make mistakes; the important thing is to use the language.	1	2	3
7	Whenever you meet an English-speaking person, you should always try to speak to them in English.	1	2	3
8	The teacher can help, but learning English is *your* problem.	1	2	3

Now add up the numbers you have noted down.

2 On the right are three possible scores:

	SET 1	SET 2	*Difference*
STUDENT A	20	12	8 (Set 1 is high)
STUDENT B	12	20	8 (Set 2 is high)
STUDENT C	16	16	0 (The sets are equal)

Work out your score and decide which of the three students you are most similar to, and read the descriptions below:

Student A (or near A)
You seem to be a cautious learner. You don't like taking risks; you want everything to be planned in advance and predictable. If you persist, you will learn well, but you need to relax more, and not rely too much on the teacher to do everything for you. Good learners take chances, because learning can be quite unpredictable!

Student B (or near B)
It sounds as if you are a risk taker, so you may improve your speaking skills quite quickly. But remember that any language is a complicated network, and that it takes a lot of hard work to sort it all out if you are to have a good knowledge of the language.

Student C (or near C)
You look like a 'middle-of-the-road' person. You like to be orderly and systematic, but you are willing to take chances. It sounds like a good combination.

3 Discuss the descriptions with a partner. Do you agree with the description that applies to you? *Remember!* There is no such thing as a single type of good language learner. The important thing is to understand what kind of learner you are, develop your strengths and overcome your weaknesses.

4 Read this description of language learning:

> These four characteristics of good learners have been identified.
>
> - **Risk taking** This is a highly visible quality, and is sometimes an indication of a good learner – but the noisy student at the front may not be the best one.
>
> - **Confidence** This is important; every psychologist knows that thinking you can do something is halfway to doing it. But quiet students can be confident too.
>
> - **Persistence** Perhaps this is the most important quality, as learning a language really well takes a long time.
>
> - **Orderliness** Most learning goes better if you are systematic about how you go about it. But learning is not the same as putting papers in a filing cabinet; it's more like little flashes of illumination.
>
> So perhaps that imaginary perfect learner is a confident risk-taker who is orderly and persistent!

With a partner or in groups, discuss these characteristics of good learners, and say if they fit with your ideas about language learning.

Talking about words and grammar

Words 'When *I* use a word,' Humpty Dumpty said in a rather scornful tone, 'it means just what I choose it to mean – neither more nor less.'

1 Here is a word: **chair**
Is it a thing?   Is it a verb?
Is it a person?   Is it a noun?

With a partner or in your group, discuss briefly what you think it is.

This is a chair.   She is the chair.

2 Now look at the three pictures on the right:

She chaired the meeting.

What can you say about the word **chair** in these three pictures?

3 Look at the words below, copy the table into your notebooks, and say what part of speech you think each word is:

Noun	Verb	Adjective	Preposition / adverb

up   away
go   green
picture flower

4 Now read these sentences, and say what part of speech the word in **bold** is:

They've **upped** the price of milk again.
Come on Mark, why don't you have a **go**?
The roses are **flowering** beautifully this year.
I can **picture** the scene; it must have been astonishing.
The **Greens** won 23 seats in the European parliament.
The football team has played three **away** games this season.

5 With a partner, discuss these questions:
- Was the word in **bold** in the above sentences used in the way you were expecting?
- Do you think any word can be used as any part of speech?

6 Look at the words in **bold**, discuss them with a partner, and decide what part of speech each one is in these sentences:

1 He had a good **look**.
2 He gave a great speech and **floored** the opposition.
3 Can you **book** three seats for tonight?
4 We went for a long **run** this morning.

12   STARTING OUT

Grammar

> I am the Roman Emperor, and I am above grammar. *Emperor Sigismund, 1361–1437*

... but if you are *not* a Roman Emperor, you will find these grammatical terms useful when you are using this book. They all appear in the Grammar boxes in the Grammar part of the book (pages 121–81):

1 Here are six ways of describing words used in different ways. Discuss them with a partner and match them to their descriptions A–F:

linker
article
multi-part verb
past perfect
modal verb
adverb

A a word usually used to modify the meaning of a verb
B a verb tense describing an event before another past event
C an auxiliary verb which adds meaning (e.g. permission) to the main verb
D a verb and particle (a preposition or adverb), usually with a special meaning
E a word which joins two or more ideas
F a word which goes before a noun, making it definite or indefinite

2 On the right are six grammatical expressions. Discuss them with a partner and match them to their descriptions A–F:

relative clause   reported speech   comparative / superlative

A used to tell someone what someone else has said
B a clause which tells you more about a noun or noun phrase
C used to say that one thing is more or less than another

passive   tag question   conditional

D a clause added on to the end of a sentence, to ask for confirmation
E used when one part of a sentence is true if the other part is true
F used to make the object of a sentence into the subject

3 Match the **bold** items with the grammatical expressions:

1 She ran **quickly** downstairs.
2 He **says he'll** be there.
3 They **got on** the bus.
4 The city **was founded** in 1436.
5 He went home **because** he was tired.
6 You know him, **don't you**?
7 I chose **the** hotel with **a** swimming pool.
8 I **had read** the book before I saw the film.
9 He's **the oldest** and **the best**.
10 She **might** come, but he certainly **will**.
11 **If you go I'll go**.
12 That's the car **(that)** I like best.

A conditional
B linker
C relative clause
D tag question
E multi-part verb
F reported speech
G modal verb
H comparative / superlative
I passive
J article
K past perfect
L adverb

The right language for the right situation!

1 Here are four pictures of Philippa in different places, having different conversations. Look at the pictures, read the dialogues, and match each dialogue to the right picture:

C In the office

A A pair of new shoes

D Lending money

B Buying a camera

Dialogue 1
PHILIPPA: Could you give me some idea of the prices?
ANOTHER: They range from £28 for the basic economy model up to £650 for the deluxe model.

Dialogue 2
PHILIPPA: Can't you wait for a bit?
ANOTHER: Oh come on! You promised to let me have it by today.
PHILIPPA: Tell you what, I'll give you half now and the rest later.

Dialogue 3
PHILIPPA: I was wondering if you could wait a few days for delivery.
ANOTHER: Well, I was expecting the supplies next Wednesday.
PHILIPPA: We could let you have part of the order by then but could you give us a few extra days for the rest?

Dialogue 4
PHILIPPA: How much were they?
ANOTHER: I think they were about £20 but I'm not sure.

2 Decide whether each dialogue is formal or informal. What is the *function* of each dialogue? Is it:
- persuading someone to wait?
- asking about prices?

Give your answers on a table like the one here.

Dialogue	Formal or informal	Function
1		
2		
3		
4		

3 In groups, talk about the four dialogues and the pictures. Discuss the differences in:
- clothing
- 'body' language
- expressions on the faces
- language

14 STARTING OUT

Keeping records

It is useful to keep a record of what you study. There are many ways in which this can be done. One method is to keep *two* kinds of records: one for your work, and one for your feelings about the course.

Keeping a record of your work

1 A loose-leafed folder is a good place to keep your records. Make up a table of contents showing how you could organise your folder, and what you would put in it. For example, in the Skills section you could put in the letters and paragraphs you write. Discuss your ideas with a partner.

Recording your feelings: keeping a learner diary

What is it?
It's a record of your *feelings* about your learning.
- You can describe the class activities, books, etc., and say what you feel about them. Are you doing what you want to do?
- You can describe how you are progressing, and how you feel about that. Are you doing as well as you would like?

Why do it?
Learning something new requires clear thinking and concentration. You'll do it better if you 'think about your thinking'.

How often?
Once a week is common. Think about what you have done and how you feel about it; then write it down. You can look back at past entries to see if your feelings are changing.

Who sees it?
That's up to you. Some students think a learner diary is private, others use it to express their feelings to the teacher.

What is it like?
Here is a sample:

> Monday was a good day. We practised talking in groups; it was useful. We described our own towns. Then we did a dictation. I thought that was helpful, but sometimes I think the dictations are too long. The teacher didn't spend enough time checking our work.
>
> I studied on Tuesday evening (40 minutes) and Thursday (half an hour). I'm not sure how to study best. I read over my grammar notes and try to think of sentences, and then I repeat all the new words in my vocabulary lists. Is that the best way to learn? I will ask the teacher about this next week.

2 Think about what *you* have done in the last week in your English classes and write an entry for a learner diary.

STARTING OUT 15

SKILLS

The **Skills** part is designed so that it can be worked through in order, although teachers may adjust this to suit students' needs. The units are cross-referenced to relevant units in the **Grammar** and **Vocabulary** parts.

	page		page
1 WRITING		**6 PEOPLE ON THE MOVE**	
Books and writers	18	A way of life	48
Choosing something to read	20	Living away from home	50
Descriptions	22	Journeys	52
2 PRIVATE LIVES		**7 HEALTH**	
Romance and friendship	24	Staying healthy	54
Parents and children	26	Getting enough sleep?	56
Family matters	28	A healthy body	58
3 FEAR		**8 BUSINESS**	
Is fear good for you?	30	The right job?	60
Overcoming fears	32	Applying for a job	62
Describing fear	34	Dealing with companies	64
4 SPORT		**9 POWER**	
Women and sport	36	Power in conversation	66
Sport and violence	39	The power of the way you look	68
Sport and politics	40	The power of advertisements	70
5 DISCIPLINE		**10 HUMOUR**	
Children and discipline	42	The cartoonist	72
Discipline in society	46	Jokes	74
		Telling stories	76

1 WRITING

Books and Writers

Discussion

1 Look at the book cover on the right.

1 Describe the picture.
2 What kind of book do you think it is? Why?
3 What kind of reader do you think the book is written for?

ANNE MELVILLE has won an enthusiastic following with the *Lorimer* series, *The House of Hardie* and *Grace Hardie*. In *The Dangerfield Diaries* she breaks new ground with a powerfully moving story of a distinguished old lady's extraordinary past rising to haunt her.

What is she to do with the diaries which chart her stormy relationship with Gil Blakey, the poor boy from her own village who devoted his life to the exposure of scandals? Written while she was still practising as a doctor, the diaries record other people's secrets as well as her own.

'Girls can't keep secrets.' Gil Blakey said that to Ainslie Dangerfield when she was only five years old. Her life has proved him wrong – but has the time come when to remain silent about the truth is as deceitful as to lie? Should she, or should she not, destroy the Dangerfield Diaries?

Reading

2 Now read extracts from the blurb (short description of the book) on the left, and answer these questions:

1 Were you right about the kind of book it is?
2 Who do you think the people on the cover above are?
3 What kind of secrets might the diaries contain?
4 What might the effect be of publishing the diaries?
5 Do you think the old lady will publish them? Why (not)?
6 Would you read the book? Why (not)?

Listening to an interview

Anne Melville has written romantic novels, historical sagas and children's books under a number of different names. Many of her books have been translated into other languages. You are going to hear her talking about how she writes adult fiction.

3 Before listening

1 When you write a long text like an essay or a story, in English or in your own language, what are the different stages that you go through? Do you just pick up a pen and write until you have finished? Discuss with your partner what you do.
2 In which order do you think Anne Melville might do each of the following?
   A write a first version
   B get a general idea
   C do background research
   D work out the story in detail
   E ask for comments
   F make changes to her work
   G decide on a title

4 First listening

Listen to see whether you were right about the order in which Anne Melville carries out each stage of her own writing process.

5 Second listening

1 She mentions one source of ideas for stories. What is it? Can you think of other possible sources?
2 Which chapter does she write first? Why?
3 How many times does she rewrite a novel? What kind of changes do you think she makes? (For some ideas, look at the changes made to the manuscript below.)

SEE ALSO: Vocabulary (Writing, lists A and D), pages 80–1; Grammar (Modals 1 and 3), pages 142–3 and 146; Tapescripts, page 187; Teacher's Book.

1 WRITING

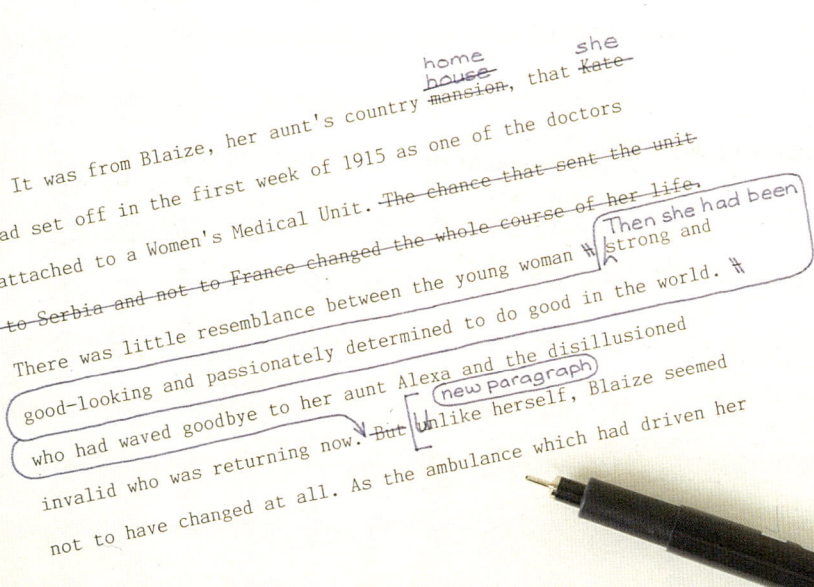

SKILLS 19

1 WRITING

Choosing something to read

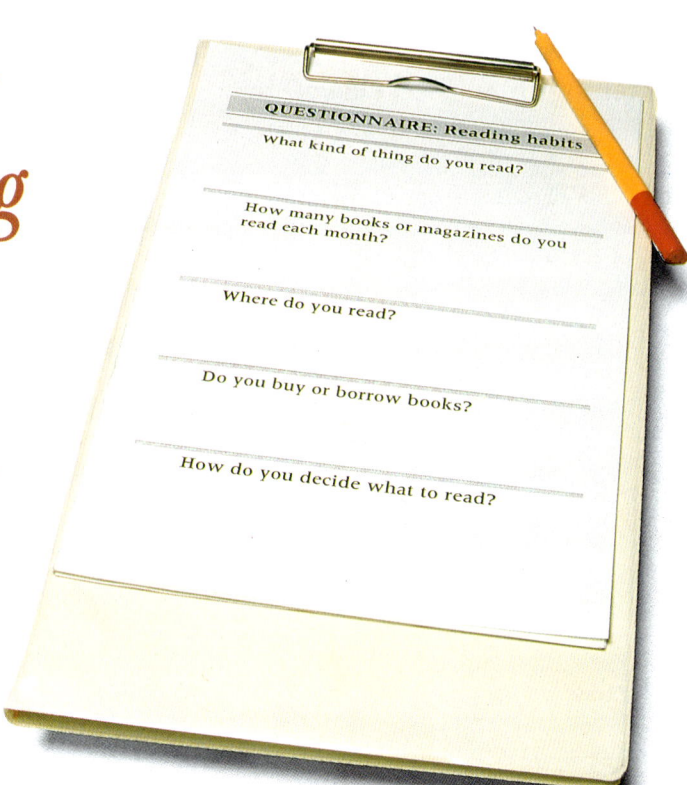

Making notes

1 Ask your partner questions about the books and magazines he or she reads. Make notes on a piece of paper, and then compare the answers with those given by other members of the class.

Reading reviews

2 Look at the extracts from reviews of five new books. Make guesses about the content of each book.

1 What type of book is it?
2 Can you make any predictions about the story and characters?
3 What kind of ending would you expect?
4 Which book would you most want to read?

Listening to a conversation

3 Listen to Victoria talking to friends about how she chooses a book to read.

1 Which of the following does she look for?
   A books on economics
   B good dialogue
   C something new
   D something surprising
   E a familiar subject

2 Why does she choose a particular book?
   A A friend has recommended it.
   B The blurb interests her.
   C She likes the picture on the front cover.
   D She's enjoyed another book by that writer.
   E She's read a good review of the book.

A ... the excitement of the search for lost treasure in the Brazilian jungle is made more vivid by ...

B ... when the hero becomes aware that the house is haunted by the spirit of his dead aunt ...

C ... as good as any Agatha Christie, and with many, many more bodies ...

D ... set on the planet Mars 200 years from now, this exciting tale of a new society ...

E ... an unforgettable love story of two people torn apart by the French Revolution ...

20 SKILLS

Emphasising important words

4 Look at this extract from Victoria's speech. List the words which are most important in expressing what she wants to say.

> 'But when I look in bookshops, I really – I think I look for surprise elements on, when I read the blurb on the back of the books. I look for something that's sort of, that surprises me, that I didn't know much about before, unless of course it's about, you know, economics or something . . .'

5 Now listen to the tape and see if you were correct. Were you surprised by any words that she stressed? Why do you think she stressed them? Try to read the extract in the way that Victoria spoke.

SEE ALSO: Vocabulary (Writing, lists A–C), pages 80–1; Grammar (Tenses 1), page 136; (Modals 1 and 3), pages 142–3 and 146; Tapescripts, page 187; Teacher's Book.

Listening and speaking
Making suggestions and recommendations

6 Listen to a conversation in which one person is recommending a book to the other. What questions does the man ask his friend?

7 Suggest to a partner a book they might like to read (or a film they might like to see). Give reasons for your recommendation: tell them about the kind of book / film it is; the author / director; the plot (but not the ending!), and the characters.

You may find these phrases useful:

Can you recommend . . . ?	It's about . . .
Have you read / tried . . . ?	It's set in . . .
Why don't you try . . . ?	It's based on . . .
A book I enjoyed very much was . . .	The main characters are . . .
	The hero / heroine is . . .
How about reading . . . ?	The reason I enjoyed it is that . . .
Do you know a book called . . . ?	
I can really recommend . . .	Other books by the same author are . . .
What's it like?	

SKILLS 21

1 WRITING

DESCRIPTIONS

Reading

1 Descriptions of places are common in fiction, but they can also be found in other kinds of writing. Can you think of any? Look quickly at the description below. What kind of publication do you think it is taken from?

2
1 Look at the photograph, and then read the description of a small holiday resort. List any parts of the description which are not correct.

> **T**HE HOTEL is a stunningly attractive new building standing completely alone in an isolated bay. Immediately in front of the hotel is a long golden beach, where cool drinks and local snacks are always available. You can relax in the bright sun or under the free umbrellas, while your children play safely in the warm, emerald-green sea. Behind the hotel, tall mountains rise dramatically towards the clear blue sky.

2 What changes would you make to the description to make it more accurate? Is there anything you would want to add?
3 In which order does the writer describe:
   A the beach   C the sea
   B the mountains D the hotel
Why do you think the writer chose this order?
What tense is used in this kind of publication?

Preparing for writing

3 Look at the description above again. Take out as many descriptive words as you can, but keep each sentence grammatical. Start like this:

   The hotel is a building . . .

Now discuss with a partner all the possible adjectives you could use to make your skeleton text more interesting.

4 Imagine you went on holiday to the resort and now you are writing to a friend explaining why you hated it. Think about the tenses and adjectives you might use.

Example:
The hotel was a(n) modern / shabby / old / characterless building . . .

22 SKILLS

1 WRITING

5 Think about how your senses respond to a place.

Examples:
*The hotel **looked like** a small railway station.*
*The inside **smelt like** a hospital.*
*The food **tasted like** the meals we were given as children at school.*
*The receptionist **sounded like** my teacher.*
*The beds **felt like** blocks of stone.*

Use one of the expressions in **bold** in the examples to describe your response to:
1 waves breaking on a beach   3 soup
2 a museum   4 a hat

6 Another way of comparing something new with something more familiar is to say:

*The hotel **reminded me of** my grandmother's house in Wales.*
*He **reminded me of** my father.*

What might these remind you of?
1 an underground station   3 mountains
2 a shopping centre   4 a sitting-room

7 You can also describe how you feel about something.

Examples:
*I **disliked** the hotel **because of** its ugliness.*
*I **loved** the hotel **for** its charm.*

Which other words could you use in the place of **disliked** or **loved**?

Writing

8 Write a description of a place that you have visited. Include in your description:

- descriptive adjectives
- the responses of one or more of your senses
- comparison with other places that you know well
- your feelings about the place

Think about the order in which you are going to describe the place. Here are two possibilities:

- Give a general impression (for example, of scenery), followed by a description of important features (for example, the hotel, the beach).
- Start by describing a central feature (for example, a hotel), and then move outwards to describe its surroundings (for example, the beach, the hills).

9 Exchange descriptions with a partner. Ask additional questions about the place your partner has described.

Examples:
In what way was the valley beautiful?
How did you feel while you were there?
Did it remind you of anywhere else?

> SEE ALSO: Grammar (Comparative adjectives), page 130; (Tenses 2), page 137, (Linking ideas with phrases), pages 176–7; Teacher's Book.

SKILLS 23

2 PRIVATE LIVES

Romance and Friendship

Discussion

1 What sort of qualities do you look for in a partner – a boyfriend / girlfriend or a wife / husband?
Do you look for the same qualities in a friend?

Listening

2  A woman is talking about finding a suitable partner. Listen to the tape, then answer the following questions:

1 What does the speaker look for in a partner? What qualities does she think are important and unimportant?
2 She mentions two ways of falling in love. What are they?
3 She says she is looking for 'someone who is compatible . . . who leads a compatible lifestyle'. What do you understand by this? Which of the people in the pictures above might lead a lifestyle compatible with your own?

Text structure and intonation

3 Look at the phrases on the left. Match each one with the kind of information (on the right) that you expect to follow it:

1 first of all
2 in fact
3 it may sound strange, but . . .
4 it's easy to say . . . but . . .

A a more specific comment which emphasises something already said
B something surprising
C a contrasting opinion
D a main point followed by a number of others

4  Listen again to the tape. Were you correct? Are the phrases stressed? Why / Why not?

24 SKILLS

Discussion

5 Look at the extract from an advertisement for *Dateline*.

1 What do you think *Dateline* does?
2 Do agencies like this exist in your country?
3 Would you use a service like this? Why / Why not?
4 If you do not use a service like this, how do you meet new friends?

"Joining Dateline was the best thing I have ever done." When Wendy met Andrew "it was love at first sight to be honest. I went to work the next day and said, 'Well this is it, I've found the man for me'. 'It'll blow over' they said, but I knew it was right!" It most certainly was and they will be married this autumn.

'We met through *Dateline*'

You too can find love

2 | PRIVATE LIVES

Reading

6 Here are a number of advertisements written by people who want new partners. Work in pairs and match the people according to their interests and the kind of person they say they are looking for. Are there any problems?

MALE

1 TALL, DARK, RICH AND HANDSOME? What a pity, not me! I'm 40, single, a bit shy, medium height and weight. Interested in music and the countryside. Looking for a romantic lady of any age with a sense of humour. Non-smoker.

 ARE YOU an attractive, single, slim lady, 21–27? I'm single, 27, slim, attractive, quite tall, fair hair and blue eyes. Interests include cinema, jogging, sports. Relaxed personality and good sense of humour. Smoker trying to stop!

 FARMER. Non-smoker, divorced, 35. Seeks female, any nationality. Child, horses and pets welcomed.

FEMALE

A Jennifer. Attractive professional (33) with wide interest in the arts, literature and countryside. Seeks male company.

B Tired of working too hard. I'm 40, fair, medium build, quite good company, hate loud music and crowds. Looking for sincere man (non-smoker). Prefer professional.

C LONG-HAIRED AND SLIM. Graduate, 25, quite short, seeks tall, slim male graduate for sincere relationship. Interests include music, cinema, theatre, travel, sports.

SEE ALSO: Vocabulary (Private lives, lists A and B), page 82; Grammar (Modals 1), pages 142–3; (Linking ideas with phrases), pages 176–7; Tapescripts, page 187; Teacher's Book.

SKILLS 25

Parents and children

Discussion

1 Have relationships between parents and children changed? Think of your parents and grandparents.

1 Did your parents and grandparents live near their families when they were first married?
2 Did / Do / Will your parents look after your grandparents in their old age?
3 What about you? Do / Will you live near your parents? Do / Will you look after them?

Reading

2 Now read 'Anthea's story' and 'Stephen's story'.

1 What are the main differences between Bill and Anthea's relationship with their parents and Jill and Stephen's relationship with theirs?
2 What are the differences between Anthea's relationship with her children and Jill's relationship with hers?
3 Do you think the changes that have taken place between the generations are *good* changes for everybody? How have they affected:
   a old people?
   b middle-aged people?
   c young people?

ANTHEA'S STORY

WE WERE MARRIED in 1946 when Bill came out of the army, and we lived with his parents for two years, until we found a house of our own. We didn't go far though, because we wanted to be near our families. After the children were born, my mother came to my house every day. She was a great help. As they grew older I had more time to help my sisters with their kids. Bill never had much to do with the children as babies, but he was a good father . . . he always managed to bring in enough money to keep the family going. By the time the children were old enough to look after themselves, Bill's parents and my own were getting old and I had to start looking after them. When my father died, mum moved in with us. She lived another ten years and it was hard work for us because she was ill for most of that time. Both our children married young – in their early twenties – and they lived with us for the first few years after they were married.

2 PRIVATE LIVES

26 SKILLS

STEPHEN'S STORY

JILL AND I MARRIED in 1967. We were both 20 and we had known each other for about four years. We lived with my mum and dad at first, but it was all a bit difficult – Jill and my mother just didn't get on. As soon as Jill became pregnant we moved out into our own place. In fact we moved a long way – to the north-east of Scotland where I got a job in the oil industry. We had a daughter a year after the first child, and when the children were both old enough to go to school, Jill started work. We've both worked ever since. Jill is a manager in a factory and I work as an electrician. Both of our children have left home. Barbara's gone to college in Liverpool and Denis is working in London. We're lucky if we see them twice a year now. They both want a career and show no signs of getting married. My father died two years ago and my mother is in an old people's home in the town where she has lived all her life. I feel bad about it, but I know we couldn't look after her here.

2 PRIVATE LIVES

Listening

3 Listen to a short dialogue between a father and son. As you listen, answer these questions:

1 How old do you think the boy is? Why?
2 What does the father want? Does he get it?
3 What does the boy want? Does he get it?

Intonation

4 Listen to the following sounds. They are taken from the dialogue above, but the words have been removed.

1 Do you think they represent the speech of the boy or the father? Give reasons for your answers.
2 The father ends the negotiation by saying 'all right'. What does he mean?
He could also have used 'OK' or 'if you must'. Practise saying these, using the same intonation pattern.

SEE ALSO: Vocabulary (Private lives, list C), page 83; Grammar (Comparative adjectives), page 130; (Tenses 1, 3 and 5), pages 136, 138–9 and 141; (Multi-part verbs), pages 148–9; Tapescripts, page 187; Teacher's Book.

Speaking

5 Now make up dialogues for these situations:

A A teenager wants to go to a party that finishes late. His mother wants him to come home by 10 o'clock, but the teenager wants to stay until midnight. How can he persuade his mother?

B A father wants his 18-year-old daughter to go on holiday with her parents. She doesn't want to go . . . she would prefer to go and stay with her friend. How can she persuade her father?

6 Listen and compare your conversations with those on the tape.

SKILLS 27

family matters

2 PRIVATE LIVES

Reading

1 Read the letter once quickly. Summarise in your own words what it tells us about the writer.

> 3 Castle Street,
> Exeter
> EX5 7RU
>
> 10 August 1992
>
> Dear Brian,
> We're back from holiday, and I can't tell you how glad I am to be home. The whole family went this time, and Penny and I felt as if we were in prison – no discos, no fun, no excitement. All we did was visit boring ruins and walk around the city. Can you imagine anything more tedious than looking at the outside of places of so-called interest and sitting in cafés making awkward conversation with your parents? The evenings were no better. One night we went to a ballet which was so silly and dull that I fell asleep. Another evening we went to a concert of classical music... It was two weeks of absolute misery, counting the days until the flight back to England.
>
> Dave

2 Read the letter again and answer the following questions:

1. Which words and phrases tell you that the writer did not enjoy his holiday?
2. Which two adjectives have a similar meaning to 'boring'?
3. Which phrase means 'great unhappiness'?
4. Explain in your own words why the writer felt as if he was in prison.
5. What kind of music do you think he enjoys?
6. What kind of holiday do you think he would prefer?

Preparing for writing

3 In pairs or groups, make a list of words that can be used to describe a *good* holiday. Think particularly about feelings, activities and companions.

28 SKILLS

Writing

4 Imagine that you are one of the parents of the bored teenager in exercise 1. For you the holiday was a great success because the family was able to spend two weeks together doing things that interested you. Write a paragraph for a letter to a friend.

5 Read through what you have written, and consider these questions:

- Does the paragraph have a clear structure? Do you introduce the topic in the first sentence? Is there some kind of conclusion in the last sentence?
- Have you expressed clearly your feelings about the holiday? Would a reader be sure that you enjoyed the holiday and know the reasons for your enjoyment?
- Could the language be improved? Can you use a more precise word or a more suitable structure?
- Are you sure of the spelling of each word? Have you checked difficult words in the dictionary?
- Is your punctuation appropriate?

Make any changes that you think will improve your work.

6 Exchange paragraphs with your partner and make suggestions for improvement. Then write a final version which takes into account the changes your partner suggests.

SEE ALSO: Grammar (Modals 3), page 146; (Linking ideas with phrases, by reference and with general words), pages 176–81; Teacher's Book.

2 PRIVATE LIVES

3 FEAR

Is FEAR good for you?

Discussion

1 Look at the photographs above.

1 Describe the fears they show.
2 Have you ever been in any of the situations shown in the photographs? Describe the situation and how you felt.
3 Some fears are useful: for example, fear of busy roads can stop a child getting hurt. Others are not so useful. Make a list of all the types of fear you can think of. Then decide whether they are *useful* or *not so useful*.

Listening

2 You are going to hear some extracts from an interview with Angela Phillips, a professional actress. In Part 1, Angela is talking about her fears before a performance. While you listen, answer these questions:

1 What does she call the fear that actors get?
2 Does she think this fear is common among actors?

3 Now listen again and answer these questions:

1 How do actors show their fear? Which of these does Angela mention?
  A They cry.   E They shout.
  B They sweat.   F They feel ill.
  C They talk a lot.   G They argue.
  D They go to the toilet.   H They tremble.

2 Does the fear continue on stage? Why / Why not?
3 How does she say actors feel at the end of a performance?

4 🔊 Now listen to Part 2. While you listen, answer these questions:

1 What do actors do to try to overcome their fears before going on stage?
2 What does Angela do?
3 She feels that fear can be a positive emotion for actors. In what way?

5 Angela uses a lot of special words connected with the theatre. Match the words on the left with the definitions on the right:

1 stage   A the period just before the performance begins
2 script   B the side of the stage, where the actors stand just before coming on
3 half   C the written lines of a play
4 scene   D the place where actors get changed and put on their make-up
5 wings   E the raised platform on which the actors perform
6 dressing room F a part of a play

Intonation

6 Angela says this:

(Some people) like to talk . . . I prefer to be quiet.

She stresses the words underlined because she is *contrasting* them. Practise saying the sentences below. Find the words that are being contrasted, and emphasise them as you speak.

Example:

The red one, not the green one.

1 His brother, not his sister.
2 Don't turn left; turn right.
3 Jane's father, not Sara's father.
4 I wanted three, not four.
5 It arrives at 11.15, not 10.15.
6 I need his new address, not his old one.
7 It's the director I want to speak to, not his assistant.

7 🔊 Now compare what you said with the sentences on the tape.

SEE ALSO: Vocabulary (Fear, lists A–D), pages 84–5; Grammar (Tenses 1, 3 and 4), pages 136, 138–9 and 140); Tapescripts, pages 187–8; Teacher's Book.

3 FEAR

Overcoming fears

Speaking and listening

1 How can we overcome our fears? Choose *one* of the fears shown in the photographs on page 30 and, working in groups, discuss all the ways you can think of to overcome it. One person should take notes and be prepared to report the group's ideas to the rest of the class.

2 When people are afraid, they often need the help of other people. Here are two situations:

A Your friend has to make a short speech to a large group of people and is terrified. Try to encourage him! Give him some useful advice.

B You see a child of about 11 years old sitting alone and crying in a railway station. You discover that her uncle has failed to meet her. Speak to her and try to make her feel better.

Have the conversations in pairs. Here are some useful expressions you could use:

Is there something wrong?	Can I help?
Everything will be fine!	Calm down!
I'm sure things will be OK!	It's all right!
Are you all right?	Don't worry!

3 Now listen and compare what you said with the conversations on the tape.

3 | FEAR

32 SKILLS

Reading

4 Look at the newspaper article 'Putting fear to flight'. Read the headline and try to predict what you think the article is about. Then read the article and see if you were right.

Putting fear to flight

The statistics on the safety of flying are immensely comforting. One expert has estimated that more people in the world are kicked to death by donkeys than die in plane crashes. The chances of being involved in an accident are a million to one – the equivalent of flying safely every day for 95 years. Nevertheless, fear of flying is widespread. An American survey put it as the fourth most common fear (jointly with visits to the dentist) preceded only by snakes, heights and storms and well ahead of illness and injury.

Psychologist Maurice Yaffe runs seminars at Guy's Hospital in London for those who want to try to overcome their fear of flying. Yaffe explains the principles of flight and its effects on the body, before moving on to techniques of relaxation and 'right thinking'. He believes that most fears about flying are irrational, so he tries to encourage people to look at the evidence and find positive alternatives to their negative fears. For example, a passenger who is terrified in the middle of a flight because the air hostesses have disappeared is encouraged to think positively: air hostesses have to have tea breaks, and would tell us if there were a crisis. As well as substituting good for bad thoughts, Yaffe also teaches 'thought stopping'. A person concentrates on an unwanted thought (we're going to fall out of the sky!) for a few seconds before saying the word 'stop' quietly. Included in the cost of the seminar is a short air trip to Paris and back.

It seems to work. Yaffe has had nearly 500 clients in the last decade. Only one person ever refused to board the plane. He believes his success rate is about 80 per cent, success being measured not so much in terms of enjoyment as in a willingness to fly again. He treasures a stack of postcards sent by former sufferers from all corners of the world.

Adapted from an article in The Times

5 Which three sentences summarise the article best? Choose one from each column to summarise each paragraph:

1	2	3
Very few people die in air crashes.	Dr Yaffe's courses help people overcome their fear of flying.	Twenty per cent of people fail to overcome their fears.
A lot of people die in air crashes.	You can stop bad thoughts if you really try.	After the seminar, 80 per cent of people enjoy flying.
Fear of flying is very common.	Most fears about flying are irrational.	Most people can successfully overcome their fears.

6 The correct answers to exercise 5 are main points from each of the three paragraphs. Now find a *supporting point* in the text for each of the main points and write it in your own words.

Example:
Paragraph 1 – Fear of flying is very common.
     It is the fourth most common fear.

SEE ALSO: Vocabulary (Fear, lists B–E), pages 84–5; Grammar (Articles 1), page 123; (The passive), page 147; Tapescripts, page 188; Teacher's Book

7 Look back at paragraph 1 and order these fears from most to least common:

A snakes   B illness   C flying   D heights   E storms   F dentists

DESCRIBING FEAR

Reading

1 Read the extract below, which is taken from a short story.

THE PICTURE was a simple drawing in black and white, of the kind which is found in colouring books. It showed a *single-decker bus* whose driver stared woodenly ahead over the steering wheel. Two passengers were already sitting on the back seat: a man who wore a motor-cycling helmet and a woman with a bulging shopping basket. Just stepping on to the *platform* was a football supporter: a young man in a striped woollen hat, with a rosette pinned to his anorak. An elderly gentleman with his scarf flying was hurrying towards the bus, waving his hand to stop it. It was a perfectly ordinary scene. There was nothing in the picture which could possibly explain why a mist of horror should rise from its thin black lines like poison gas to envelop Andrew, to smother him, to snatch his breath away.

He stood up, not hearing the crash as his chair toppled sideways and the pencil fell on to the floor. He was not aware of anything except the need to escape from the picture.

The room was too small. A single step backwards was enough to bring him against the wall. His mouth was dry and his heart seemed to have stopped beating and instead to be swelling like a balloon inside his chest. Round the edges of his head there was a roaring sound, but in its centre was a small white circle of terror. He pressed backwards against the shelves of books, his hands stretching sideways to find some secure grip, for he knew that he was going to fall.

From 'The Boy on the Bus' in *Snapshots* by Anne Melville, Severn House, 1990

> *single-decker bus* = a bus with all the seats on one level
>
> *platform* = the open part of a bus, where passengers get on and off

34 SKILLS

Discussion

2 Without looking back at the extract, discuss the following:

1 Try to describe to a partner the picture which frightened the boy.
2 Try to remember how the boy reacted.
3 What do you think the reason for the boy's terror could be?

Word study

3 From the last sentence in the first paragraph until the end of the extract, the writer uses a lot of words and phrases to convey different ways in which we respond both emotionally and physically to fear. Working in small groups, write lists of words and phrases that are used in the text to describe at least *two* of the following:

- feelings
- space
- movement
- taste
- breathing
- sound

Speaking

4 Now imagine yourself in a terrifying situation. Write down all the words and phrases you can think of to describe your emotional and physical responses. Then describe the situation and your fears to your partner.

SEE ALSO: Vocabulary (Fear, lists B and C), pages 84–5; Grammar (Joining nouns: 's, *of* and ∅), page 131; (Modifying the noun), pages 132–3; (Linking ideas by reference and with general words), pages 178–81; Teacher's Book.

Writing

5 Look at the short text below. It is a neutral description of a sequence of events that take place in an isolated house in the country. The person in the story is alone in the house. Your task is to make the story more interesting. Add words, phrases, or even whole sentences to give it suspense and drama by telling the reader what the person in the house is *feeling*. Change any part of the text. Use some of the vocabulary from exercise 3.

3 FEAR

IT WAS AROUND MIDNIGHT. I was lying in bed, reading. Suddenly I heard a sharp noise coming from the back garden – like a small stick breaking. I got out of bed and went downstairs quietly. As I entered the kitchen, I saw a shadow move across the window. I stared at the handle of the back door and watched as it turned. Then I heard some low whispers; so, there were at least two of them. The footsteps moved away from the door and round to the window of the dining room. A few moments later there was a soft tapping on one of the windows, then a loud crash as the glass fell inwards on to the dining room floor.

4 SPORT

WOMEN AND SPORT

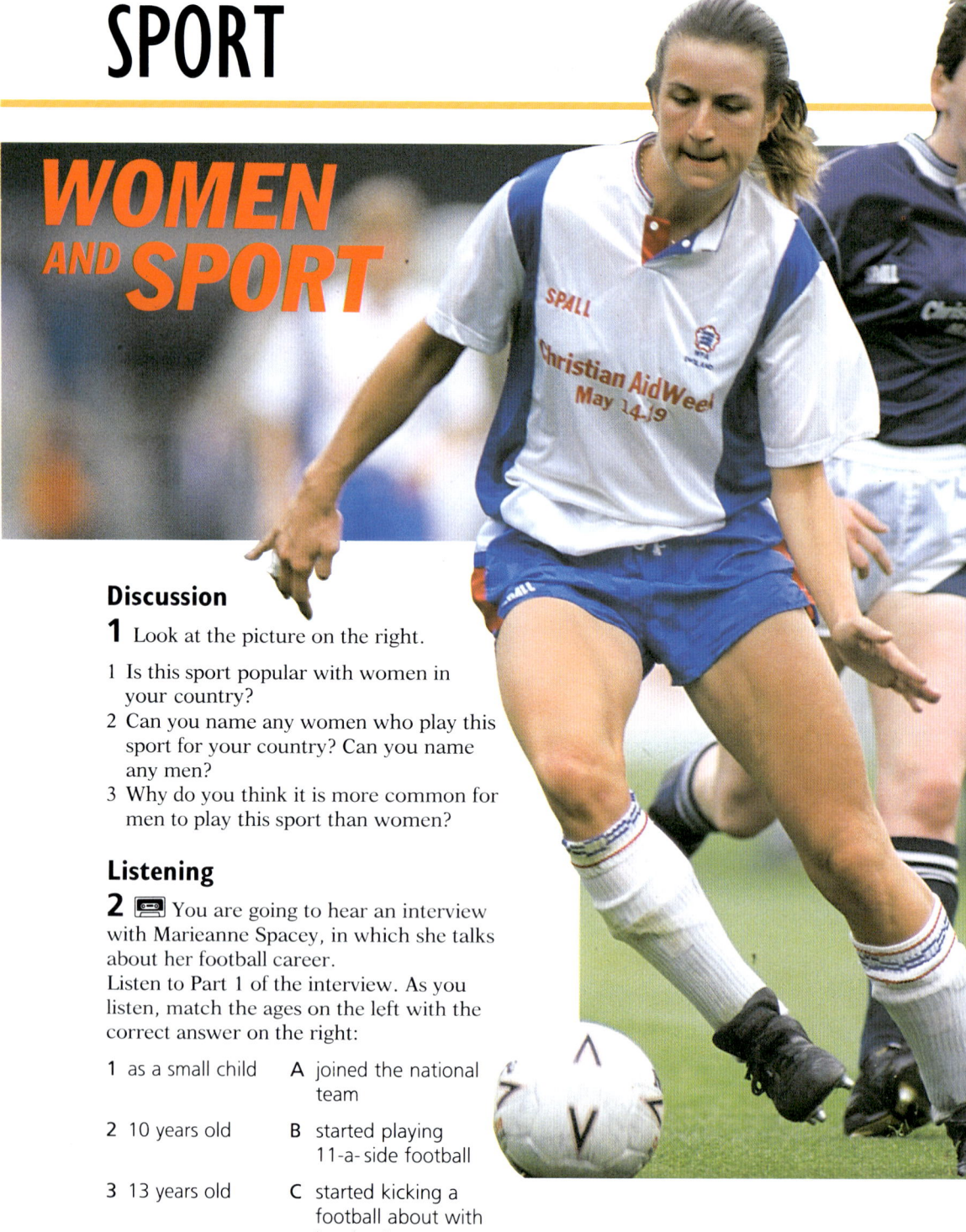

Discussion

1 Look at the picture on the right.

1 Is this sport popular with women in your country?
2 Can you name any women who play this sport for your country? Can you name any men?
3 Why do you think it is more common for men to play this sport than women?

Listening

2 You are going to hear an interview with Marieanne Spacey, in which she talks about her football career.
Listen to Part 1 of the interview. As you listen, match the ages on the left with the correct answer on the right:

1	as a small child	A	joined the national team
2	10 years old	B	started playing 11-a-side football
3	13 years old	C	started kicking a football about with her family
4	13 / 14 years old	D	joined a five-a-side team
5	18 years old	E	started playing for Friends of Fulham

Why did she continue playing football as she got older? At school, did she play football with boys or with other girls?

36 SKILLS

3 🔊 Now listen to Part 2 of the interview. Marieanne compares women's football in Britain with the same sport in other countries.

1 Name the other countries she refers to.
2 What two differences does she mention between crowds attending women's football matches in Britain and in these other countries?
3 Marieanne mentions some differences between men's and women's football. Which of the following does she say?
   A Women's football is more physical.
   B Men's football tends to be faster.
   C Women players tend to be more sporting.
   D Women rely on skill rather than strength.
   E Women are more emotional.
   F Men's football is not as skilful.
   G Women are not paid to play.

Speaking

4 Look at these names of sports and match them with the pictures:

basketball   athletics
skating   boxing
horse racing
motor racing
synchronised swimming
hockey   gymnastics
archery

5 Now describe how each sport is played.

Example:
In basketball, you have to throw a ball into a basket.

6 Say whether each sport is played in your country by men or women or both.

Examples:
Archery is for both women and men.
Boxing is only for men.
A lot of women race horses.

7
1 Are there any good reasons why some sports are played by men more than women?
2 Are different sports more popular with women now than in the past in your country? If so, why?

SEE ALSO: page 38 for references to other parts of the book.

4 SPORT

SKILLS 37

Reading

8 Read the article quickly and list all the sports that are mentioned in it.

WOMEN AND SPORT
Changing attitudes?

In nineteenth-century Britain, sport was not considered a suitable pastime for a woman. It was associated with male physical strength and intense competition, whereas women were expected to be much gentler and less energetic. Middle-class women were, however, spectators at events like horse racing and cricket matches, and they did play slow games of tennis, badminton and croquet. If they played with men, the men were careful not to hit the ball too hard and to give the ladies every possible advantage. Richer women had the opportunity to take up sporting hobbies such as riding and hunting, as long as they behaved in a feminine manner.

As women's clothes became looser and lighter towards the end of the century, cycling became very popular with women of all social classes. Special sportswear was designed for other games; it carefully hid the body's real shape so that women would remain respectable.

With the new century, many more women participated in a much wider range of sports – cricket, golf, hockey and swimming, among others. On the whole, though, they played separately from men, and it is still true today that mixed sports are common at a social level but not in competitions. Many women, like myself, favour the development of mixed participation, and believe that in many sports women could compete successfully with men if they had the same opportunities and training.

Adapted from an article by J. Hargreaves in *Sport and Leisure*, 7 August 1990

9 Look at these questions, and then read the article again more carefully to find the answers:

1 What is the purpose of the article? (There may be more than one correct answer.)
   A To list all the sports that women have traditionally played.
   B To complain that women have been badly treated in the past.
   C To give the historical background to women's participation in sports.
   D To explain why men are stronger and more athletic than women.
   E To show why women and men rarely compete against each other in sports.
2 Is the writer a man or a woman?
3 Find any sentences in the article that give the author's *opinion*. What does the rest of the article give us?

Making notes

10 Ask an older woman about opportunities for women to play sports when she was young. Make notes on what she says. Then report back to the class, and discuss whether the situation has changed.

SEE ALSO: Vocabulary (Sport, lists A–D), pages 86–7; Grammar (Quantities 2), pages 126–7; (Comparative adjectives), page 130; (Tenses 3), pages 138–9; (Reporting statements), page 150; (Modifying the verb 2), page 153; Tapescripts, page 188; Teacher's Book.

Sport & Violence

Listening and speaking

You are going to hear three extracts from a conversation between a group of friends. They are talking about football supporters.

Before listening

1 Discuss the following questions:

1 How would you describe spectators at football matches in your country? What are they like? How do they behave?
2 Is there any violence at football matches? If so, what causes it? If not, why do you think other countries have this problem?
3 What about other sporting events? Are the attitudes and behaviour of spectators different from football supporters? In what ways?

2 Now listen to all three extracts and answer these questions:

Part 1
1 In your own words, explain what the speaker finds difficult to understand.
2 Describe the speaker's neighbours
   a as they usually are.
   b after a football match.

Part 2
3 In what way is Brazil said to be different from England and some other countries?

Part 3
4 What two differences are there between a tennis tournament at Wimbledon and a football match?

Discussion

3 Most people would like to be able to watch their favourite sport in safety, without the threat of trouble and violence. But different groups of people have different points of view about how this should be arranged. Imagine you are going to a meeting to try to solve the problem of violence at football matches in your town. Working with two or three other students, take on the role of one of the groups below and decide what you would want to say at such a meeting:

- police
- local politicians
- people who live near the football ground
- football supporters
- football players

Now choose a chairperson and have the meeting. Keep talking until you arrive at a solution that everyone can accept!

SEE ALSO: Tapescripts, page 188; Teacher's Book.

4 SPORT

Sport and politics

Reading

1 Read the letter below, which was written to a newspaper. Which of the following are the writer's opinions?

A Politics and sport should be kept separate.
B Staying at home is a good way for small countries to express their opinions.
C Sports people who cannot go to the Olympic Games should protest.

3 Hawthorn Avenue,
Manchester M12 8PR

4th March 1992

Dear Sir/Madam,

I am writing in support of those countries that have decided for political reasons not to send teams to the Olympic Games this year.

In my opinion, you cannot separate international sport from politics. I feel strongly that we should respect the right of people from other countries to express their political beliefs in this way. It is often very difficult for smaller countries in particular to get an audience for their views. By refusing to attend an international sports event, they can be sure that they will get some world attention.

Of course the situation is unfortunate for the individual athletes who will not be able to take part in the world's greatest sporting competition. However, they must accept that the interests of their country come first and that political protest is more important than gold medals.

Yours faithfully,
Caroline Sykes

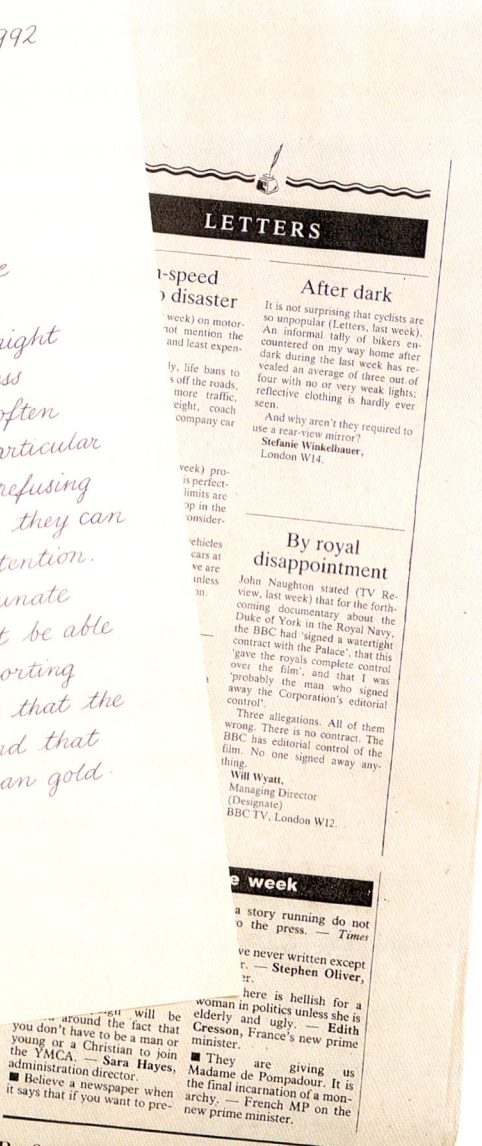

Preparing for writing

2 Read the letter again and answer these questions:

1 In the first paragraph, the writer makes her main point and gives her main reason for writing. Look at these beginnings of sentences. Do you think the writer is going to agree or disagree with a point of view?
   A I am writing to protest . . .
   B I am writing to express my dissatisfaction . . .
   C I am writing in support of . . .
   D I am writing to say how disgusted I am . . .
   E I am writing to complain . . .

2 In the second paragraph, the writer gives her opinions. Find two expressions used at the beginning of sentences to introduce the writer's opinions. Can you think of other ways?

3 In the third paragraph, the writer mentions an opposing argument, but then summarises her own again. Which word tells the reader that a point is being made which is in disagreement with the previous point?

SEE ALSO: Grammar (Linkers), page 170; (Linking ideas with phrases and by reference), pages 176–9; Teacher's Book.

Writing

3 You have recently read about a new proposal that *all* sports teams in schools should be mixed (girls and boys together). Working in pairs, write a letter to a newspaper expressing your opinion.

Before writing
- Work with your partner and list all the ideas you can think of for and against the proposal.
- Select the *two* strongest points in support of your argument, and *one* point against it that you think you can answer.
- List all the words that you think will be useful in your letter.
- Plan what you are going to say in each paragraph. Use the letter in exercise 1 to help you. Structure your letter like this:

   Paragraph 1:
   State your reason for writing and give your general position.

   Paragraph 2:
   Write two sentences giving points in support of your argument.

   Paragraph 3:
   Make one point *against* your argument. Then tell the readers why this is not as important as your previous points.

- Remember to *begin* with 'Dear Sir / Madam,' and to *end* with 'Yours faithfully'. (These words are usually omitted when the letter is printed in a newspaper.)

After writing
- Check that your letter is organised according to the pattern above.
- Check that you have stated your opinions clearly and strongly.
- Check grammar, spelling and punctuation.

4 SPORT

5 DISCIPLINE

children and

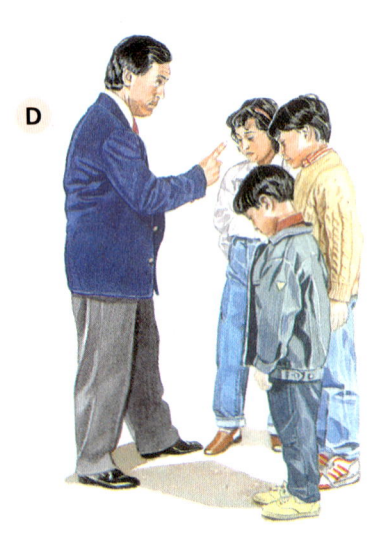

A

B

C

D

E

F

42 SKILLS

discipline

Discussion

1 How do parents teach their children good behaviour? What is the parent doing in each of the pictures opposite? Match the sentences with the appropriate pictures:

1 He's praising his son.
2 She's smacking the child.
3 He's trying to bribe his daughter.
4 She's kissing her son.
5 He's telling the children off.
6 She's sending her children to bed.

Can you think of any other ways of developing good behaviour in children?

Listening

You are going to hear a child speaking about the ways parents punish children.

Before listening

2 Working in pairs, discuss this question with your partner:

What kinds of punishment do you think are most effective with children?

3 🎦 Now listen and answer these questions:

1 Which kind of punishment does the child think is most effective? Why?
2 How does this child feel if he thinks the punishment is unfair?
3 How does he respond to being smacked?

Intonation

4 🎦 Listen again to the tape for exercise 3. Listen carefully to the interviewer's last question and decide whether his voice goes *up* or *down* at the end. This is what he says:

So that's better than being smacked?

What does the interviewer expect the child's answer to this question to be?

Now look at these questions and decide whether the speaker's voice should go *up* or *down* at the end.

(Expects *yes*)
So you enjoy playing football?

(Doesn't know what to expect)
You can come to the party tonight?

We can ask questions by using intonation alone, without using a question form like 'Do you . . .?'. Make questions for the situations below *without* using a question form.

Example:
You want to know if someone wants a cup of tea.
You want a cup of tea?

1 You want to ask if someone is feeling ill. (You are sure they are.)
2 You want to ask if you have to change trains at Oxford. (You are not sure whether you do or not.)

5 🎦 Listen to the tape and compare your answers.

SEE ALSO: page 45 for references to other parts of the book.

5 DISCIPLINE

SKILLS 43

How can parents discipline children?

A REWARDS

Although it is much more enjoyable to reward than punish, most parents are much better at recognising bad behaviour than they are at noticing the good things a child has done. Rewards are important as the following list shows.

- *Giving attention*   This is the most effective of all rewards, especially if it is given without interruption. Even a few seconds of undivided attention can be rewarding.
- *Praise*   Praise is a particular form of attention that uses words and pleasure. Most parents are good at giving praise for the first few years of a child's life, but as their child gets older, they generally give less and less praise.
- *Special treats*   Treats are no substitute for attention or praise. It is, however, much easier to hand out a sweet or a toy than to devote time and energy to giving attention.
- *Special privileges*   These cost nothing and are useful because they are easy to arrange. An example might be letting a child go to bed a little later than usual.
- *Bribery*   Bribery is offering the child a reward on condition that they do what the parent wants.

B PUNISHMENTS

In theory, it should be possible to avoid all punishments by only rewarding good behaviour. In practice it is very difficult. Just as parents praise too little, so they usually punish too much. Here are some examples.

- *Smacking*   It is very easy to smack a child. It doesn't require much effort and usually has an immediate effect. As children grow older, however, smacking becomes less effective and may actually make things worse. Children who are smacked a lot often grow up to believe that their own problems can be solved by punching or hitting others.
- *Shouting*   Raising your voice is only effective if it is reserved for serious situations. If you shout all the time, your child will take little notice.
- *Removing attention*   This is one of the most effective means of punishing a child. But be very careful not to do it for too long.
- *Loss of privileges*   Examples are sending a child to bed early, or forbidding them to watch television.
- *'Telling off'*   This is only effective if you have your child's full attention and the child takes seriously what you say. Be clear, firm and confident.

Adapted from *The Kids Workout Guide for Parents* by Dr John Pearce (Thames Television), Thorsons, 1987

Reading

6 Read the extract on page 44, taken from a book that gives advice to parents on how to teach their children good behaviour at home.

1 As you read, complete the diagram opposite.
2 Read the extract again and put a tick against each technique in the diagram that you know is used in *schools*. Then tell a partner about any personal experiences of these methods.

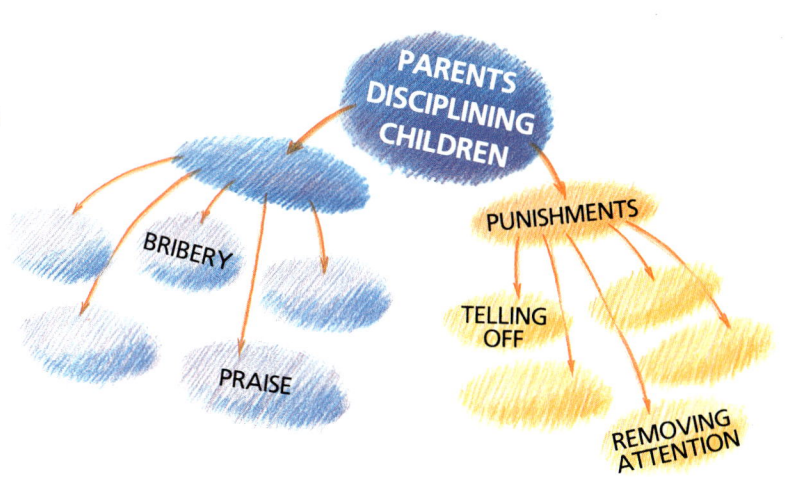

Listening and speaking

7 Listen to the tape. You are going to hear three short extracts in which a parent is punishing a child. Compare the different methods used on each occasion. Are they all mentioned in the article opposite? Which is most / least effective, do you think? Why?

8

1 The parent in extract 3 says, '*How many times have I told you not to* play near other people's houses?' Use this construction in these situations:
   a a child eating with her fingers
   b a teenager coming home late
   c a child playing with matches

2 In extract 3 the parent threatens the child by saying, '*If you ever do this again. . .*'. Make threats like this for the last two situations in 1 above.

9 A teenage girl has just hitch-hiked home in the dark. One parent threatens punishment; one parent tries to make her understand why she was foolish. Work in groups of three and have a conversation.

10 Compare your conversation with the one on the tape.

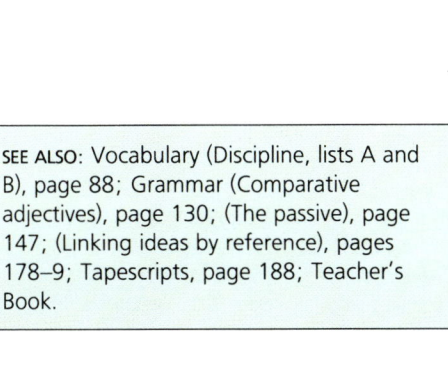

SEE ALSO: Vocabulary (Discipline, lists A and B), page 88; Grammar (Comparative adjectives), page 130; (The passive), page 147; (Linking ideas by reference), pages 178–9; Tapescripts, page 188; Teacher's Book.

PARENTS DISCIPLINING CHILDREN

BRIBERY

PRAISE

PUNISHMENTS

TELLING OFF

REMOVING ATTENTION

SKILLS 45

5 DISCIPLINE

DISCIPLINE IN SOCIETY

Discussion

1 Different countries deal with young people who offend against society in different ways. Look at the pictures.

1 Describe each different type of discipline. Can they all be called 'punishment'?
2 What happens to young people in your country if, for example, they are caught stealing or are involved in football violence?

Speaking
Giving opinions

2 When we want to give our opinions, we can use the following phrases:

In my opinion, . . .   I think . . .

I believe . . .   I feel (strongly) that . . .

I have no doubt at all that . . .

What do you think should happen to young people who offend against society? Give an opinion and a reason for each of the cases below:

Example: *(steal)*
In my opinion, young people who steal should be sent to prison because that will force them to think about what they have done.

1 (drive dangerously)
2 (take drugs)
3 (damage property)
4 (steal money, using violence)
5 (paint graffiti on trains)

SEE ALSO: Vocabulary (Discipline, lists C–G), pages 88–9; Grammar (Modifying the noun), pages 132–3; (Tenses 3 and 4), pages 138–9 and 140; (Modals 1 and 2), pages 142–5; (The passive), page 147; (Reporting statements), page 150; (Conditionals), pages 168–9; (Linkers), page 170; Teacher's Book.

5 DISCIPLINE

46 SKILLS

Reading and writing

3 Read the information below. The first box gives details about a young man who is in trouble with the police. The three boxes that follow contain comments made by people who know him. This information is about Jeffrey Roberts. As you can see, he has had a short but difficult life. He has been in trouble with the police on a number of occasions and has now been accused of stealing from a supermarket. What do you think should happen to him? Write a short essay in two paragraphs:

Paragraph 1: Describe Jeffrey's past, and his present situation.
Paragraph 2: Give your opinions on what should happen to him. Make sure that you *give reasons* for your opinions.

NAME: Jeffrey Alan Roberts   **AGE:** 18

EDUCATION: Left school at 16; no qualifications

EMPLOYMENT: Unemployed since leaving school, except for a few months of temporary work

FAMILY: Youngest of five children. Parents divorced when he was three. No contact with father since then. Two brothers in trouble with the police recently

POLICE RECORD: Stole a bicycle (age 12) - given a warning

Stole from a shop (age 14) - sent to a special school

Stole from a shop (age 17) - fined £200

CURRENT CHARGE: Theft of food from a supermarket (value £16.50)

CURRENT SITUATION: Homeless. Sleeps on the streets

Head teacher: Jeffrey would be fine if only he would make a fresh start. His problem is that nobody will give him a job with a background like his.

Social worker: Jeffrey's problem is the same as that of many young people. He has nowhere to live. He can't get a job until he has an address; he can't get anywhere to live until he has a job. It's a vicious circle.

Supermarket manager: Kids like Jeffrey need a shock when they are young to prevent them from becoming criminals for the rest of their lives.

5 DISCIPLINE

6 PEOPLE ON THE MOVE

A way of life

Discussion

1 Look at the photograph above and the one on page 49.

1 Describe what you see in them.
2 What do you think are the advantages and disadvantages of this kind of life-style, in which you never spend long in one place?
3 What kind of life do you think the children lead?

Reading

2 Read texts A (below) and B (at the top of the next page) about gypsies (also known as Romanies or travellers). Who do the writers expect to read them? What is the purpose of the writer in each case?

A

Strictly speaking, gypsies belong to a group who left India for Europe many centuries ago. They have their own language, as well as a life-style and values which are very different from those of most house-dwelling Britons. In England alone there are 11,000 caravans belonging to people – gypsies among them – who, traditionally at least, are constantly on the move.

The gypsy way of life is changing now for a number of reasons. With the development of new agricultural machinery, there is less temporary work on farms. At the same time, many stopping-places have disappeared as cities expand into rural areas. In addition, county councils now have a duty to provide sites for travelling people, in order that they should not have to park beside the roads (which can lead to complaints from local residents and from drivers). Until enough sites have been provided, however, councils are recommended to respect gypsies' need to stop in other public places and not to move them on unless it is absolutely necessary.

Adapted from *Gypsy Sites* by the Association of County Councils, November 1986

48 SKILLS

B

WHEN GYPSIES move into an area, people living nearby often feel threatened by a life-style they do not understand, and try to persuade the authorities to move them on – as is currently happening in Turntock. The gypsies, however, have their own complaints: shopkeepers refuse to serve them; they find it difficult to get jobs; their children are teased or ignored by other children. Worse still, stones are thrown at the windows of their caravans. It is time that we all started behaving like civilised human beings, accepting our differences and living together in harmony.

3 In which text (A, B, or both) are the following points made? Try to remember, and then look back to check your answers:

1 Local residents often complain about gypsies living near them.
2 Gypsies are having to adapt to a new life-style.
3 Gypsies may have problems finding work.
4 Sometimes violence is used against them.
5 Traditionally, gypsies have not lived in one place for long.
6 They have habits which are very different from those of people who live in houses.
7 Councils are providing special places where gypsies can park their caravans.

SEE ALSO: Vocabulary (People on the move, list A), page 90; Grammar (Modifying the noun), pages 132–3; (The passive), page 147; Tapescripts, page 188; Teacher's Book.

Listening

4 You are going to hear a song, written and sung by a gypsy. It is called *Stuck on a Permanent Site* and it describes how he feels about living in one place for the first time. Listen, and note down the words that are missing from the lyrics below.

Stuck on a Permanent Site

I was born a travelling feller
And I took me a travelling wife,
For all of our people were needies
And followed the travelling _____.
Such ways they's hard but they's _____,
For there's plenty of fun on the way;
You don't have to _____ of tomorrow,
Just think of the living today.
So give us a honk on your horn, bruv,
When you're _____ by day or by night,
For no more shall we be a-travelling;
We're stuck on a _____ site ...
... If one day you went a bit 'ungry,
The next there'd be _____ to eat;
If sometimes you're down when you're travelling
You're _____ back up on your feet ...
Now these sites, they seem just like _____ –
And the life here is terrible hard.
Not as free as the side of the road, lads,
Or stopping in some _____'s yard.
Though there's 'lectric and plenty of water,
There's all these _____ to obey.
If I only 'ad some place to pull to,
I'd 'itch on and leave 'ere today.
So _____ us a toot on your hooter
And maybe a flash of your _____,
And if you want to live long and happy,
Stay _____ these permanent sites.

6 PEOPLE ON THE MOVE

SKILLS 49

6 | PEOPLE ON THE MOVE

Living away

Discussion

1 What is it like when you have to leave your home suddenly; when you arrive in a strange country where you have no friends and you don't speak the language? Discuss the following questions:

1 What is a refugee? Why do people sometimes have to leave their home countries?
2 What sort of difficulties do you think you would face arriving and settling in a strange country?

Reading

2 Read what a young refugee told a reporter and find answers to these questions:

1 Where is he from?
2 Is he alone?
3 When did he come to Britain?
4 Do you think he had travelled abroad before?

A refugee speaks

'I WAS NERVOUS and even a little frightened when I first arrived in Britain. Everything was strange. I had never been on a plane before and I couldn't speak much English, so it was difficult talking to the officials at the airport. What I remember being most shocked about was the time. The clock in the airport was completely different from my watch – and I remember thinking that even the time in Britain was different!

I was surprised by many things. I thought everyone in Britain would be rich, but of course it's not true. Some are rich, but there are quite a lot of poor people too. Of course the food was a problem at first, but it's not so bad now. It took me a long time to get used to shopping and catching buses, but the most difficult thing of all was dealing with officials and forms – paying electricity bills, registering for this and that.

My father and mother and two sisters are with me and we've been here for two years now. We know quite a lot of other people from Vietnam and my sisters and I have some English friends. But I think it's much more difficult for my parents to settle into life here and make a new start – they're older and they haven't learned much English. We are all homesick. We miss our relatives and we've left behind everything we had. Although we have a place to live and enough to eat, we are poor. Some British people are unfriendly – they think we are going to take their jobs. Some are just against anyone who has a different culture and different-coloured skin. But most of them are quite friendly.

I hope we'll be able to visit Vietnam in a few years when the situation in our country has changed. I know my parents will want to go back and live there, but perhaps by then my sisters and I will have found a new life here. I don't know . . .'

50 SKILLS

from home

6 PEOPLE ON THE MOVE

3 Are these statements true or false? Give reasons for your answers:

1 His parents have settled easily into life in Britain.
2 They don't see many people from their home country now.
3 He and his sisters hope to return to live in the country where they were born.

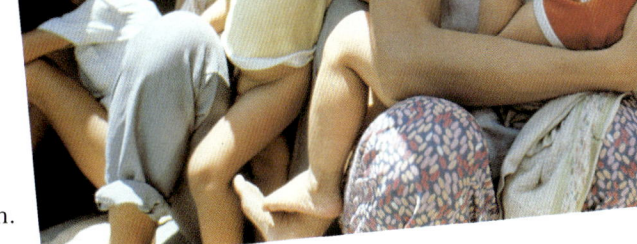

4 List the words used in the text to describe the writer's feelings.

Example: *nervous*

Listening

5 You are going to listen to a Mexican woman, who has also come to live in Britain. As you listen, think about the ways in which it was probably easier for her than for the refugee to adapt to life in Britain. Why do you think this was so?

6 Listen again, and make notes in answer to these questions:

1 What does she find difficult about life in Britain?
2 What does she not find difficult?
3 What does she not like about the British?
4 What do the speaker's comments tell you, indirectly, about Mexico and Mexicans?

SEE ALSO: Vocabulary (People on the move, lists B and E), pages 90–1; Grammar (Modals 1), pages 142–3; (Conditionals), pages 168–9; (Infinitives and gerunds), page 173; (Linking ideas by reference), pages 178–9; Tapescripts, pages 188–9; Teacher's Book.

Speaking

7 In what ways do foreigners find it easy or difficult to adapt to life in your country? Think particularly about:

- people (attitudes and relationships)
- language
- facilities
- customs and habits
- climate

Do you know any foreigners living in your country? How do they feel?

8 If you do not know many foreigners, you may be uncertain about how they feel. How can you express this uncertainty when you speak? Look at these comments about foreigners in London:

They are **probably** shocked by the dirt.

They **may well** find the transport system unpleasant.

It is **likely** that life will be expensive for them.

I **should think** that they would be impressed by the theatres and galleries.

I **wouldn't be surprised** if they were lonely at first.

Use these constructions to make sentences about foreigners in your country.

SKILLS 51

6 PEOPLE ON THE MOVE

Journeys

Listening and speaking

1 Look at this announcement.

1 Where might you see it?
2 What form of transport does it refer to?
3 How would you respond to it?

2 Describe the places shown below. What happens at each of them?

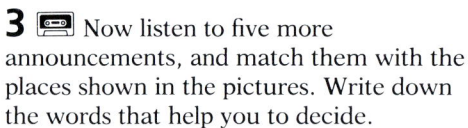

> LONDON TRANSPORT regrets that the Central Line between Oxford Circus and Holborn is closed until further notice due to tunnel repairs.

3 🖭 Now listen to five more announcements, and match them with the places shown in the pictures. Write down the words that help you to decide.

4 Look again at the announcement at the top of this page. 'London Transport regrets . . .' is a very formal way of apologising. Here are some other ways of saying sorry:

A I'm very / terribly / extremely / so sorry (that) . . .

B I'd like to apologise for . . .

C Please accept my apologies for . . .

Which of these is the most formal? Which would you say or write to somebody you do not know well? And to a friend?

Reading and speaking
Apologising and making excuses

5 Some people give excuses for coming to work late that are extremely hard to believe. Find the excuses mentioned in this article, then use them in a conversation with a partner. Plan what you are going to say. Your partner will almost certainly ask you for more information, so make some up!

Sorry I'm late, there is an elephant in the road

By PAUL CROSBIE

BRITISH workers are the most creative in the world – when it comes to dreaming up excuses for being late at work.

Among classic excuses given to a survey were the worker who rang in to say his hand was stuck in a cornflakes packet, the accountant with no clean socks and the man whose mother burnt his toast.

Another man blamed his late arrival on an elephant that had blocked the road.

Yet another couldn't attend a meeting because his dog had eaten important documents.

From the *Daily Express*, 13 December 1990

52 SKILLS

6 PEOPLE ON THE MOVE

Preparing for writing
Letters of apology and explanation

6 What is the function of each of the paragraphs in this letter? Put them in the order in which they occur:

A explanation
B main apology
C secondary apology

7 The opening sentence states the *purpose* of the letter. You can use 'I'm writing to . . .' to begin any letter. What would you write if you wanted to:

1 ask for information?
2 complain about something?
3 congratulate someone?

8 Notice that 'apologise' is followed by: **for** + verb + **-ing** (or **for** + noun phrase). Make sentences beginning 'I am writing to apologise . . .' for these situations:

1 You arrived late.
2 You forgot a meeting.
3 You didn't meet someone when you had arranged to.
4 You behaved badly at a party.

9 The *explanation* in the second paragraph of the letter gives a reason for the writer not being able to attend. Here are some other reasons. What would you write if:

1 you had had a car accident?
2 you had broken your leg?
3 your child had suddenly become ill?

Note:
Letters that begin with 'Dear Mr / Ms' etc. end with 'Yours sincerely'. Letters that begin with 'Dear Sir / Madam' end with 'Yours faithfully'.

SEE ALSO: Vocabulary (People on the move, lists C and D), page 91; Grammar (The passive), page 147; (Linking ideas by reference), pages 178–9; Tapescripts, page 189; Teacher's Book.

---

37 Victoria Road,
Cambridge CB3 4FE

2 May 1992

Dear Mr Thomas,
I'm writing to apologise for not attending your daughter's wedding last week. I was so sorry to miss it, but there was a very good reason which I am sure you will understand.
Unfortunately, on the evening before the wedding, my mother was taken into hospital after a nasty fall and I went to Wales to be with her. I stayed until she was able to go back home three days later. She's much better now.
Once again, I'm sorry. Please give your daughter and her new husband my best wishes for the future.

Yours sincerely,
P. Matthias
Patrick Matthias

Writing

10 Now write a letter of apology and explanation for one of the following situations:

● You were unable to attend an important meeting yesterday in a town 70 kilometres from your home. Your train broke down between stations and you were stuck for two hours. When the train was repaired, it returned to the station where you had started your journey. You were unable to contact anyone by phone.

● You are a student who has been late for morning classes again and again. You have been asked to write a letter of apology to the Principal (or Head Teacher) explaining your lateness. Your problem is that you have had to take your younger sister to school for the last two weeks because your mother has been ill. She is better now and there should be no problem in future.

SKILLS 53

7 HEALTH

STAYING HEALTHY

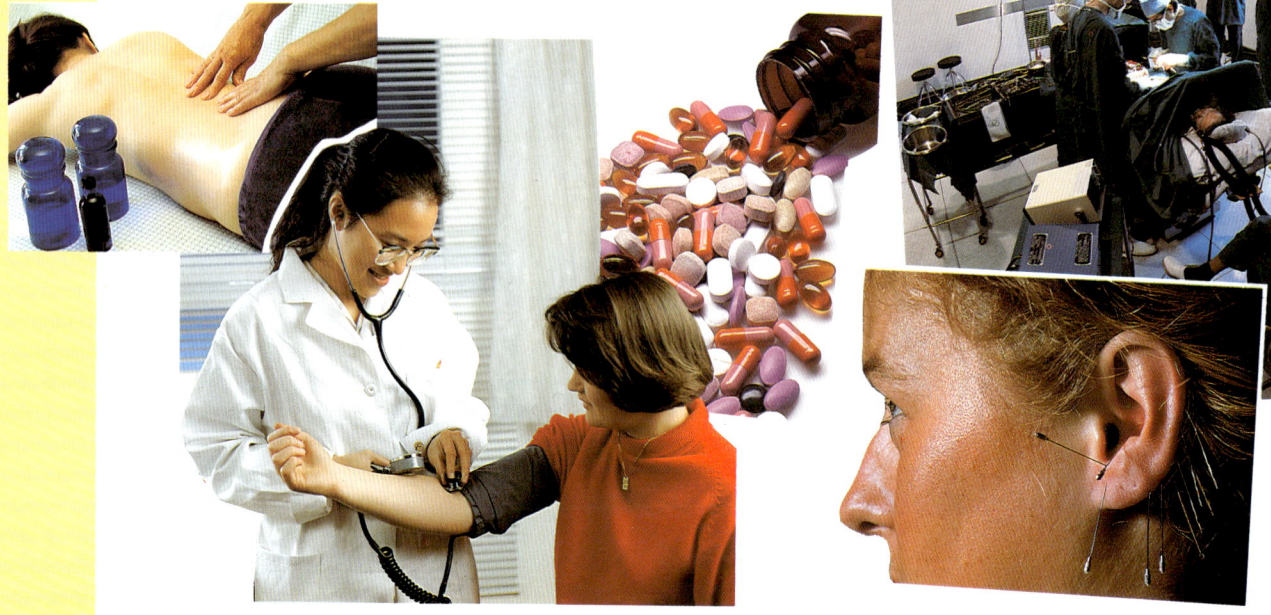

Discussion

1 Look at the pictures, and talk about the different kinds of treatment being offered.

1 What sort of treatment do you prefer when you are ill? Why? How successful is it?
2 Is there any kind of treatment which you have heard about and would like to try?

Listening

You are going to hear two doctors talking. One practises 'conventional' Western medicine; the other is an 'alternative' doctor who uses the ancient Chinese form of treatment known as acupuncture.

Before listening

2 Find out what these mean:

GP   massage   prescription
NHS   arthritis

3 Listen to both extracts, and answer these questions briefly:

1 What differences are mentioned between the two forms of treatment?
2 To what extent does each doctor agree that the other form of treatment is useful?

4 Listen again and answer these questions:

1 What does the 'alternative' doctor mean by a person's 'whole being'?
2 What example does she give to show what she means by treating the whole being?
3 Does she feel that drugs are ever useful in treating patients?
4 What does the 'conventional' doctor mean by treating people 'in a whole sense'?
5 Why is this more difficult for a GP to do?

Intonation

5 Listen to two sentences contrasting conventional and alternative medicine, using 'whereas' to emphasise the contrast. Listen particularly to the stress patterns. Practise saying these sentences. Then make sentences with 'whereas' to compare the two types of medicine in terms of:

1 time
2 money
3 methods of treatment

Are these contrasts true of medicine in your own country?

54 SKILLS

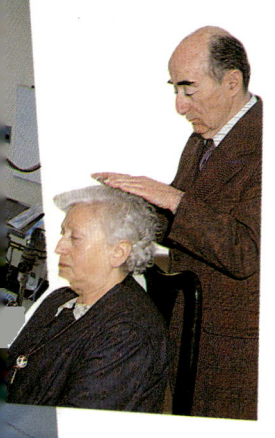

Discussion

6 In the listening extract, the second doctor says that one view of conventional medicine is: 'Here is a prescription, there is the door; go away and take it.' Is this your experience of doctors?

Reading

7 Read this extract from a magazine article and summarise, in your own words, the writer's main point.

Stop telling us to stop it

Many years ago, when I was a boy, a cartoon in *Punch* magazine pictured a young housewife addressing her small daughter and saying: 'Go and see what Johnny's doing and tell him to stop it.' I suspected that the lady was a doctor taking time off from her career to start a family, for her words were pure doctor-speak.

Now I'm all for health education, and *preventive medicine*, and healthy living, and I agree that it's stupid to spend enormous quantities of money and effort on attempting to cure diseases which ought never to have happened in the first place, but need doctors make us feel quite so sinful and guilty?

Doctors have some positive advice to give, such as eating lots of fruit and vegetables, and going for long walks, but most of the time what they are saying is 'Stop it'! Stop drinking. Stop eating salt. Stop worrying. Stop spreading butter on your bread. And most of all, of course, stop smoking. All good advice, maybe, but must they make it a *moral issue*?

In short, doctors should learn to serve rather than to direct.

Adapted from *New Scientist*, 27 October 1990

8
1. What does the writer mean by 'doctor-speak' at the end of the first paragraph?
2. How do doctors make us feel guilty?

preventive medicine = medical treatment which is given to healthy people to make sure that they do not become ill

moral issue = a question of right or wrong

Discussion

9 Read the article again quickly.

1. The writer lists things doctors tell us *not* to do. Why are these things bad for us? Have they become 'a moral issue' in your own country? (Think, for example, about attitudes to smokers.)
2. Is a doctor's duty to serve the public or to direct people's behaviour? Give reasons for your views.

SEE ALSO: Vocabulary (Health, lists A–C), page 92; Grammar (Comparative adjectives), page 130; (Modifying the verb 2), page 153; (Verbs followed by *to* + inf. / noun *to* + inf. / clause *that*), pages 154–5; Tapescripts, page 189; Teacher's Book.

GETTING ENOUGH SLEEP?

Reading and speaking

1 Do you ever have difficulty getting to sleep? Look at these people. Why can't they sleep? Can you think of any other possible reasons?

2 Now read this case study about a woman who has difficulty sleeping. Answer the questions *using your own words*:

1 What stops Mrs M. sleeping?
2 How are her personality and behaviour affected?
3 What possible solutions can you suggest for her problem?

3 In pairs, act out a conversation between Mrs M. and a friend. Use this structure to help you:

MRS M.: I feel dreadful! I just can't seem to get to sleep at night!
FRIEND: Oh, I know. It's terrible when you can't sleep. What do you think the problem is?
MRS M.: (*Give details, explain how you feel.*)
FRIEND: (*Make a suggestion.*)
MRS M.: (*Explain why that's not a good idea.*)
FRIEND: (*Make another suggestion.*)
MRS M.: (*Agree to try, thank friend.*)

4 Now listen to one way of having this conversation.

A CASE STUDY

Mrs M. is 56 years old and has been suffering from insomnia for a long time. When she goes to bed at 11 o'clock, she lies awake for an hour or two, while the events of the day and problems go round and round in her head: frictions with her co-workers, a large dentist's bill that will soon have to be paid, her mother's poor health. She is unable to relax, and instead keeps mulling over all these things, so that sleep refuses to come. Every night when Mrs M. goes to bed, she is afraid that she will not be able to get to sleep again. Her alarm clock rings at 6.30 in the morning. She has to get up, even though she feels miserable and exhausted. During the day she cannot keep her mind on her work; she is grouchy, short-tempered, and nervous.

Adapted from *Secrets of Sleep* by Borbely, Penguin Books

7 HEALTH

Listening and speaking

5 🔊 Listen to a conversation between a doctor and her patient and complete this summary. Listen again to check your answers.

The patient's problem is _____. He is worried because this has now lasted for _____. The doctor asks him whether _____. He replies that he _____. The doctor advises him to _____. If the problem continues, he should _____.

Asking and persuading

6 Now imagine that you are the patient. You are desperate to sleep and you insist on being given sleeping pills. Try and persuade the doctor (another student) to give you some. Some useful expressions are given on the right.

Patient:
I need . . .
I'm desperate . . .
Look, I really must insist that . . .
Would it not be possible . . . ?
I'm afraid I can't accept that . . .

Doctor:
I'm afraid I can't . . .
You don't need . . .
Have you tried . . . ?
Why don't you . . . ?

Describing, making comparisons

7 We asked 10 people in each of the age groups below to tell us about their own and their children's sleeping habits. The figures in the chart show an *average* for each group. Study the chart carefully and compare the different age groups. Use words and phrases like these:

Generalising	Comparing	Noting similarities
in general	compared with	just as
on average	while, whereas	about the same
on the whole	in contrast to	similar
generally speaking	however, but	too, also, as well

SEE ALSO: Vocabulary (Health, lists A, B, C, and F), pages 92–3; Grammar (Comparative adjectives), page 130; (Reporting statements and questions), pages 150–1; (Modifying the verb 2), page 153; Tapescripts, page 189; Teacher's Book.

7 | HEALTH

Example:
Children aged between one and five sleep about 12 hours a day on average, while teenagers sleep for about eight hours a day.

HABITS

Age	<1	1 - 5	6 - 10	11 - 20	21 - 50	51 - 70	71+
Total hours of sleep	14	12	10	8	7	8	7
Number of times a day	3	2	1	1	1	1	3
Time of day/night	a.m. p.m. night	p.m. night	night	night	night	night	p.m. night
Feelings on waking	unhappy and hungry	wide awake	wide awake	don't want to get up except on weekend		drowsy and bad tempered tired	
Techniques for getting to sleep	feed rock sing music	read play	read drink	read music TV	drink relax read TV	read pills	read pills

SKILLS 57

A healthy body

Listening

1 🔊 Look at the drawings below while you listen to the tape. A teacher is giving instructions. In which order does she describe these positions and movements?

A B C D E F G H I J

Understanding and giving instructions

2 🔊 Now listen again, and this time do the exercises yourself. (If you are not well, or are not accustomed to exercise, watch while the other members of the class try to follow the tape.) Then *you* try to give the instructions to your partner.

3 Which muscles do you think each exercise is designed to strengthen? Remember which part of your body you could feel while you were doing each exercise, and make sentences like the example below.
Here are some words you may need for parts of the body:

thighs   back   waist   chest
stomach   shoulders   arms

Example:
Exercise D is designed to strengthen the back muscles.

Speaking

4 In pairs, look at the pictures of different strokes in swimming. Choose one and discuss the instructions you would give someone who does not know how to do the stroke. Think about what they should do, and how they should do it.
Here are some useful words:

raise   lower   bend   push   pull   kick
stretch   move   turn

5 Join another pair and tell them your instructions. Ask them to guess which stroke you are describing, and to tell you how the instructions could be made clearer.

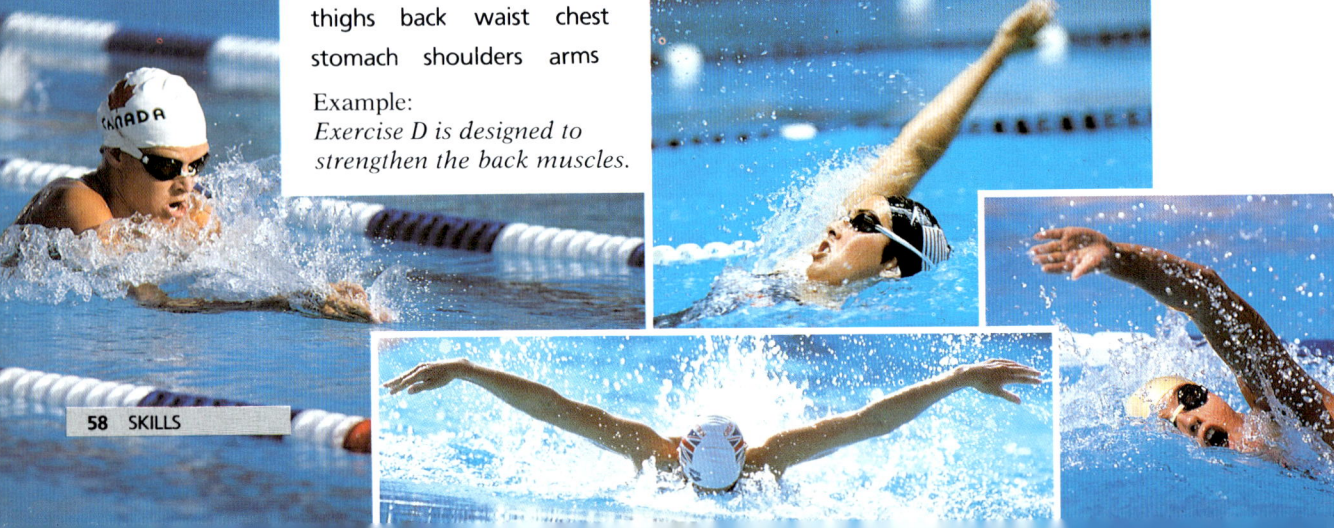

7 | HEALTH

58 SKILLS

Reading and speaking

6 Look at the instructions below, and try to identify:

- the place and situation
- the speaker / writer
- the listener / reader

1 Keep warm, and drink plenty of liquid.

2 Add 15 and 23, and then take away 7.

3 Bake at a low temperature for 45 minutes.

4 Open your mouth – and a little wider!

5 Please switch machine off after use.

6 Photographs: Do not bend!

7 Keep both hands on the wheel . . . that's right . . . and stay close to the kerb . . .

8 Keep out of direct sunlight, and water not more than once a week.

9 Listen when I'm speaking to you, boy!

10 Put your feet up and relax!

7 HEALTH

Writing

7 The pictures show you how to do a simple yoga exercise.
Write a list of the verbs and nouns that you need to describe the movements. Ask another student or your teacher if you are not sure of a word.

Examples:
  Nouns: floor, legs
  Verbs: sit, stretch

8 Write careful, detailed instructions for a reader who wants to try the exercises. When you finish your first draft, you will find it helpful if you can persuade a friend to do the exercise following your instructions. You will then know what additional information you need to include in your corrected version.

SEE ALSO: Vocabulary (Health, lists D and E), pages 92–3; Grammar (Multi-part verbs), pages 148–9; Tapescripts, page 189; Teacher's Book.

SKILLS 59

8 BUSINESS

The right job?

Discussion

1 Look at the photographs.

1 What jobs are the people doing?
2 What kinds of skills are needed for each of these jobs? In other words, what does each person have to be *good at* to be effective in the job?

Listening

You are going to hear an interview with the manager of an estate agency. Estate agents help people to buy and sell property, and then they take a percentage of the sale price.

2 What kind of skills do you think are needed by:

1 an estate agent?
2 the manager of a small business?

3 Now listen to a man who is both an estate agent and the manager of a small business. As you listen, write down the skills that he mentions under these headings:

'People' skills
Special knowledge
Organisational skills

60 SKILLS

4 🎧 Listen again and match each of the expressions underlined in the sentences with one of a similar meaning below:

financial records   encourage   confidence   about   are likely to

1 ... the skills that are to do with dealing with people ...
2 It's terribly important that I win people's trust.
3 ... I have to motivate all the people who work in the office to sell as many houses as possible.
4 ... I have to keep my own accounts ...
5 ... they tend to sell in the spring and summer.

5 Using what the estate agent said about his business, and any similar experience you have, what qualities do you think he looks for in his employees?

Reading and discussion

6 How do you work with other people? Do you know your own personal strengths and weaknesses? Look at these 'types' below and decide which you are. (Most people feel they are a combination of at least two.) Then ask your partner. Find out *why* your partner considers him / herself to be a certain type.

Type	Qualities
A	Well-organised, practical, hard-working, unwilling to change.
B	Calm, self-confident. Good at encouraging others, but few new ideas.
C	Active and creative, but impatient with others.
D	Intelligent, imaginative but often impractical. Finds it difficult to work with others.
E	Enthusiastic about new tasks and good at communicating with others, but interest soon disappears.
F	Unemotional and careful. Good at analysing situations and able to take hard decisions. Bad at communicating with other people.
G	Sensitive and good at working with other people. Has difficulty making quick decisions.
H	Well-organised and concerned with detail. Worried that everything should be perfect.

7 Which type or types of person do you think would be good at:

1 chairing meetings?
2 working on a committee?
3 running a small company?

SEE ALSO: Vocabulary (Business, lists A–C), pages 94–5; Grammar (Tenses 1), page 136; (Linkers), page 170; (Linking ideas with general words), pages 180–1; Tapescripts, page 189; Teacher's Book.

Applying for a job

Reading and speaking

1 Look at these job advertisements. Which job would be suitable for someone who:

1 enjoys travelling?
2 has business experience and wants responsibility?
3 can't work during the day?
4 has good telephone skills?
5 can't work in the evenings or at weekends?

2 Stephen Baker has applied for the job of Marketing Assistant. He telephoned the number in the advertisement and was sent further details about the job. Then he sent in his application form and was invited to go for an interview.

Look at the application form and the job details below. Make notes on the following:

1 What questions do you think Stephen needs to ask at the interview to find out more about the job?
2 What questions do you think the interviewers will want to ask Stephen?

PART TIME
SALES CONSULTANT

required for our store in Oxford selling distinctive clothes for women and children. Hours: 16 per week. 8.45 am–5.45 pm. Two days per week. Rate of pay £3.50 per hour.

If you would like to join a lively energetic team, please telephone Jane Brown on 0865 672418 for further details and an application form.

Supergear, 45 South Street,
Oxford OX1 39Y

OFFICE CLEANER

A vacancy exists for a central office in London. Only mature, reliable and conscientious, hardworking persons need apply. Hours 5.30–8.30 am Monday to Friday inclusive.

In return we offer
£3.50 per hour.

Apply to:
Mrs M. Brown,
London & South East
Haulage Company,
Camden Road,
London NW1 3TU
Telephone:
071 398 2788

MARKETING ASSISTANT

Enjoy working within this small team, liaising with clients and co-ordinating travel etc.

Good communication and word processing skills needed plus enthusiasm and cheerfulness. Good salary and some foreign travel.

Call Sylvia White on Manchester (061) 272 9485 now for immediate attention.

Opening soon
BRISTOL'S NEWEST NIGHTCLUB

invite applications for the post of
MANAGER

Applicants must have had experience in this field and possess good organising skills

Apply in the first instance by telephone to Mr Ryan on Bristol (0272) 714360

JOB DESCRIPTION
JOB TITLE:
MARKETING ASSISTANT

The Marketing Assistant will work in the Marketing Department with responsibility for arranging trips and shows, sending out publicity, keeping records of clients and providing secretarial support to two marketing managers. There is some evening and weekend work, especially on overseas trips.

NAME: Stephen Baker
AGE: 23
MARITAL STATUS: Single

QUALIFICATIONS:
'A' level French, English
Completed first year of university course
Diploma in word processing

WORK EXPERIENCE:
1 year as a waiter in France
1 year as administrative assistant in a small company in London

8 BUSINESS

62 SKILLS

Listening

3 Now listen to the interview. Check to see if your predictions were correct, then answer the questions below:

1 The interview had three main stages. Which order were they in?
  A Stephen's questions
  B general questions to Stephen
  C questions about Stephen's application form
2 Which was the main tense or verb structure used at each stage of the interview? Write down one question from each stage.
3 What does the interviewer say when she asks Stephen if he wants to ask any questions?
4 Do you think Stephen is a good person for the job? Why / why not?

Speaking

4 Here are the details of two other people who applied for the job. Interview one or both of them. Before you begin, prepare the questions you want to ask at each stage. The person taking the role of the interviewee should add to the details any others that may be necessary.

SEE ALSO: Vocabulary (Business, list C), page 95; Grammar (Tenses 1 and 3), pages 136 and 138–9; (Reporting statements and questions), pages 150–1; (Conditionals), pages 168–9; (Questions and answers 1), page 171; Tapescripts, pages 189–90; Teacher's Book.

NAME: Sally Jeffreys
AGE: 27
MARITAL STATUS: Single
QUALIFICATIONS: BA in History
Typing certificate
Certificate in Marketing
WORK EXPERIENCE: 3 years as an air hostess
2 years as a trainee manager in a supermarket

NAME: Arthur Peacock
AGE: 34
MARITAL STATUS: Married
QUALIFICATIONS: Secondary school Certificate (ordinary level)
Typing certificate
WORK EXPERIENCE: 3 years as a driver
5 years as a bank clerk
6 years running own shop

Dealing with companies

Listening and speaking on the phone
Being polite

1 📼 When we speak to people we don't know on the telephone, we use polite phrases. Try to make this conversation more 'polite'. Then listen to the conversation on the tape and compare.

SECRETARY: Hello? Who's that?
CALLER: My name's Smith. I want to speak to Mr Jones.
SECRETARY: Why?
CALLER: Because he asked me to call him.
SECRETARY: OK. Wait a minute . . . No he's busy . . . Call back later if you want.

Getting through

2 📼 Dealing with companies on the phone can be annoying. It's often difficult to find the person you want to speak to. Listen to another phone conversation, then answer these questions:

1 What's the problem?
2 Can you think of any other reasons the secretary could give for not being able to put the caller through?

Practise the conversation with your partner, using different reasons for not connecting the caller.

Making an appointment

3 Make these sentences more 'polite':

1 I want to make an appointment with Ms Brown.
2 What do you want to see her about?
3 You can see her at 4 o'clock on Tuesday.

4 📼 Now listen to the conversation. Were your improvements to the sentences above the same as those used in the conversation?

5 Working in pairs, one of you is the caller and wants to make an appointment with the manager; the other is the manager's secretary. Use the diaries below to arrange a time.

CALLER'S DIARY

9-12 Meeting then lunch.

10 Meet Peter at airport. Rest of day holiday.

a.m. Managing Director's visit.

8-10 Breakfast meeting. Lunch with staff.

Training Day

MS BROWN'S DIARY

MONDAY 19th
Meeting all day

TUESDAY 20th
9-10 Visit exhibition
p.m. Staff meeting

WEDNESDAY 21st
Holiday

THURSDAY 22nd
9-11 Interviews
2-4 Interviews

FRIDAY 23rd
8 a.m. Leave for Poland

8 | BUSINESS

64 SKILLS

Preparing for writing
A letter of complaint

The language in the conversations opposite is quite formal. We also use formal language when we *write* to companies and organisations, for example to make a complaint.

6 Look at this letter and match the paragraphs to these descriptions:

Request for action   Reason for writing   The problem

> 22 High Street
> Birmingham
>
> 22nd March 1992
>
> The Manager
> Home Shopping
> Corn Street
> Birmingham
>
> Dear Sir / Madam,
>
> I am writing to complain about a radio I bought in your shop last Saturday. When I got home, I turned the radio on. At first there was no problem, but after a few minutes I noticed that it was becoming very hot. Soon after, smoke began to come out of the back of the radio so I rushed to take out the plug.
>
> I am returning the radio with this letter and a copy of my receipt. Please send me a full refund as soon as possible.
>
> Yours faithfully,
> George Thompson
> George Thompson

Writing

7 Now you write a letter of complaint to a company. Choose one of the following situations. Use the model in exercise 6 above to help you.

- You buy a music cassette. You find there is nothing on it!
- You buy a book. You find there are some pages missing!
- You buy a table. When it is delivered you find it is damaged!

SEE ALSO: Vocabulary (Business, list D), page 95; Grammar (Modals 2), pages 144–5; (Verbs followed by *to* + inf. / noun *to* + inf. / clause *that*), pages 154–5; Tapescripts, page 190; Teacher's Book.

8 BUSINESS

SKILLS 65

9 POWER

Power in conversation

Discussion

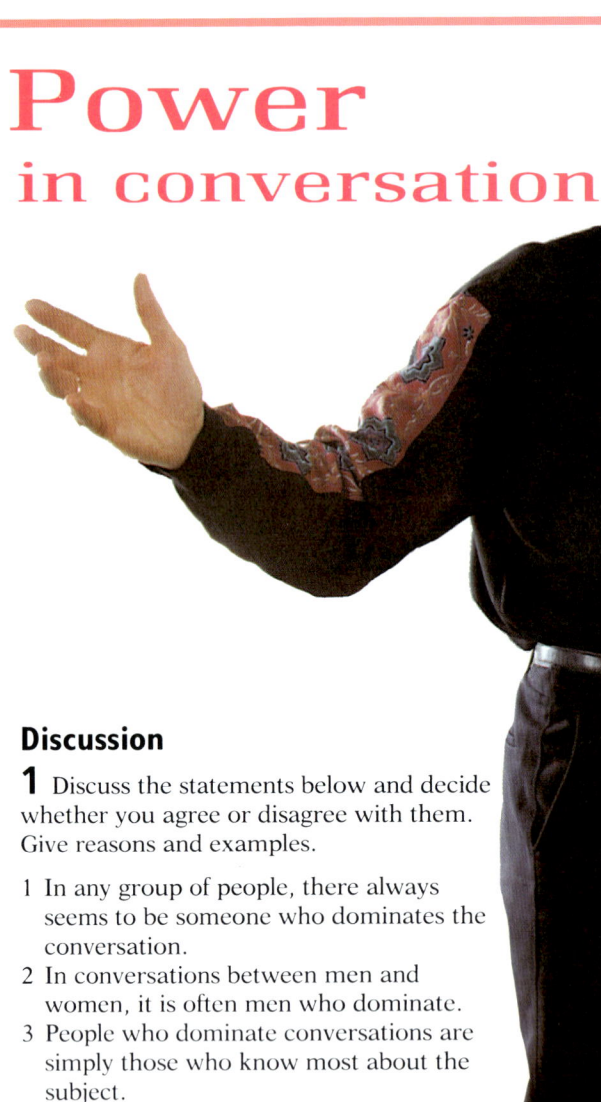

1 Discuss the statements below and decide whether you agree or disagree with them. Give reasons and examples.

1 In any group of people, there always seems to be someone who dominates the conversation.
2 In conversations between men and women, it is often men who dominate.
3 People who dominate conversations are simply those who know most about the subject.

Listening

2 Listen to a group of people having a discussion about how people dominate others in conversation, and then answer the following questions:

1 According to the speakers, how do individuals dominate conversations? For example: they talk loudly.
2 What differences are mentioned between the ways men and women speak? For example: women are said to be 'good listeners'.
3 Do you agree with the opinions expressed? Can you think of any other ways in which people dominate conversations?

Speaking

Interrupting politely

In any language, there are rules for politely interrupting someone who is speaking. In one-to-one conversation, we usually wait until someone has finished. But what do we do in a larger group of people?

3 There are a number of useful expressions for interrupting politely. Which of these are polite?

A Excuse me . . .
B May I say something . . . ?
C I don't agree . . .
D Could I interrupt you for a moment . . . ?
E You're quite wrong . . .
F Just a moment . . .
G I'm sorry, but I feel I have to speak . . .
H Sorry, but . . .

In fact, these expressions are only *really* polite if they are said when the speaker has finished making a point, but you may have to wait a long time!

Intonation

4 Listen to the tape. For each extract, decide whether the speaker has finished making a point (and therefore it is polite to interrupt) or not.

1 It was terrible . . . the rain was pouring down, the wind was blowing, it was so cold I could hardly move my fingers . . .
2 She asked me to get something from the shops for her . . .
3 He told me he couldn't come . . .
4 Nobody understands what she means . . .
5 So there he was, standing all alone in the street . . .

What do you notice about the speaker's voice at the end of each of the above extracts? Can you make a rule?

5 The teacher will give a short talk which you may interrupt with polite questions. However, the teacher will *not* pay any attention to interruptions that are impolite. Use one expression from each of the two boxes below when you interrupt. And don't forget, only interrupt when the speaker has finished making a point.

Attracting attention	Excuse me . . . I'd like to ask a question . . . May I ask something . . . ? Could I interrupt for a moment . . . ? Sorry, but . . .

Asking for repetition	Could you repeat . . .
Asking for clarification	Could you explain . . .
Asking for an example	Could you give an example . . .
Asking for more information	Could you give us some more information . . .

SEE ALSO: Vocabulary (Power, lists A and B), page 96; Grammar (Tenses 1), page 136; Tapescripts, page 190; Teacher's Book.

9 POWER

SKILLS 67

THE POWER OF THE WAY YOU LOOK

Discussion

1 Look at these pictures and decide what each person's job is:

1 TV personality
2 Teacher
3 Politician
4 Librarian
5 Office worker
6 Shop assistant

What features of their personal appearance affected your decisions?

Listening

2 Listen to some more extracts from the conversation you heard earlier. What features of people's appearance do the speakers think may affect a person's power over others?

3 Listen again.

1 One of the speakers says 'Sad, isn't it!' What is sad?
2 What do you think 'props' are?
3 What does the American survey show?

Listening and speaking

4 Listen to your teacher.

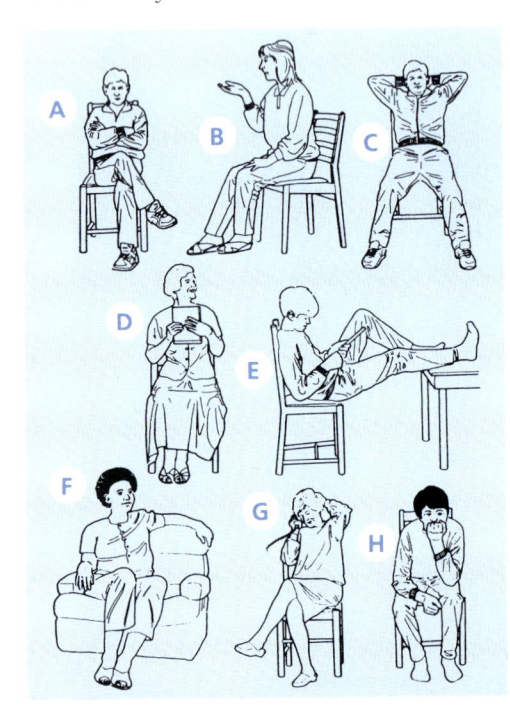

9 POWER

68 SKILLS

Reading
Body language

5 Do our bodies give away information about what we're really feeling? A lot has been written about 'body language' in the United States, but are the claims true for people in other parts of the world? Read the newspaper article on the right and think about your own country. Decide for yourself!

YOUR BODY – do you know what it's saying?

Body language experts claim that they can tell a lot about us by the way we stand, the way we sit, the way we greet each other. Are they right?

■ **PERSONAL SPACE**

Do you feel uncomfortable when someone you don't know very well stands too close? Experts say that 50 centimetres is about the minimum distance we need between ourselves and others. And anyone who comes closer than that (except for family and close friends!) is showing signs of wanting to dominate us. When you take a seat on a bus or train, do you find the largest unoccupied space and sit in the middle of it? Most people apparently do.

■ **GREETING PEOPLE**

When you shake hands with someone you meet, which way does your palm point? Offering the hand with the palm upwards shows openness; the palm facing downwards is a sign of dominance. Other signs of dominance include any other touching while shaking hands – for example, holding a person's shoulder or arm with your other hand.

■ **BARRIERS**

Do you cross your arms or legs when you speak? Do you sometimes hold papers or a book in front of you? Do you prefer to sit behind a desk when talking to people? We use all of these as barriers to protect us from possible threats.

■ **SHOWING AGGRESSION**

Do you ever stand with your legs slightly apart and your hands on your hips? Do you ever sit with your legs apart and your hands together behind your head? If you do, you are showing signs of aggression!

6

1 What do you think of the claims made in this article? Are they true, in your experience?
2 What is going on in the pictures below . . .
  a according to the text?
  b according to people's behaviour in your own country?

SEE ALSO: Vocabulary (Power, list C), page 97; Grammar (Joining nouns: 's, *of* and ∅), page 131; (Modifying the noun), pages 132–3; (Tenses 1), page 136; (Modals 1 and 3), pages 142–3 and 146; Tapescripts, page 190; Teacher's Book.

A   B   C   D   E

THE POWER OF

Discussion

1 Look at these three advertisements.

1 Describe the pictures.
2 What are they advertising?
3 Why are the advertisements like this? Why do you think they might make people buy the products?
4 How do advertisers try to persuade people? Make a list of all the techniques you can think of.

A

It doesn't bear thinking about

The thought of child injury is horrifying. Yet thinking about it is exactly what wise parents do. Because in the security of the home lie many dangers for babies and toddlers.

Stairs are just one example. And 'I didn't think he'd go near' is the sad cry after countless accidents.

So all round the house, Hago products protect.

Carefully designed to keep children safe, with thought for adults too. Our sturdy Stair Gate has a conveniently wider centre opening and lower step-over. With an easy-fit extension if needed. Simple to fit and remove from stairways or doors, keeping the most determined toddler from danger areas.

Wherever inquisitive fingers and unsteady limbs put young children at risk, Hago safeguards them. Against dangers, in every room.

HAGO
SAFEGUARDING YOUR FAMILY

Hago
– safeguarding your family

B

C

The rich guys shouldn't have all the fun.

9 POWER

70 SKILLS

ADVERTISEMENTS

Dream of a garden so fragrant that you'll never want to leave.

Reading and speaking

2 Look at some of the techniques that advertisers use, listed on the left below. Match them with the correct explanation on the right.

1 Repetition
2 Reward
3 Imitation
4 Envy
5 Agreement with values
6 Punishment

A You want to be like the people in the advertisement.
B You find the argument in the advertisement sensible and convincing.
C You see the name of the product many times.
D You see an ideal situation that you would very much like to be in yourself.
E You feel you deserve a product like that.
F You will feel guilty if you don't buy the product.

3 Now look again at the three advertisements in exercise 1. Which of the techniques listed above are being used in each?

Writing

4 Look at the picture below. It is taken from an advertisement for the Post Office which encourages us to send letters to our friends and relatives overseas. The words have been removed from the advertisement. Write about 50 words that could go with the picture and encourage people to use the service.

Before you write
- Think about all the possible reasons why people should use the postal service.
- Think about the techniques that advertisers use (listed in exercise 2 above).

After you have written
- Read the original text from the advertisement, which is in the Key (page 183). How does it compare with yours?

le Jardin
MAX FACTOR

le Jardin
The incurably romantic fragrance.

SEE ALSO: Grammar (Modals 1), pages 142–3; (Linkers), page 170; Teacher's Book.

9 POWER

SKILLS 71

10 HUMOUR

The Cartoonist

Discussion

1 Look at the cartoon on the right.

1 Do you find it amusing?
2 Describe the situation. What can you say about the two people? What are the words that are usual in this situation in your country? Do you know what they are in Britain?
3 What does the cartoon tell us about cartoonists?

Reading

2 You are going to read part of the introduction to one of Mel Calman's books. Before you read, discuss what you think a day in the life of a cartoonist is like. Then read the extract and find something which surprises you.

> I get up about 8.30 a.m. – reluctantly. I eat a small breakfast and shave a small portion of my face. I dress and drive to my studio. I look at the clutter of years of old drawings and magazines, and shudder. Must tidy all this tomorrow, I say to myself. I sharpen pencils, read my mail, put on some music, then go out for a second breakfast.
>
> During the day I grapple with bits of advertising work, illustrate articles and think of jokes. At the end of the afternoon on four days of the week, I go to *The Times*. I consult the oracles about the choice of subject. There is nothing funny happening in the world. I try to find a fresh approach to the same old problems. I read the papers, I listen to the radio, I even talk to journalists. I hope to find a joke lurking somewhere among the clutter of my desk and mind.
>
> I never planned to be a cartoonist. It happened to me over the years, in the same way that one acquires a mortgage and grey hairs.

From *What Else Do you Do?* by Mel Calman, Methuen, 1986

3

1 Summarise in your own words how the cartoonist spends his day.
2 What does the text tell you about his character?
3 Where do his cartoons appear?
4 Where do his ideas come from?
5 How did he become a cartoonist?

4

1 Find a word in the passage which means:
   a letters that arrive through the post
   b people who can give good advice
   c a room where artists work
   d without enthusiasm
   e work hard to do something difficult
2 Find these words. What part of speech are they? What do you think they mean?
   a shudder
   b a fresh approach
   c clutter
   d lurking
   e mortgage (This is connected with your house or flat.)

5

1 Most of the passage is written in one tense. What is it? Why?
2 Find two words, phrases or clauses which show that the passage is intended to be amusing.

Listening

6 You are going to hear Mel Calman talking about his work. Look first at how he begins:

'If you can say something that's mildly shocking that isn't in such bad taste that it frightens people, or – no, sorry – distresses people, that can also be funny . . .'

1 Does the cartoonist want to:
   A shock people slightly?
   B offend people?
   C frighten people?
   D make people unhappy?
   E amuse people?
2 Why does he say 'no, sorry'?

7 Look at the words below, which he uses to talk about a story that was in the news. What do you think happened? (Check any new words in your dictionary.)

spaghetti restaurant
terrorism   siege
hostages   surrender
release

8 Now listen to what he says, and then answer these questions:

1 What was Mel Calman's cartoon about the spaghetti restaurant siege? Describe the picture. What was written in the cartoon?
2 Why did people find it amusing?
3 Why do you think he waited a week before doing the cartoon?

SEE ALSO: Vocabulary (Humour, list C), page 99; Grammar (Tenses 1), page 136; Tapescripts, page 190; Teacher's Book.

10 HUMOUR

SKILLS 73

jokes

Discussion

1 Look at these jokes.

1 Which ones do you find funny? Why?
2 Which do you not find funny? Why?
3 Describe the jokes. First describe the cartoon picture; then try to explain why it is supposed to be amusing.

A

'We had the Brown family for dinner on Monday evening.'

B

'WANTED – MAN TO WASH DISHES AND TWO WAITRESSES.'

C

THE YUPPIES by ANNIE TEMPEST

WHAT ARE YOU WOMEN GOSSIPING ABOUT?

DON'T TELL ME! LEG WAXES, BABIES AND BOYFRIENDS?

NO, TONY. THE SECOND LAW OF THERMODYNAMICS.

© Associated Newspapers Ltd. 1990

10 HUMOUR

74 SKILLS

The terror of a man who thinks he is going bald

"ONE SNIGGER AND YOU'RE DEAD!"

"DOCTOR, I THINK I'VE CAUGHT SOMETHING"

SEE ALSO: Vocabulary (Humour, lists A–C), pages 98–9; Grammar (Modifying the noun), pages 132–3; (Tenses 3), pages 138–9; (Linking ideas by reference), pages 178–9; Tapescripts, page 190; Teacher's Book.

Listening and speaking

2 Listen to a man telling a joke. This is the last line:

'I had a car like that once.'

Do you find it funny? If so, why?

3 Try to answer these questions. Then listen again to check your answers:

1 Where are the two men in the joke from?
2 In what way are their two farms different?
3 How does the second man describe his farm?

4 Listen to the joke again. Listen carefully to the part where the Englishman is describing the area his farm covers.

1 What happens to the speaker's intonation at the points underlined? This is what he says:

'Well, it goes up to the house over there, you see, and then back across to those trees, then down here to this little stream, and back to where we're standing.'

What does the intonation tell us at each point? Practise saying the sentence yourself.
2 Now we hear the Texan speaking. Which words does he stress most when he speaks? Why does he stress these words?

'Man,' he said, 'in my spread back in Texas, in my car it takes me a whole day just to drive around it!'

5 The joke is told by an Englishman. Which of the two people in the joke is being laughed at? Are there similar jokes in your own country? What other groups of people, situations or things are the subjects of jokes?

6 Listen. Here is another joke, just for fun. It is set in a supermarket. Do you find it funny? If so, why?

10 HUMOUR

SKILLS 75

TELLING STORIES

Preparing for writing

It is very common for people to tell or write stories about amusing things that have happened to them. Below is a true story about a wedding.

1 Before reading, discuss this question: When people get married in your country, is it usual for friends to play jokes on them? If so, describe what they do.

2 While reading, answer these questions:

1 Do you think this story is told well? Why / why not?
2 How is the story organised? Divide the text into three parts according to these categories:

The amusing part
Background information
Events

> It was about a few years ago, I think... Barry and Julie, they're old friends of mine, they were getting married. And I decided... well not only me, there was a group of other friends too... we thought we'd decorate their car. You know, spray it with foam and tie all sorts of things to the back... that sort of thing. Of course, we didn't want them to know about it so we thought we'd do it just after the wedding... we knew they'd be busy talking to guests then.
>
> Anyway, after the wedding, everyone went to a hotel... it was quite near... for the reception. Barry and Julie parked their car... I remember it very well, it was a blue Fiat... they parked it in the street outside the hotel and we all went in. About an hour later we crept out and started on the car. We sprayed foam hearts on the windscreen and the back window, and put more foam on the side windows... then we tied a bunch of balloons and some ribbons to the aerial... oh, and a few more ribbons here and there to make it look colourful – they were pink, you see. Then someone found one of the doors was unlocked... so we opened it up and poured a mountain of confetti on the front seats!

10 | HUMOUR

76 SKILLS

By the time we'd finished, that car was a right mess! We quickly went back into the hotel and waited to see Barry and Julie's faces when they saw the car!

At the end of the reception everyone was getting ready to leave and all the guests went outside ... you know, to wave goodbye to the happy couple.

To our horror, Barry and Julie walked towards a taxi waiting outside the hotel entrance. As they passed us, Barry turned to me, glanced at the blue car and said with a grin – 'You'd better start cleaning my brother-in-law's car ... he's not going to be very pleased when he sees it!'

3 The story is written as somebody *said* it. If we wanted to *write* the story, we would need to make a lot of changes. Working with a partner, produce a written version of the first paragraph of the story.

4 Now tell the story again, *either* from Barry's point of view *or* from the brother-in-law's point of view.

SEE ALSO: Vocabulary (Humour, list D), page 99; Grammar (Modifying the noun), pages 132–3; (Linking ideas with phrases, by reference and with general words) pages 176–81; Teacher's Book.

Writing

5 Look at the cartoon sequence below. Imagine you are the man. Work with a partner and tell the story from that character's point of view.

6 *Write* the story, still imagining that you are the man. Write short paragraphs that describe what happened. Divide the text like this:

Paragraph 1: Pictures A, B and C
Paragraph 2: Pictures D and E
Paragraph 3: Picture F

VOCABULARY

This part of the book is for presentation, practice and reference. It looks at vocabulary – that is, words and phrases – in two sections:

WORD GROUPS

pages 80–99

A double-page unit for each of the ten themes in **Skills**. The words and phrases are listed by area of meaning.
Some important problems of pronunciation are also presented in each unit.

KEY WORDS

pages 100–17

A selection of problem words with practice exercises.

THE DICTIONARY – EXTENDING ITS USE
Exercises on using a dictionary

pages 118–19

WORD GROUPS

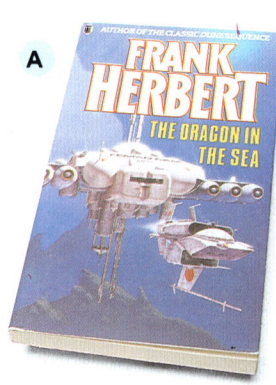

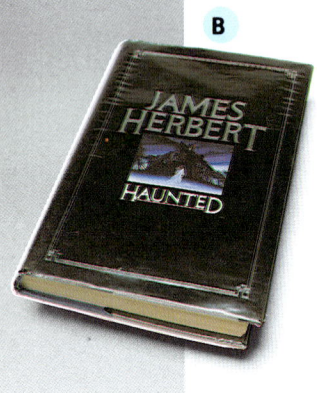

1
WRITING

A What kind of book is it?

fiction
a romantic novel
a detective story
a historical novel
a play
a textbook
non-fiction
science fiction
a ghost story
a collection of short stories
a collection of essays

B What's the story like?

exciting
frightening
interesting
ridiculous
terrifying
extraordinary
moving
humorous
boring
sad
funny
thrilling
dramatic
dull

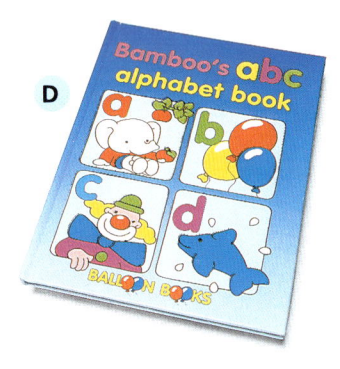

1 Grouping and matching

Look at the words in list A and then at the book covers. Are the books fiction (F) or non-fiction (NF)? What kind of book do you think each one is?

2 Selecting

Which words in list B mean that:

1 you did not find the story interesting?
2 you laughed as you read it?
3 you were impatient to find out what happened?
4 the story was in some way different from others you have read?
5 it made you feel like crying?
6 it made you feel afraid?
7 a lot happened in the story?

Look at the book covers again. In pairs, choose one adjective from the list which might describe each book or your feelings about it. Be prepared to explain your choice to the rest of the class.

VOCABULARY

WORD GROUPS

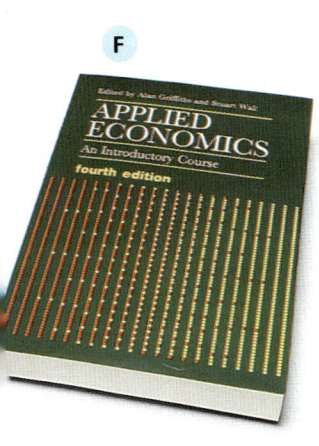

1
WRITING

C What does a story consist of?
plot
characters
narrative
description
dialogue
events
climax
ending
background
murder
mystery
romance
suspense

D How is a book organised?
front cover
back cover
title
blurb
biographical details
contents page
index
bibliography
reviews
chapters

F

G

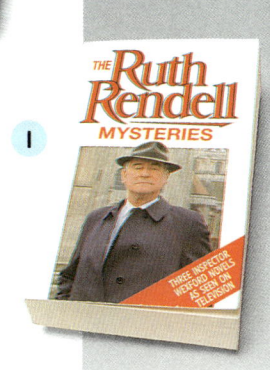

H

I

3 Completing a report

Use words from list C to complete the book report:

I have just read a book which I enjoyed very much. The main _____ are two men and a woman who is married to one of them. It's a _____ story because the woman is killed, but there is also some _____ since the single man is in love with the married woman and she tries to be kind to him. The _____ is quite complicated and very exciting. The _____ of the story comes when the husband kills his wife, thinking that she is going to leave him. My only criticism of the book is that there is not enough _____ between the characters, which would have broken up the long paragraphs of _____ and made it easier to read.

4 Matching

You want the information below. Which part of a book (list D) would you look at to see if it is suitable for your purposes?

1 the author's name
2 information about the writer's life
3 a brief summary of the contents to interest possible readers
4 suggestions for further reading on the same subject
5 a paragraph on a very specific point
6 the topic of each chapter

PRONUNCIATION
Running words together

1 🔊 Here are some words that occur in this unit. Listen to them carefully. What happens to the parts of the words in **bold**? Then repeat.

tex**t**book   ghos**t** story   fron**t** cover

The same thing happens in conversation. Listen.
You must be Andy.
That could be true.
Is that picture sold?
He's such a good boy!

2 🔊 Here are some more words from the unit in which a possible sound often disappears in conversation. Write down these words and circle the part of the word that is not sounded. Then check with the tape.

interesting   frightening   different

SEE ALSO: Skills, pages 18–23;
Tapescripts, pages 190–1;
Workbook, pages 6–7;
Teacher's Book.

VOCABULARY   81

WORD GROUPS

2 PRIVATE LIVES

A How do we want a partner to be?

warm	honest
affectionate	tidy
kind	sincere
open	friendly
loving	gentle
strong	patient
helpful	generous

B What interests do you have?

theatre	cinema
fashion	painting
literature	walking
architecture	building
driving	pottery
sports	travel
computers	music
countryside	flying

1 Gapfilling

Finish these sentences with words from list A:

1 John gets so angry when little things go wrong. I wish he were more _____ .
2 She never hides anything. She is such an _____ person.
3 I believe everything he says. He's very _____ .

2 Matching

Now find four words in list A that are similar in meaning.

3 Finding opposites

Find words in list A that mean the *opposite* of:

weak   mean   deceitful   messy

4 Words that go together

Look at the words below. Which of the words in list B do they go with?

Example: *fields – walking, countryside*

film	wings	plate
brush	shoes	bricks
gymnastics	actor	poem
passport	building	model
orchestra	program	car

5 Putting words into sentences

Make sentences for each of the words in list B as shown in the examples. Say what you really feel:

Examples:
I enjoy going to the theatre.
I am not interested in fashion.
I prefer driving to flying.

82 VOCABULARY

WORD GROUPS

C **How can we refer to groups of people?**

children	toddlers
teenagers	adults
middle-aged people	pensioners
	young people
babies	retired people

D **How do we refer to individuals?**
Mr (mɪstər)
Mrs (mɪsɪz)
Ms (/mɪz/ or /məz/)
Madam
Sir
Dad
Mum

2
PRIVATE LIVES

6 Putting words in groups

1 Two of the words in list C are general words. Together, they refer to all people. Which two words are they?

2 Write down all the words that refer to:
- people under eighteen
- people who have finished their working lives.

7 Putting words in order

Put these words in order of the age they refer to from youngest to oldest:

teenagers   toddlers   babies
pensioners   middle-aged people

8 Addressing people

Look at the words in list D and find the following:

1 one word that suggests a woman is married
2 two words that mean these people have children
3 an informal way of addressing your mother
4 two words that are very formal (usually used in formal letters or shops / restaurants)
5 two words that do not indicate whether a woman is married or has children

PRONUNCIATION
Running words together

The pronunciation of words on their own often changes when the words occur in normal running speech. Here are two useful areas.

1 *Words ending with **n** followed by words beginning with **b / p***
Listen. What happens to the sounds at the end of the words on the left when they occur in the contexts on the right? Then repeat.

eleven	Eleve**n p**eople are waiting outside.
one	There's only o**ne b**ag in the room.
can	I ca**n b**e there at six.

2 *Words ending with **n** followed by words beginning with **c / k***
Listen. What happens to the sounds at the end of the words on the left when they occur in the contexts on the right? Then repeat.

in	I'll see you i**n cl**ass tomorrow.
can	She ca**n g**o if she wants to.
again	You can see him agai**n, c**an't you?

SEE ALSO: Skills, pages 24–9;
Tapescripts, page 191;
Workbook, pages 8–9;
Teacher's Book.

VOCABULARY 83

WORD GROUPS

3
FEAR

A What frighten(s) you?

open spaces
old age
motorways
public speaking
crowds
heights
rats
ghosts
moths
flying
spiders
water

B How do you feel?

frightened
terrified
nervous
petrified
hysterical
worried
uneasy
anxious

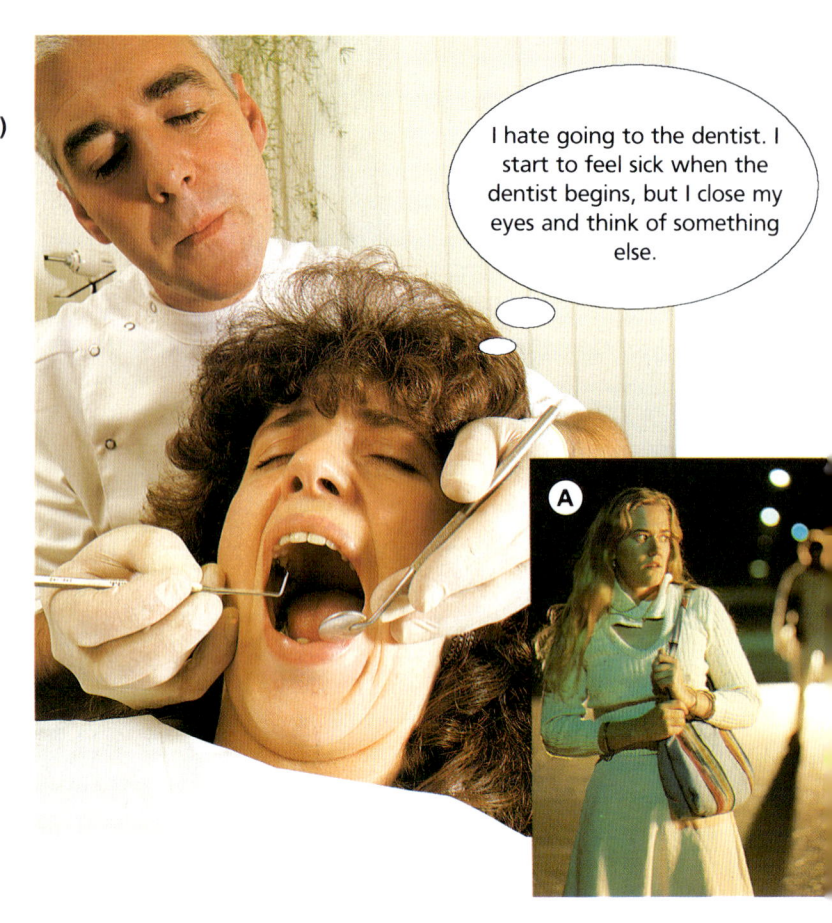

I hate going to the dentist. I start to feel sick when the dentist begins, but I close my eyes and think of something else.

1 Discussion

Look at list A:

1 What else are people commonly afraid of?
2 What is it about each of these things or situations that some people find frightening?
3 Divide the fears into those that are *rational* and those that are *irrational* in your opinion. Give reasons.

2 Putting words in order

Can you put the words in list B in order from the weakest (a little bit frightened) to the strongest (very frightened indeed)? Some words are of equal strength.

3 Gapfilling

Complete these sentences. Include *something you are frightened of* and *how you feel*. Use the expressions in lists A and B to help you:

Example: *I become anxious when I fly.*

1 _____ makes me _____ .
2 I am _____ of _____ .
3 Most people become _____ when they _____ .
4 I feel _____ when I see a _____ .
5 Some people are _____ just thinking about _____ .

84 VOCABULARY

WORD GROUPS

E How can other people help?
reassure
calm
listen
hug
understand
advise
recommend
cuddle
comfort
support

C What is your response to fear?
run away
sweat
feel sick
scream
cry

D How can you try to overcome your fears?
talk to a friend
try to relax
ignore them
see a doctor
be sensible

4 Speaking

Look at lists C and D. What other possible responses and solutions are there to fear?

5 Discussion

Discuss the situations illustrated above with your partner. Then, using the words from lists C and D, write briefly on how you respond in each situation and how you deal with any fear you have. An example has been done for you (the woman at the dentist's).

6 Putting words in groups

1 Which words in list E always involve:
- physical closeness?
- words?
- either of the above?

2 Which words from list E describe what the following speakers are doing?
   a Don't worry. It won't hurt you!
   b Yes. I know exactly what you mean.
   c You really should see someone about this.

PRONUNCIATION
Word stress — weak forms

1 Copy these sentences. Then listen to the tape and underline all the (ə) sounds:

   a The bags are in the car.
   b She can come tomorrow.
   c I've got some dollars.
   d He was so naughty!

2 The (ə) sound occurs very often. It occurs on *un*stressed words and parts of words. Try saying these sentences. Note the (ə) sounds and then check with the tape:

   a The man has been sent to prison.
   b There are some large birds in the garden.
   c Children have an advantage if they come from happy family backgrounds.

SEE ALSO: Skills, pages 30–5; Tapescripts, page 191; Workbook, pages 10–11; Teacher's Book.

3
FEAR

WORD GROUPS

A What kind of sport do you play?
- tennis
- hockey
- rugby
- athletics
- ice hockey
- gymnastics
- football
- badminton
- swimming
- squash

B Where are sports played?
- pitch
- court
- stadium
- track
- pool
- field
- rink

4 SPORT

1 Putting words in groups

1 Which of the sports in list A are played with a ball?
2 Which of the sports are usually played in *teams* and which by *individuals*?

2 Discussion

Which of the sports in list A do you play? Can you think of any others to add to the list?

3 Matching

Which words from list B are being referred to in the following sentences?

1 It *must* be grass.
2 These *can* be grass but need not be.
3 This is cold!
4 You run around this in a race.

4 Gapfilling

Finish these sentences with a word from list B:

1 Tennis is played on a _____ .
2 Ice hockey matches are held on an ice _____ .
3 Most swimming _____ in the UK are indoors.
4 Big events, such as important football matches or athletics meetings, are held in a _____ .
5 Most public parks have football _____ and running _____ that anyone can use.
6 Pitch and _____ are similar in meaning, but the first can be inside or outside, while the second can only be outside.

5 Putting words into sentences

Now write sentences similar to the example:

Example: *Football is a team sport that is played on a pitch.*

1 squash
2 tennis
3 ice hockey
4 rugby

86 VOCABULARY

WORD GROUPS

C What kind of equipment do you need?

bat	socks
shuttlecock	net
vest	cap
shorts	stick
pads	shoes
helmet	shirt
racquet	puck
ball	trousers
boots	

D What kinds of actions are common in sports?

throwing	saving
passing	catching
hitting	tackling
serving	kicking
jumping	running

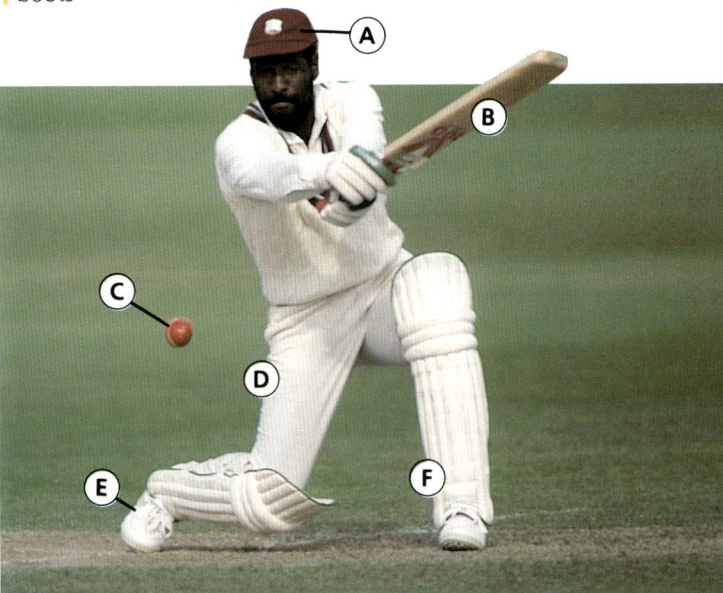

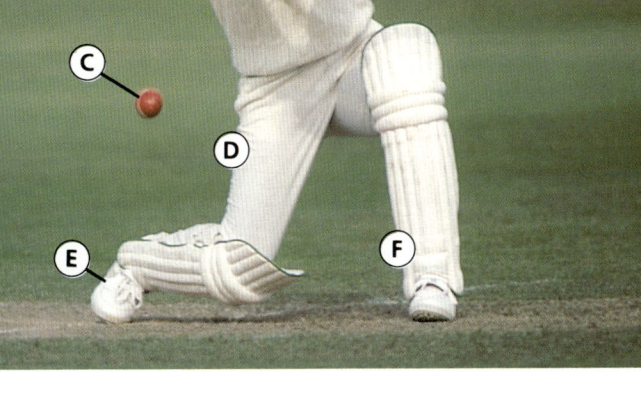

4
SPORT

6 Labelling

Look at the three pictures and label them with words from list C.

7 Describing actions

Match the words in list D with the drawings on the right.

PRONUNCIATION
Problem words

Some spelling patterns in English present severe pronunciation problems for learners. One particular area is words which contain **-ough-**.

1 Look at the words containing **ough** on the left below and match them with the words they sound like on the right:

| enough | through | off | two |
| cough | though | low | stuff |

Now compare your answers with the tape.

2 What about these words? How are they said? Check with the tape.

tough   although   rough

3 Can you think of any other words with **ough**? How are they said?

SEE ALSO: Skills, pages 36–41;
Tapescripts, page 191;
Workbook, pages 12–13;
Teacher's Book.

VOCABULARY 87

WORD GROUPS

A How can you punish children?
turn off the television
smack them
shout at them
take away their toys
send them to bed
tell them off

B How can you reward children?
cuddle them
praise them
buy them presents
give them sweets
give them extra attention

C What happens in a law court?
charge
defend
accuse
sentence
judge
prosecute
convict

D Who's who?
defendant
jury
judge
lawyer
witness

E What's the judge's decision?
guilty
innocent
sentence
not guilty
verdict

5 DISCIPLINE

1 Gapfilling

The words below often occur with 'discipline'. Put them into the sentences:

badly-   well-   self-   lack of

1 He's very _____ disciplined. He gets up early every day and runs 5 kilometres before breakfast whatever the weather.
2 Young people today have a terrible _____ discipline. A few years in the army would solve that!
3 Liverpool football team win regularly because they are such a _____ disciplined team.
4 It's difficult being a manager with _____ disciplined workers.

2 Adding words

What other responses are there to the questions in lists A and B?

3 Matching

Match a comment on the left with an explanation of what is happening:

1 'Come here at once and hold out your hand!'
2 'If you're good when the visitors come, I'll buy you some sweets tomorrow.'
3 'If you do that again you'll be in trouble!'
4 'Your exam results are excellent. Well done!'
5 'You naughty boy! Don't play football in the house!'

A She's praising him.
B She's threatening him.
C She's smacking him.
D She's telling him off.
E She's trying to bribe him.

WORD GROUPS

F What punishment can a criminal receive?
fine
prison sentence
community service
probation
the death penalty
warning

G What kinds of crimes are there?
theft
vandalism
assault
murder
smuggling
arson
fraud
burglary

4 Gapfilling

Fill in the gaps with words from lists C, D and E. If you use a verb, make any necessary changes to its form:

1 The _____ was found guilty.
2 There are 12 people on the _____ .
3 The lawyer called the first _____ .
4 The judge _____ him to 6 months in prison.
5 The woman has been _____ with theft.
6 The leader of the jury stood up and delivered their _____ .
7 If you break the law you will be _____ .

5 Describing and explaining

Look at the words in lists F and G. What does each form of punishment and each crime involve?

Example: *A fine involves paying money to the court.*

6 Combining words into sentences

Select three parts of sentences, one from each column, to express what is true in your country:

1 People convicted of arson,	for example, parking in a NO PARKING area,	are usually given community service.
2 People convicted of assault,	for example, stealing from a supermarket,	are usually sent on a training course.
3 People convicted of murder,	that is, attacking another person,	are usually fined.
4 People convicted of burglary,	that is, setting fire to someone's property,	are always sent to prison.
5 People convicted of traffic offences,	that is, killing someone,	are usually sent to prison.
6 People convicted of small thefts,	that is, breaking into someone's house,	are sometimes given a warning.

PRONUNCIATION
Word stress and parts of speech

1 🔊 The word **convict** can be said in two ways. Listen and read:

(convíct) He was convicted of murder.
(cónvict) The convict was taken from the court to prison.

What part of speech is **convict** in each of the sentences?

2 🔊 There are a number of other words that have the same spelling as nouns and verbs but differ in the position of the stress. Check the meanings of these words in a dictionary, then make sentences using them first as nouns, then as verbs. What general rule can you make about the word stress in relation to the part of speech? Check with the tape.

export	increase	contract
record	insult	produce
import	decrease	extract
escort	transport	rebel

SEE ALSO: Skills, pages 42–7;
Tapescripts, pages 191–2;
Workbook, pages 14–15;
Teacher's Book.

5
DISCIPLINE

VOCABULARY 89

WORD GROUPS

6
PEOPLE ON THE MOVE

A Where can you spend the night?
hotel
guest house
youth hostel
night shelter
campsite (tent)
rented flat
friend's house
the open air

B How do you feel when you're away from home?
lonely
homesick
isolated
depressed
frightened
down
miserable
scared
alone

1 Putting words into groups

Look at the words in list A and answer these questions:

1 In which places would you have to pay?
2 Where would you stay if you were homeless and had no money?

2 Matching

Find all the words from list B that refer to:

1 feeling afraid.
2 being without friends and the company of people.
3 feeling sad or upset.

3 Speaking: giving advice

What advice would you give to people who are suffering from the emotions in list B?

Example: *(lonely)*
Why don't you join a club of some kind?

4 Words that go together

1 Which prepositions can we use in front of the words in list C?

Example: *We go by bus*
We travel in (or on) a particular bus.

2 Instead of saying 'I'm going by bus', we can say 'I'm going by **road**'. What can we say for the other words in list C?

90 VOCABULARY

6 PEOPLE ON THE MOVE

WORD GROUPS

C How do you travel?
bus
train
foot
car
boat
plane

D What are the problems of travelling?
cancellations
crowds
traffic jams
delays
hold-ups
breakdowns
accidents

E Why do people move?
unemployment
divorce
cheaper housing
better schools
unpleasant neighbours
bigger house
change
marriage
fear
climate

5 General and specific

Two of the words in list D are general words that refer to *lost time*. The others are *specific reasons*. Which are which?

6 Speaking: giving reasons

Make sentences using words and phrases from lists C and D:

Example: *I hate going to work by car because there are always traffic jams.*

7 Finish the sentences

Make sentences beginning 'People move as a result of . . .' or 'People move because they want . . .'. Use the words in list E or any related words:

Example: *People move as a result of unemployment.*
or *People move because they want to find a job.*

Can you think of any other reasons for moving?

PRONUNCIATION
Word stress — compound nouns

1 🔲 Compound nouns are nouns that are formed from two or more words that can occur separately. Here are some examples from this unit:

guest house   youth hostel
hold-ups   traffic jams
night shelter campsite
breakdowns

Listen to the tape and notice again where the main stress lies for each compound. What rule can you make?

2 🔲 Now test your rule on these compounds:

teapot   sports car
typewriter   grandfather
notepaper   son-in-law
coat hanger

Say them to yourself, and then check with the tape.

3 🔲 Listen to two expressions stressed in two different ways. How does the meaning change? Which ones are the compounds?

SEE ALSO: Skills, pages 48–53; Tapescripts, page 192; Workbook, pages 16–17; Teacher's Book.

VOCABULARY 91

WORD GROUPS

7
HEALTH

A What do doctors do?
examine
treat
cure
diagnose
prescribe

C What's the treatment?
pills
tablets
injection
surgery
cream
medicine

B What's the problem?
spots
pain
swelling
deep cut
infection
ache

D Which part of your body needs exercising?
ankle   stomach
neck   wrist
waist   thigh
shoulder   elbow

1 Identifying words that go together

Which of the verbs in list A can be followed by each of these nouns:

1 medicines   2 patients   3 illnesses

2 Putting words into groups

1 Which of the problems in list B can be seen on the outside of your body? What do you see in each case?

2 Which words refer only to what you feel? Which word is stronger?

3 Gapfilling

Use a form of one of these verbs to complete each sentence:

have   take   apply

1 He's got to _____ an operation on his knee.
2 I'm _____ pills to stop the infection spreading.
3 You'll need to _____ some injections before you travel.
4 _____ the cream twice a day, and rub it in well.
5 She's given me this medicine to _____ .

4 Labelling

Label the diagram of a human body with words from list D.

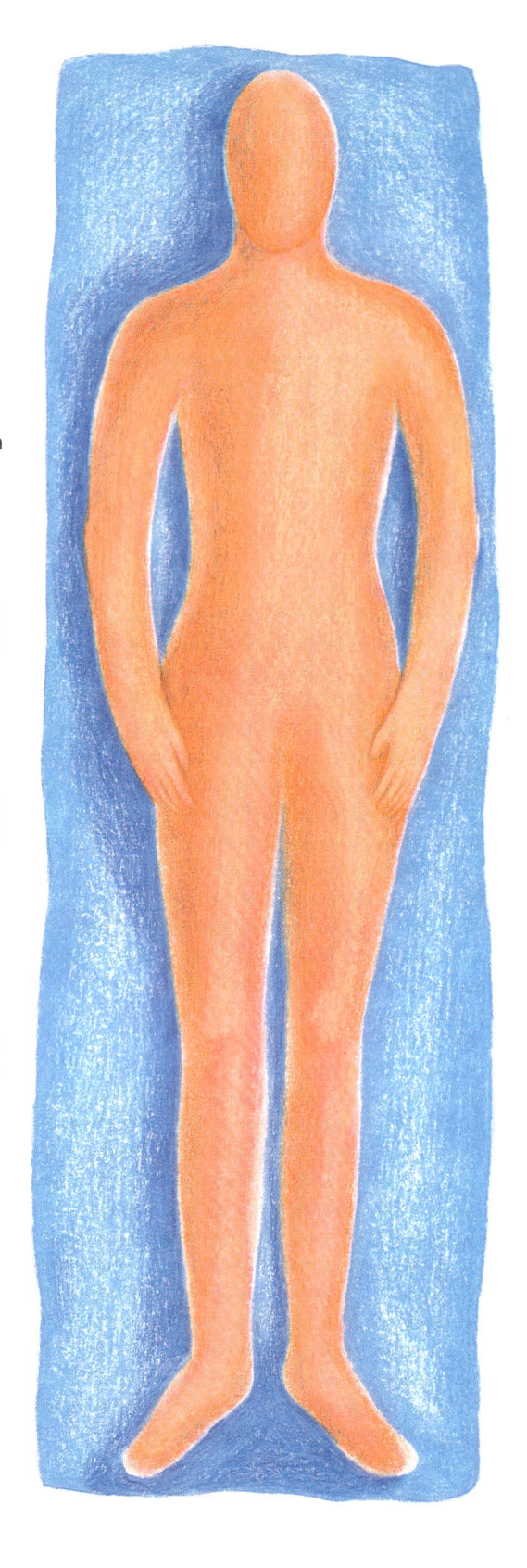

WORD GROUPS

7 HEALTH

E How can you move parts of your body?
raise
tense
lower
rotate
straighten
relax
bend
turn
stretch

F How do you feel in the morning?
sleepy
irritable
wide awake
exhausted
short-tempered
unsociable
refreshed
drowsy
alert
happy

5 Describing

Look at the words in list E and the pictures labelled A to F. Describe what the person is doing in each picture.

6 Words with similar and opposite meanings

Which pairs of words in list E have similar or opposite meanings?

7 Matching

Find expressions in list F that match the descriptions below. Sometimes more than one expression will be suitable:

1 You feel it's time to go to bed.
2 You feel slightly angry when you wake up.
3 You don't want to see anyone.
4 You've had plenty of sleep and you're ready to start the day.

PRONUNCIATION Silent letters

It is sometimes hard to come up with rules of English spelling that are of general use. In the case of 'silent letters' it is better simply to learn common words in which they occur. Below are some of the most common. Listen to the tape and repeat.

Letter	Common words
B (usually final)	thumb lamb bomb tomb
K (usually initial)	knee know knife knot knickers
W (often initial)	write wrong wrist wrinkle answer two
H (usually initial)	hour honest honour exhausted
L (usually middle)	would could should

SEE ALSO: Skills, pages 54–9;
Tapescripts, page 192;
Workbook, pages 18–19;
Teacher's Book.

VOCABULARY 93

WORD GROUPS

8
BUSINESS

A What do businesses provide?
goods
services

B What do company departments do?
interview and select staff
prepare budgets
arrange staff holidays
contact customers
collect debts
train staff
prepare brochures
draw up staff contracts
prepare accounts
advertise goods and services
deal with petty cash
attend exhibitions

1 Discussion

What kind of goods or services do these businesses provide?

1 a car manufacturer
2 a petrol station
3 a language school
4 a publisher
5 a cleaning company
6 a supermarket
7 a computer maintenance company
8 an insurance company

2 Putting words into groups

What do these departments do? Use the expressions in list B and any others you can think of:

1 the Finance Department
2 the Personnel Department
3 the Marketing Department

So, in general, which department:

4 manages employees?
5 deals with money matters?
6 tries to find new customers?

94 VOCABULARY

WORD GROUPS

C What are your colleagues like?
intelligent
imaginative
tolerant
enthusiastic
sensitive
patient
punctual
loyal
practical
formal

D What do you do on the phone?
make a call
take a call
hear the engaged signal
pick up the receiver
put down the receiver
listen for the ringing tone
connect someone
put someone through
dial a number
ring someone
hold the line

3 Putting words into groups

Are the words in list C *always* positive, or might they be disadvantages in some jobs? Can you give any examples?

4 Using prefixes to change word meaning

Which prefix can be added to each of the words in list C to give an opposite meaning?

Example: *unenthusiastic*

5 Putting words and phrases in groups

Which of the actions in list D are done by:

1 the caller?
2 the person receiving the call?
3 the telephonist (or switchboard operator)?

6 Putting things in order

List, in order, the stages of making a phone call to a number that is engaged. Use the expressions in list D.

PRONUNCIATION
Word stress — prefixes

1 🔲 If you completed exercise 4 correctly you will have come up with the list of words below. Listen to them on the tape and mark the position of the main stress for each word.

unintelligent   unenthusiastic
unimaginative   insensitive
intolerant   impatient
unpunctual   impractical
disloyal   informal

What general rule can you form about these prefixes?

2 Now think of some more words with the prefixes **un-**, **in-**, **dis**, and check in a dictionary to see whether your rule works.

★ Of course, we can choose to stress prefixes if we wish – for example when we want to make a contrast. Look at this:

Example: *I think he's a very sensitive man.
No he's not. He's completely insensitive!*

8
BUSINESS

SEE ALSO: Skills, pages 60–5;
Tapescripts, page 192;
Workbook, pages 20–1;
Teacher's Book.

VOCABULARY 95

WORD GROUPS

A What do we do when we speak?
insist
disagree
promise
advise
correct
add
inform
request
explain

B What are we communicating?
advice
information
argument
explanation
promise
request

9
POWER

1 Selecting

Choose a word from list A which describes what each of the speakers below is doing:

1 'What I mean is that . . .'
2 'Yes, and another point is that . . .'
3 'At that time, the economy was in a terrible state.'
4 'I'll do it tomorrow, honestly.'
5 'It wasn't Gandhi; it was Nehru.'
6 'I think you should . . .'
7 'I don't think you're right about . . .'
8 'Would you mind helping me . . .?'
9 'That really is what she said.'

Can you think of other ways of doing any of these things when you speak?

2 Defining

Choose a word from list B and add an appropriate verb to make an expression that means the same as the verbs below:

Example: *to advise* = to give advice

1 to argue =
2 to promise =
3 to explain =
4 to request =
5 to inform =

3 Explaining

With a partner, try to explain what these words mean:

argue   interrupt   dominate

As you explain them together, *do* what it is you are explaining. Argue, for example, about the meaning of **argue**!

4 Describing

Write three sentences describing what you think each of the people in the photographs labelled A–C is doing. Use suitable words from any of the lists.

96 VOCABULARY

C How do we look?

good-looking	aggressive
overweight	decisive
bearded	depressed
smart	intelligent
stunning	charming
balding	strict
healthy	shy
attractive	kind
slim	tired
scruffy	friendly
confident	cheerful

5 Selecting

Use words from list C to describe the people in the two photographs. Use a dictionary to check any words that you do not know.

6 Speaking

Choose a person who is well-known nationally or internationally, and describe that person to a partner. Your partner should guess who it is that you are describing, if necessary by asking additional questions like:
How tall is she?
What colour is his hair?
Does she have a warm personality?
How does he dress?

PRONUNCIATION
Word stress — suffixes

1 On the left below are some verbs that have occurred in this unit. Check where the main stress falls in each word, and practice saying them.

2 On the right are nouns associated with the verbs. Listen to the tape and write in the main stress for each one.

explain	explanation
inform	information
dominate	domination
add	addition
interrupt	interruption
correct	correction
insist	insistence
disagree	disagreement

a What do you notice about the position of the stress in the nouns?

b What is the difference between the stress patterns in the top and bottom groups of words?

WORD GROUPS

9
POWER

SEE ALSO: Skills, pages 66–71;
Tapescripts, page 192;
Workbook, pages 22–3;
Teacher's Book.

WORD GROUPS

10 HUMOUR

A What's in a joke?
humour
punch line
national stereotypes
pun
embarrassment
suspense
sexism
religion
sex
toilets

B How do we show that we find something funny?
laugh
chuckle
giggle
clap
smirk
grin
smile
snigger
titter

1 Matching

Which words in list A may relate to a joke about:

1 English people?
2 a woman with a well-developed figure?
3 judgement at Heaven's gate?

2 Discussion

Which of the ingredients in list A do you find amusing in a joke? Which do you find offensive? Give reasons for your answers.

3 Defining

Which word in list A means:

1 a play on two meanings of the same word, or on two words with the same sound?
2 the last line of a joke, which makes the joke funny?
3 the drama in a joke which makes you continue listening?

4 Putting words into groups

Look at list B and, working with a dictionary, decide on the following:

1 Which words suggest that a *noise* is made?
2 Which words are most often associated with children?
3 Which words suggest that the amusement is unpleasant in some way?
4 Which word does not involve the mouth?

Now try doing each of them, in the way your dictionary describes!

5 Matching

Which of the words in list C might describe these stories?

1 a very good joke
2 a report of a bad accident
3 a description of what your friend had for lunch
4 your sister's story about being chased by a man with a knife
5 a very good mystery story

98 VOCABULARY

WORD GROUPS

C What kinds of stories are there?
amusing
sad
exciting
terrifying
embarrassing
tragic
boring
shocking
hilarious
interesting

D What makes people laugh?
mimicking
clowning
playing a practical joke on someone
making fun of someone
pulling someone's leg
playing the fool
impersonating
taking someone off
teasing

6 Related words

How do you feel when someone tells you a story? If it's a *boring* story you would probably feel *bored*. What about these kinds of stories?

1 amusing   2 exciting   3 shocking   4 interesting   5 tragic

7 Choosing the best expression

Look at the pictures above, labelled A–E. Match them with the descriptions below and then choose an expression from list D which fits the description:

1 'He was being very amusing – you know, making funny faces and silly noises . . . and he was dressed in the most ridiculous clothes.'
2 'She was very good. Not only did she sound like Margaret Thatcher, she even looked like her. It was hilarious.'
3 'Everyone laughs at his hairstyle when he's only trying to cover his bald patch. It's a bit cruel really.'
4 'Here he comes now. I hope the water falls on his head.'
5 'I pretended I'd forgotten to buy him a birthday present . . . but I couldn't keep up the pretence for long. He was so pleased when I gave it to him!'

PRONUNCIATION -ed endings

1 Put these words into three groups according to whether the **-ed** endings are pronounced /ɪd/, /d/ or /t/.

amused   excited   shocked   embarrassed   promised
waited   landed   begged   tasted   amazed

2 Now listen to the words on the tape and check to see if you were correct. What rule can you make for the pronunciation of **-ed** endings? (Clue: listen carefully to the consonant sound just before the **-ed** ending.)

SEE ALSO: Skills, pages 72–7;
Tapescripts, page 192;
Workbook, pages 24–5;
Teacher's Book.

10
HUMOUR

VOCABULARY 99

KEY WORDS

see

look at

watch

hear

listen to

LOOK

A I **saw** a man in the crowd.
B I **looked at** him carefully.
C I **watched** him walk into a shop.
D **Listen to** me when I'm talking to you.
E I **heard** a loud noise, and ran outside.

CHECK

1 Which of the following explanations go with each of the verbs in **bold** in LOOK above?

1 to use your eyes to follow something that is moving
2 to be aware of something with your eyes
3 to be aware of sounds with your ears
4 to direct your eyes to a particular place
5 to pay attention in order to hear something

PRACTICE

2 Which of these sentences sound wrong? Discuss with a partner *why* they sound wrong, and make any necessary changes:

1 Look at that boy! He's standing on his head.
2 We left in a great hurry, and listened to the clock striking 3 o'clock.
3 She sat down, put the radio on, and heard music all evening.
4 He always listens to his mother's advice.
5 I had a lazy day yesterday. I saw television all day.

3 Look at the pictures and work with a partner to tell the story:

4 Now complete the text. Use the past tense form of one of the key word verbs:

Tessa was lying in bed one night when she _____ a noise. For a few minutes she stayed in bed and _____ the sounds of someone moving around below. Then she got up and walked very quietly down the stairs. On the bottom step she stood still as she suddenly _____ , through the kitchen doorway, a man sitting on a stool and eating a banana. Tessa _____ him until he finished the banana, but at that moment the man turned and noticed her. They _____ each other for a minute in silence before the stranger jumped up and ran out of the house. He left a bag of Tessa's cassettes on the kitchen floor.

SEE ALSO: Grammar, page 137; Workbook, page 26; Teacher's Book.

100 VOCABULARY

LOOK

A B C D

George IV **went** *mad*.
Look, the weather**'s getting** *better*.
The leaves **are turning** *brown*.
She **became** *an architect*.

1 Which sentence belongs to each picture?

CHECK

1 Which key word verb belongs with each of these pairs of sentences?

1 The milk will _____ sour if you don't put it in the fridge.
  The sky is _____ grey.
2 Let's hurry before it _____ dark.
  My cat's _____ too old to catch mice.
3 At the age of 46 he _____ prime minister.
  These delays are _____ a bit of a bore.
4 Men often start _____ bald after 40.
  Michael doesn't seem to hear me. I think he's _____ deaf.

WORD STUDY

- The four key word verbs describe *change*.
- They are used with different adjectives, and one of them (**become**) is regularly used with nouns.
- **Become / turn** are more formal. **Get / go** are neutral.
- The following expressions are common:

get	get / become	become
old	angry	famous
lost	cloudy / sunny	
well / ill	cold / warm	a doctor
better / worse	light / dark	a driver
married	worried	President
ready		Minister of...

go	go / turn	turn
mad	bad	nasty
blind	sour	
deaf	pale	
bald	grey	
	brown	
	red	

KEY WORDS

become (an architect)
go (deaf)
get (cold)
turn (brown)

PRACTICE

2 Complete these sentences with an appropriate form of a key word verb, and discuss alternatives:

1 I think our poor old dog is _____ blind.
2 The food's _____ cold.
3 The dog was friendly at first, but suddenly he _____ nasty.
4 He's _____ better after his illness.
5 He first _____ Chairman of the company in 1987.
6 If I stay here much longer I'll _____ mad.
7 The leaves curled up and _____ yellow.
8 After many years of effort he _____ a great pianist.
9 She's _____ ready to go out.

3 Make up sentences about changes in your life / family etc., using the expressions in the WORD STUDY box, like this:
Example: *Where I live, it'll get cold next month.*

For informal sentences use **get** or **go**; for more formal sentences use **become** or **turn**.

SEE ALSO:
Workbook, page 26;
Teacher's Book.

VOCABULARY 101

KEY WORDS

have
take
give

LOOK

She **had** a long sleep that night.
They sat down and **had** a long talk.

He didn't **take** any chances.
They **took** care of the baby.

I don't like **giving** speeches.
They **gave** us a warm welcome.

CHECK

1 Complete these phrases with **have**, **take** or **give**:

1 to photograph = _____ a photograph
2 to chat = _____ a chat
3 to kiss her = _____ her a kiss
4 to lecture = _____ a lecture
5 to lead = _____ the lead
6 to rest = _____ a rest

PRACTICE

2 Complete these sentences with an appropriate form of **have**, **take** or **give**:

1 He didn't do it, but he _____ the blame anyway.
2 You must _____ an account of your actions.
3 She _____ me a kiss and left the room.
4 Don't let's _____ a quarrel.
5 They _____ a long talk.
6 She didn't _____ part in the debate.
7 She _____ me a long look.
8 She _____ a good cry and felt better as a result.
9 He _____ a picture of her.

3 Put each phrase into the right sentence, using **have**, **take** or **give**:

| power   faith   a rest   a decision |
| a short interview   10 lectures |

1 The prime minister _____ to the press.
2 Why don't you sit down and _____ ?
3 He has to _____ a term at his college.
4 The generals have been running the country since they _____ in 1983.
5 The Americans _____ in their economic strength.
6 She _____ to give up smoking.

SEE ALSO:
Workbook, page 27;
Teacher's Book.

WORD STUDY

Common examples of nouns with **have**, **take** and **give**:

have
a chance
an accident
a headache / a pain / an illness
an idea / a thought

a party
a rest

take
a chance
an action / a risk / an exam
medicine / a pill

a photo / a picture

care (of somebody)
place

give
(someone) a chance
(someone) a smile
(someone) a warm welcome

an order / an instruction / permission
a talk / a speech / a lecture
an opinion
information / evidence

These sentences indicate the difference between the three words:

It was obvious he wouldn't win the race; he didn't **have a chance**.
It was dangerous, but he **took a chance** and was successful.
Do you think he can do it? Let's **give him a chance**.

Have / take

British English
to **have** tea / coffee
to **have** a bath / shower / walk / swim

American English
to **take** tea / coffee
to **take** a bath / shower / walk / swim

102 VOCABULARY

LOOK

KEY WORDS

make
let
force
allow

WORD STUDY

make let		do	
	someone		something
force allow		to do	

PRACTICE

2 Rewrite these sentences using the verb in brackets. Make any grammatical changes that are necessary. The meaning will remain the same:

1 The company let her have an extra week's holiday.   (allow)
2 The nurses made me take some very unpleasant medicines.   (force)

3 Now complete this text. Use the past tense form of one of the verbs in brackets:

It was the first time I'd flown, and I didn't enjoy it! First they _____ (make / force) us wait for several hours while they prepared the plane. They finally _____ (let / allow) us to board it, but by that time we were very hungry and they didn't _____ (let / allow) us eat anything for another hour. After that it got worse. They _____ (make / force) us stay in our seats the whole time because we were flying through storms, and they _____ (make / force) us to watch the most awful film. I can't tell you how happy I was when we arrived in Kuala Lumpur and they _____ (let / allow) us leave the plane.

4 Think about the place where you work or study. What do you have permission to do? What do you have to do even if you don't want to?

Example:
The manager makes me stay late every evening.

A Why did Tim's boss **let** him leave the office?
B Why did Tim's boss **make** him leave the office?
C Tim **was forced** to go.
D Tim **was allowed** to go.

CHECK

1 After studying the sentences in LOOK above, answer these questions:

1 Which verbs in **A–D** tell us that Tim *wanted* to go?
2 Which verbs tell us that he did not want to go, but that he had no choice?

SEE ALSO: Grammar, pages 154–5;
Skills, pages 42–7;
Workbook, page 28;
Teacher's Book.

KEY WORDS

rob
steal
burgle
swindle
thief
pickpocket
burglar
crook
theft
burglary
fraud

LOOK

The **thieves robbed** the bank and **stole** £200,000.

A **pickpocket stole** Walter's wallet, and he reported the **theft** to the police.

Our house **was burgled** last week. The **burglar** hasn't been caught yet. There have been several **burglaries** in our street.

The bank manager turned out to be a **crook**. He **swindled** several people out of their life savings. He was accused of **fraud** and sent to prison.

CHECK

1 Discuss these sentences. Use forms of the key words to say who did it, what they did, and what the action is called:

1 While the family was away, he broke the kitchen window, entered the house and took the microwave.
2 She was the treasurer of the local women's group. She collected the members' subscriptions but didn't give them receipts and kept the money herself.
3 He works on the Underground, putting his hand into people's handbags and pockets and taking their wallets and valuables.
4 He takes cars which do not belong to him.

WORD STUDY

The following verbs take different objects:
1 **steal** The object is *the thing they stole*:
   They **stole** *the camera*.
2 **burgle** The object is *the building they entered*:
   They **burgled** *the house*.
3 **rob** The object is *the 'owner'* (temporary or permanent):
   They **robbed** *Brian / the bank*.

SEE ALSO:
Workbook, page 29;
Teacher's Book.

PRACTICE

2 Complete the sentences below using forms of these words. Sometimes there is more than one alternative:

burgle   burglary   crook   burglar   fraud
pickpocket   swindle

1 The _____ climbed up the drainpipe and in through the window.
2 There are plenty of _____ working in business; _____ are committed every day. Somebody is always _____ money out of people.
3 _____ are more and more frequent these days. Six houses have been _____ in this area in the last ten days.
4 Help! My wallet has gone! There's a _____ on the bus!

3 Complete these sentences with forms of these words:

thief   rob   steal

1 A group of men _____ the Central Post Office late last night. The _____ entered dressed as postmen, and _____ documents to the value of £27,500.
2 The plans for the new car were _____ from the factory on Tuesday.
3 Police! I've just been _____ !

4 With a partner, think of four different crimes that you know of and describe them, using the key words.

104 VOCABULARY

LOOK

He's **expecting** a call from his mother.
He's **looking forward to** a call from his mother.
He's **hoping for** a call from his mother.
He's **waiting for** a call from his mother.

CHECK

1 After studying the sentences in LOOK above, answer these questions:

1 Which two verbs clearly show that he *wants* his mother to phone?
2 Which three verbs show that he strongly believes his mother will phone?
3 Which verb shows that he thinks the phone call will make him happy?
4 Which verb suggests that he won't be doing anything else until his mother phones?

WORD STUDY

Other constructions:

He's expecting / hoping / waiting **to hear** from his mother.

He's looking forward **to hearing** from his mother.

He expects / hopes **(that)** she will call.

KEY WORDS

expect
look forward to
hope (for)
wait (for)

PRACTICE

2 Jane is going to the airport to meet her sister. The flight is supposed to arrive from Madrid at 8.30. Look at the pictures and complete each sentence with one of the key word verbs:

1 She's _____ a bus to the airport.
2 She's _____ seeing her sister again.
3 She _____ the plane to arrive on time.
4 She _____ her sister will bring her a present.

3 Which of the key word verbs can you use, in the present simple or progressive form, to complete these sentences? There may be more than one possible answer, but think carefully about the *grammar* of each sentence:

1 I _____ we'll be friends.
2 We _____ seeing you soon.
3 They _____ to move house.
4 A: Is there a swimming pool at the hotel?
   B: I _____ so.
5 He _____ the sun to rise in order to take a photograph.

4 Check your answers to exercises 1–3, then complete this conversation. Use a suitable tense of one of these verbs:

expect   look forward to
hope (for)   wait (for)

SUE: I'm going to the concert next week. It should be great – I _____ it for a long time. Will you be there?
TOM: I _____ so, but I haven't got a ticket yet and there may not be any left.
SUE: No, you'd better get one soon. I _____ they'll be sold very quickly.
TOM: The problem is that I _____ my friend to decide which evening she wants to go. I'll phone her tonight.

SEE ALSO: Grammar, pages 154–5; Workbook, page 30; Teacher's Book.

VOCABULARY 105

KEY WORDS

on
off
in
out

LOOK

You probably know how to use the key words in some contexts, especially to talk about *position* or *movement*:

The books are **on** the shelf.
Put the rubbish **out** in the yard.
Put the plates **in** the cupboard.
Take your hat **off** the table.

On / off and **in / out** also occur in *multi-part verbs*, often with quite different meanings:

It was late, but they **kept on** working.
She **switched off** the washing machine.
We **took** the child **in** when her parents died.
He**'s been thrown out** of the club.

CHECK

1 What do the underlined verbs mean in the sentences below? Write each verb in the correct column of the table according to the meaning contained in **on** or **off**. Two examples have been done for you:

Starting	Stopping	Continuing	Encouraging
switch on		keep on	

1 They <u>carried on</u> walking although John's legs were hurting.
2 <u>Come on</u>! We'll be late.
3 The electricity's <u>been cut off</u>.
4 I've decided to <u>stay on</u> at university for another year.
5 The match <u>has been called off</u>.
6 <u>Go on</u>! I'm sure you can do it.
7 They were going to get married but she <u>broke it off</u>.
8 Can you <u>turn on</u> the oven?

Can you think of any other verbs with **on / off** that you can add?

SEE ALSO: Grammar, pages 148–9; Workbook, page 31; Teacher's Book.

WORD STUDY

Verbs followed by: often have the sense of:
on starting, continuing or encouraging
off stopping or finishing
in including
out excluding

PRACTICE

2 Fill in the gaps in these sentences with an appropriate form of the verbs from the box below. There may be more than one correct answer:

| join   leave   get   fit   take   keep |

1 She's been _____ out of the team.
2 My son's happy at his new school. He _____ in well.
3 _____ OUT! PRIVATE PROPERTY!
4 There are some children playing football over there. Why don't you _____ in?
5 It was late and we couldn't find a hotel. Fortunately we met some people who _____ us in and gave us a bed for the night.
6 Could you _____ out of my chair so that I can sit down?

106 VOCABULARY

LOOK

KEY WORDS

up
down
away
back

She sat **down**.

She stood **up**. She went **away**. She came **back**.

1 Here are four arrows. Which best expresses the meaning of **down**, **up**, **away** and **back**?

A B C D

CHECK

1 Complete these sentences with an appropriate particle from the box:

| up down away back |

1 When he saw the policeman the boy ran _____ .
2 If you've got a temperature you should lie _____ and rest.
3 He got _____ at sunrise every day.
4 He always caught a bus to the office but he usually walked _____ to his house at the end of the day.

WORD STUDY

Up As well as direction (↑), **up** is also used in the sense of 'finish the task':
   Eat your food **up**.

Down / away As well as directions (↓ ↗), **down** and **away** are used in the sense of 'becoming less':
   The noise died **down / away** slowly.

Back has two senses:
1 'return something':
   Can you take these **back** to the library?
2 'the opposite of **forward**':
   Stand **back** and let the others see.

PRACTICE

2 Using the information in LOOK and the WORD STUDY box, complete each sentence with an appropriate verb and particle from the boxes:

| give sit put fill get | up down back away |

| look settle throw stay go | up down away back |

1 Can you _____ the suitcases _____ here on the floor, please?
2 We're hoping to _____ _____ for a few days' rest.
3 We suggest you _____ _____ and enjoy your flight.
4 You'd better _____ the petrol tank _____ . It's a long way.
5 I'd like to _____ this pen _____ to its owner.

6 If it's no good, _____ it _____ .
7 As it was New Year's Eve we let the children _____ _____ late.
8 Would everybody please _____ _____ and be quiet.
9 We had a lovely holiday. I'd like to _____ _____ there again.
10 If you don't know it, _____ the word _____ in the dictionary.

3 Here is the first sentence from exercise 2 rewritten:

Can you put down the suitcases here on the floor, please?

Three other sentences in exercise 2 can be rewritten. Which ones? Rewrite them. Discuss sentence number 6: why is it different from the others?

SEE ALSO: Grammar, pages 148–9; Workbook, page 31; Teacher's Book.

VOCABULARY 107

KEY WORDS

travel
flight
drive
tour
journey
voyage
expedition

LOOK

We **travel** a lot.
The **flight** is at 10.15.
Shall we **drive** to London?
We're planning an Arctic **expedition**.
The **journey** took an hour.
I met her on the **voyage**.
She's on a **tour** of Eastern Europe.

CHECK

1 Think about how you can use the words in **bold** in LOOK above. Use your dictionary if you are not sure. Write them in the correct place in a table like the one below:

Words that can be used as:

nouns and verbs	nouns only

Which noun is never used in the singular?

Now think about what the key words mean. Which three words tell you *how* the movement takes place? Copy the table and complete it:

Key word	Means of transport

PRACTICE

2 Complete each sentence using an appropriate form of one of the key words. There may be more than one correct answer:

1 They set off on the long _____ across the Atlantic.
2 I don't enjoy _____ , so my husband goes to Spain alone.
3 If the engine has been repaired, we'll go for a _____ in the country.
4 The _____ included three nights in St Petersburg and two in Moscow.
5 The _____ from London to Paris took about an hour.
6 He's gone on an international _____ to study wildlife in Borneo.
7 It's a short train _____ to Cambridge; you can catch a bus from there.

3 Use *nouns* to complete the chart. Add any other types of journey that you can think of:

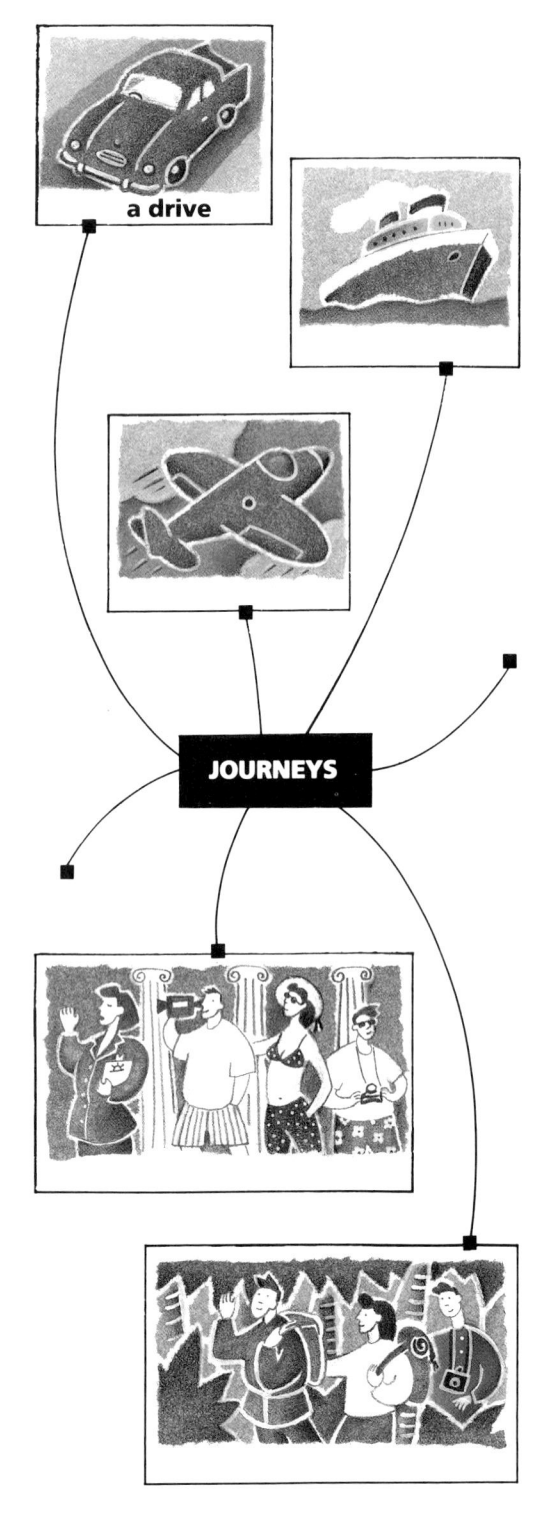

a drive

JOURNEYS

4 Describe a journey of your own, using the key words where appropriate.

SEE ALSO: Skills, pages 48–53; Workbook, page 32; Teacher's Book.

108 VOCABULARY

KEY WORDS

road
street
track
path
way
route

LOOK

We planned our **route** to the ruins, drove through the quiet **streets** of the town, and took the **road** to Mombasa. Soon we saw a sign saying 'To the Ruins', which pointed along a rough **track**. We took it and then asked an old man the **way**. He pointed along a **path**, so we left the car and walked.

CHECK

1 Attach each of these words to the best definition:

| street   track   path   road |

1 . . . for people on foot
2 . . . where vehicles can travel, especially between towns
3 . . . where vehicles can travel, especially in towns, with buildings on one or both sides
4 a narrow road, especially a rough one

| way   route |

5 a chosen line of travel which you plan or follow from one place to another
6 the (right) road, path, etc. that you need to follow in order to reach a place

PRACTICE

2 Complete these sentences with an appropriate key word:

1 Can you tell me the _____ to the station, please?
2 From the main road, a narrow _____ led to the farm.
3 Let's plan the _____ we are going to take.
4 We'll need a _____ map of Paris.
5 And let's get a _____ map of France.
6 Walk along this _____ across the fields, and you'll come to the river.
7 There's a petrol station on the edge of town, on the London _____ .
8 The shop you're looking for is in the High _____ , where all the shops are.

LOOK

Many of these words can also be used metaphorically:

He is **leading the way** in the fight to save the hospital.
Our **paths cross** from time to time.
I think we're **on the right track**.
This new car is **streets ahead** of the competition.
The road to riches is hard and risky.

PRACTICE

3 Here are some similar metaphors. Work out which is the right word. Two alternatives are sometimes possible:

| path   way   street   track   road |

1 The new hospital is on the _____ to being finished.
2 He was on the _____ to success after they published his book.
3 Have you seen John lately? No, I've lost _____ of him.
4 I don't want to stand in your _____ .
5 As a computer programmer, he's _____ ahead of Peter.
6 That idea won't work; you're on the wrong _____ .
7 'The _____ to hell is paved with good intentions.'
8 This book is confusing; I can't find my _____ through it.

4 Use the key words to describe an area you know well.

SEE ALSO:
Workbook, page 33;
Teacher's Book.

VOCABULARY 109

KEY WORDS

pay
income
salary
wages
fee

LOOK

He gets his **wages** on Friday night.
A director's **salary** is quite high.
They are negotiating a **pay** rise.
You should live within your **income**.
I can't afford school **fees** for two children.

CHECK

1 Here are five extracts from a dictionary. Using the examples in LOOK above, attach a word to each definition:

1 money you are paid each week for your work, especially if you do unskilled work
2 money that you receive every month as payment for your job, especially if you are an office worker or a professional person
3 a sum of money which you pay for professional services to a doctor, lawyer, private school, etc.
4 money which you receive regularly, usually as payment for your work or interest from investments
5 money received for work, or during absence from work (for illness, pregnancy, etc.)

PRACTICE

2 Complete each sentence with a suitable form of a word from the box. Some alternatives are possible:

| fee   wages   pay   salary   income |

1 You pay an annual _____ and they look after your accounts.
2 He gets a _____ of £25,000 per annum and a company car.
3 Half of their _____ comes from their investments.
4 _____ are paid on Friday afternoons.
5 In most companies, _____ rises are negotiated annually.
6 We offer a starting _____ of £20,000 a year.
7 The doctor's _____ are terribly high.
8 People on a fixed _____ are hurt by inflation.
9 Street cleaners get low _____ .
10 It's interesting work but the _____ isn't very good.

3 Look at these four people, and write a sentence about each one using a key word. The first one has been done for you:

£22,000 per annum
She has a salary of £22,000 a year.

investments: £75,000 p.a.
_____

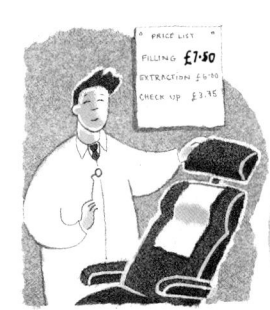

£7.50
_____

£6.00 per hour
_____

SEE ALSO: Skills, pages 62–3; Workbook, page 34; Teacher's Book.

110   VOCABULARY

KEY WORDS

work
job
career
vocation
profession

LOOK

I like **work**; I could watch other people doing it for hours!

He's got a **job** in the Post Office.
The **work** is boring, but it's steady.

She has an interesting **job** in a TV station. Most of their **work** is on news programmes.

CHECK

1 Here are definitions of the two key words in LOOK above. Which is which?

1 (uncountable) activity which uses effort and is done for a particular purpose, not for pleasure
2 (countable) regular paid employment

PRACTICE

2 Complete each sentence with **work** or **job**:

1 The factory closed down and she lost her _____.
2 He was highly praised for his _____ in genetic engineering.
3 _____ on the new tunnel will begin in January.
4 She has a good _____ in an insurance company.

LOOK

A **profession** like the law takes many years of study.

He has had a successful **career** as an architect.

She has more than an interest in the job; she has a **vocation** for it.

CHECK

3 Here are three definitions. From the examples in LOOK above, attach a word to each definition.

1 a job that you really want to do and that you have a natural ability for, usually one that helps other people
2 a job or profession for which you are trained and which you intend to follow for part or the whole of your life
3 a job that is socially respected because you need a high standard of education and also special training to do it

PRACTICE

4 Complete each sentence with a suitable word from the box. There may be more than one alternative. Discuss different meanings:

profession   vocation   career

1 He has had an outstanding political _____.
2 He's a good doctor because he has a real _____ for medicine.
3 He has a job in the legal _____.
4 She spent most of her _____ working in Edinburgh.
5 Teaching children ought to be a _____ as well as a way of earning money.
6 She's very _____-minded; she plans 10 years ahead.

5 Describe the activities of your family / friends using the key words.

SEE ALSO: Skills, pages 62–3;
Workbook, page 34;
Teacher's Book.

VOCABULARY 111

KEY WORDS

customer
client
patient
guest
tenant

LOOK

He's been a **customer** at my shop since it opened.
Most of the accountant's **clients** own small businesses.
The **patient** is out of danger now.
We often have **guests** staying over Christmas.
They've got **tenants** in their London flat.

CHECK

1 After studying the sentences in LOOK above, answer these questions:

1 Which of the words includes the idea of buying goods that you can carry away?
2 Which word can be used to refer to friends?
3 Do people pay to stay at a guesthouse? So 'guest' has two meanings. What are they?
4 Which word suggests someone who is paying for a professional service?
5 Which word refers to someone who makes regular payments for a place to live?
6 Which of the key words refer to people who probably pay
   a immediately? **b** monthly? **c** only when they receive a bill?
7 Which word refers to someone who rarely *chooses* to be in this situation?

PRACTICE

2 How many possibilities can you think of to complete the grid below?

Key word	Places	Activities	Who gets paid? (e.g.)
customer	shops		
client			
patient	surgery, clinic or hospital		
guest			nobody – or owner of guesthouse
tenant		renting somewhere to live	

3 Complete these sentences with one of the key words:

1 Each member of the tennis club is allowed to bring two _____ to the party.
2 I'm tired of being a _____ . I want to buy my own house.
3 The insurance company sends Christmas cards to all its _____ .
4 Shop assistants must remember that the _____ is always right!
5 Most doctors believe that their _____ should be told the truth – even if it is unpleasant.

SEE ALSO:
Workbook, page 35;
Teacher's Book.

KEY WORDS

talk
speech
lecture
meeting
conference

LOOK

A 1 The Labour Party is holding its annual **conference** this week.
   2 We have a weekly **meeting** on Tuesday mornings.
   3 We sat in his office and had a good **talk**.

B 1 The chairman delivered a **speech** of welcome to the new members.
   2 Students have to attend 10 **lectures** a week.
   3 Brian gave us an interesting **talk** on his life in Africa.

1 The words in **bold** in one set are about *one person speaking to a group*, and in the other about *a group of people exchanging ideas*. Which is which?

CHECK

1 Link these five words to the definitions below:

| talk   speech   lecture |
| meeting   conference |

1 a long formal meeting, e.g. between people who belong to the same political party, for the exchange of ideas
2 a gathering of people for a purpose
3 a long talk given to a group of people on a particular subject, especially as a method of teaching at universities
4 an act of speaking formally to a group of listeners
5 1 a conversation   2 an informal speech or lecture

PRACTICE

2 Complete these sentences with a suitable form of a word from the box. Sometimes more than one word is possible; you can discuss different levels of formality:

| talk   speech   lecture |
| meeting   conference |

1 The last disarmament _____ was held in Geneva.
2 I attended the union _____ last Thursday evening.
3 Her _____ on Anglo-Saxon were terribly boring.
4 I met John and had a long _____ with him about his family.
5 He gave a series of _____ on Medieval Art.
6 The text of the Minister's _____ was sent to the papers.
7 She gave a _____ on Mozart to a few people in my house.
8 The Liberal Party is holding its annual _____ next week.
9 The Queen visited the school and Jill gave a _____ of welcome.
10 He chaired the _____ , which lasted for an hour.

SEE ALSO:
Workbook, page 36;
Teacher's Book.

KEY WORDS

cloth
clothes
material
garment
dress
clothing

LOOK

Cloth is sold in rolls of 100 metres.
We use only the highest quality **material** for our **garments**.
I probably spend about £20 a month on **clothes**.
Oh no! I've spilt tea all over my **dress**.
Socks, trousers, skirts and shirts are all items of **clothing**.

CHECK

1 Study the sentences in LOOK above carefully and work with a dictionary to answer these questions:

1 Find a word that refers to an item of clothing that women wear. This word can also be a verb. What does the verb mean?
2 Find three *general* words that refer to things people wear. Which one can only be used in a plural form?
3 Find two words that refer to what clothes are made *from*.
4 Find two words that refer to a *particular* (single) item of clothing.
5 **Cloth** and **material** are usually uncountable in this sense. Which countable nouns could fill this gap?
   A _____ of cloth / material.

PRACTICE

2 Choose the correct word of the two given:

I buy cotton (cloth / clothing) and make it into (material / clothes) for myself and my family. Last winter I made a (cloth / dress), which I wore to parties, but every (clothes / garment) I make is quite different.

3 Label the pictures with all the words at the top of the page that describe them. Some words may be used more than once.

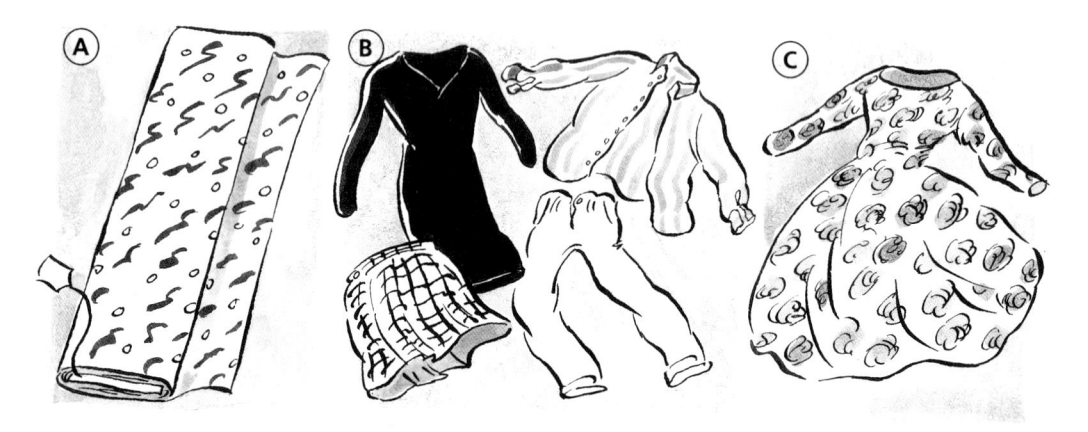

A   B   C

SEE ALSO: Grammar, pages 123–5, 128;
Workbook, page 37;
Teacher's Book.

4 Complete the text using any of the key words that you think are suitable:

Most cotton _____ is imported into Europe from Africa and South East Asia. It is then made up into finished _____ at _____ factories. Wholesalers buy in large quantities and sell to shops. Many shops now specialise in particular items of _____ . For example, the Sock Shop sells only socks, and the Shirt Shop only has shirts. There are, however, few fashion shops which sell only _____ . They usually sell other women's _____ as well.

114 VOCABULARY

KEY WORDS

next
previous
last
the last
latest

LOOK

I'm going away **next** month.
She had been there the **previous** day.
We met **last** Saturday.
They'll be here in **the last** week of August.
I'm not interested in the **latest** fashions.

CHECK

1 Which of the words in brackets can be used to complete each sentence? Why is the other one not possible?

1 _____ time you come, we'll visit the zoo. (next / last)
2 Have you heard the _____ news? We've got a new Prime Minister! (last / latest)
3 I was delighted when he praised my work, because he had not liked my _____ efforts. (previous / last)
4 _____ year we all went to Thailand. (last / the last)

PRACTICE

2 Today is *Thursday 11th April*. Using the calendar, note each day that is referred to below. An example is done for you:

Example: *next Tuesday* (●)

APRIL													
SUN	**MON**	**TUES**	**WED**	**THUR**	**FRI**	**SAT**	**SUN**	**MON**	**TUES**	**WED**	**THUR**	**FRI**	**SAT**
	1	2	3	4	5	6	7	8	9	10	11	12	13
14	15	16	17	18	19	20	21	22	23	24	25	26	27
28	29	30											

1 next Wednesday
2 the Saturday after next
3 last Friday
4 the last Wednesday in April
5 not yesterday, but the previous Wednesday
6 the Monday before last

3 Read the short newspaper report on the right and fill in the gaps using the key words:

4 Now put the following sentences in the correct order:

A The owners realised the horse was missing.
B A man was arrested.
C The horse was in its stable.
D A stranger was seen in the area.
E The area was searched.
F Nightowl disappeared.
G The police looked around the stable.

HORSE STOLEN?

Nightowl, a three-year-old racehorse, disappeared _____ Wednesday from Allington Stables in Newmarket. At first, his owners thought he had managed to get out of the stable, but after police had looked around it became clear that he had been stolen. For the _____ two days, the surrounding area was searched. When police interviewed neighbours, they heard that a stranger had been seen on a number of occasions in the _____ week. _____ night there was still no sign of Nightowl. However, the _____ news is that a man has been arrested.

SEE ALSO:
Workbook, page 38;
Teacher's Book.

KEY WORDS

very
fairly
quite
really
extremely
terribly
awfully
pretty
reasonably
absolutely
totally
completely

LOOK

It's **very** nice.
He's **fairly** good.
It's **quite** late.
That's **really** beautiful.
You're **extremely** naughty.
It's **terribly** old.
She's **awfully** kind.
It's **pretty** good.
I'm **reasonably** certain.

CHECK

1 Do the words in **bold** in LOOK above make adjectives *stronger* or *weaker*? Write them in the correct list. Two examples are given:

Stronger	Weaker
very	fairly

PRACTICE

2 Now make sentences using each of the words above with one of these adjectives:

tired	old	pleasant	serious	thin
important	interesting	boring	dangerous	

LOOK

It's an **absolutely** wonderful cake!
It's an **absolutely** awful cake!

CHECK

3 Which of the words below can be used when we want to say something is 100 per cent good or bad?

1 totally
2 fairly
3 quite
4 pretty
5 completely

WORD STUDY

1 Some words can be used before adjectives to make them *stronger* or *weaker*:
   very   fairly   quite   really   extremely
   awfully   pretty   terribly   reasonably

2 Some words can be used before adjectives when we want to say something is 100 per cent good or bad:
   It's **absolutely** awful!

★ Note that **quite** can be used in either of the ways shown above:
   The weather is **quite** good.
   Your work is **quite** perfect.

KEY WORDS

PRACTICE

4 Look at these pictures of judges giving marks out of 10 at a sports competition. Match the phrases with the pictures:

1 absolutely awful
2 very good
3 quite good
4 quite perfect
5 fairly bad

A B C D E

5 We often use the words that we have been looking at when we are giving our opinions. Look at this example:

Example: A: *Isn't that book interesting?*
B: *Well . . . I think it's <u>fairly</u> good.*

Now do the same as B. Agree or disagree with the opinion given, but use one of the key words to make it stronger or weaker.

Example: A: *Look at the price of that.*
B: *Yes. It's <u>terribly</u> expensive isn't it!*

2 A: Oh! Isn't she lovely!
B: _____

3 A: That film was quite good, wasn't it?
B: _____

1 A: Oh! I don't like that!
B: _____

4 A: What a noise!
B: _____

SEE ALSO:
Workbook, page 39;
Teacher's Book.

VOCABULARY 117

THE DICTIONARY – EXTENDING ITS USE

A monolingual dictionary gives more than just the meanings of words. It can help you to choose the right word, especially when the words are similar; it can help you put words together, for example when verbs are followed by different constructions; it can help you to use words in different ways, which are often unique to English; it can help you to check your work and correct your mistakes. It can also help you to pronounce the words.

Vocabulary – choosing the right word

You can often think of two possible words to use, and you are not sure which one you want. A dictionary will help you to distinguish between them.

1 Use the dictionary extracts to complete these sentences appropriately. If a word has a number of senses, say which number you have chosen (for example, **sensitive 2**):

1 He is much too _____; whatever you say, he gets upset.
2 The teacher realised that the boy was crying, and responded with great _____.
3 That sounds like a _____ idea; I'm sure it will work.
4 These documents are quite _____, so keep them away from the journalists!
5 My teeth are very _____ to hot or cold liquids.

sen·si·ble /ˈsensɪbəl/ *adj* reasonable and practical: *a sensible child | a sensible plan* –**sensibly** *adv*: *You acted very sensibly*
■ USAGE Do not confuse **sensible** and **sensitive**. A **sensible** person is one who is reasonable and practical, and who has good judgment. *She was very sensible in the way she dealt with a dangerous situation.* A **sensitive** person is one who is very conscious of other people's feelings and opinions: *She was sensitive enough not to ask too many questions about his unhappy childhood.* | *You shouldn't be so sensitive – I didn't mean anything bad in what I said.*

sen·si·tive /ˈsensɪtɪv/ *adj* **1** quick to show or feel the effect of something: *sensitive to cold | light-sensitive photographic paper | a sensitive pair of scales* **2** showing delicate feelings or judgment: *a sensitive performance | a sensitive actor* –opposite **insensitive** –see SENSIBLE (USAGE) **3** easily offended (a word often used to express disapproval): *For goodness sake, don't be so sensitive!* **4** needing to be dealt with very carefully: *This is rather a sensitive issue.* | *sensitive official papers* –**sensitively** *adv* –**sensitivity** /ˌsensɪˈtɪvɪti/ *n* (also **sensitiveness** /ˈsensɪtɪvnɪs/) [U]

2 Look up these words and phrases in your dictionary, and write sentences to show the differences between the words in each pair:

break / tear   bay window / french window
plump / stout   cottage / bungalow

Multi-part verbs are often confusing for students. For example, the verb **fall** forms a base for several different multi-part verbs.

3 Complete these sentences with the appropriate particle, consulting the dictionary extract if you need to:

1 He tripped on a stone and fell _____.
2 He told her a lie, and she fell _____ it.
3 It's always sad when old friends fall _____.
4 You must keep up to date with your work; don't fall _____.

fall back *phr v* [I] to move away from something: *The crowd fell back to let the doctor through.*
fall back on sthg *phr v* [T] to use something because other things have failed: *You'll always have your training as a teacher to fall back on.*
fall behind *phr v* [I] to fail to make progress as quickly as you should: *I've fallen behind with my work.*
fall for *phr v* **1** [T **fall for** sthg] to be cheated or deceived by something: *I knew it was just a trick, and I wasn't going to fall for it.* **2** [T **fall for** sbdy] to start loving someone suddenly and strongly
fall in with sbdy/sthg *phr v* [T] to agree with someone or agree to something: *I'm quite prepared to fall in with this idea.*
fall off *phr v* [I] to decrease in quality or amount: *Membership has fallen off this year.*
fall out *phr v* [I] to quarrel: *I've fallen out* **with** *my mother.* | *We fell out over money.*
fall over *phr v* [I] to fall to the ground: *She tripped and fell over.*

4 Now look up **put** and **bring** in your dictionary. Choose two multi-part verbs from each entry and use them to write sentences about yourself.

Grammar – putting the words together

Words form sentences according to the rules of grammar. Here are five abbreviated rules of grammar which you will find in the *Longman Dictionary of Contemporary English*. (Other dictionaries may express these rules in different ways.)

		Example
hope	[+ to-v]	I hope **to go**.
hope	[+ that]	I hope **that** he is going.
like	[+ v-ing]	I like **going**.
ask	[obj + to-v]	I asked **him to go**.
make	[+ obj + adj / v-ed]	The walk made **us hungry**.

5 Look at these phrases, and link them to the abbreviated rules:

1 He painted his room bright red.
2 I expect that he'll be here soon.
3 He told Susannah to wait.
4 I adore going to the ballet.
5 They are hoping to go tomorrow.

6 Now fill in the same grammatical descriptions in the missing places in the dictionary extracts on the right. The descriptions come before the sentences they relate to.

want¹ /wɒnt‖wɔ:nt, wa:nt/ *v* [*not usu. in progressive forms*] **1** [T] to have a strong desire for: *I want a drink.* | *Ask him what he wants.* | *What do you want for your birthday?* (= What present would you like?) ⊙ _____ *Do you want to go now?* ⊙ _____ *He wants you to wait here.* ⊙ _____ *I want that letter ready/typed by tomorrow.*

pre·fer /prɪˈfɜː*/ *v* -**rr**- [T *not in progressive forms*] **1** [(**to**)] to choose (one thing or action) rather than another; like better: *"Would you like meat or fish?" "I'd prefer meat, please."* | *I much prefer dogs to cats.* ⊙ _____ *I prefer singing to acting.* ⊙ _____ *He chose Spain, but personally I'd prefer to go to Greece.* ⊙ _____ *"Let me wash the dishes – or would you prefer me to dry them?"* ⊙ _____ *Would you prefer that we reschedule the meeting for next week?*

Usage – using words in different ways

The dictionary meaning is sometimes not enough to show how a word is used, so some dictionaries give usage notes where there are difficulties.

7 Read the *Usage* extracts given, and match each extract with a sentence below. Then complete each sentence with a suitable word:

1 I don't think you can say it was Michael's _____; he really wasn't to _____ for what happened.
2 Poor Sue was in a mess. She had several wasp _____, and she had been _____ by some red ants.
3 I need a _____ to store my bicycle; there isn't any _____ in my house.

■ USAGE We can use the word **bite** (verb and noun) when talking about many kinds of insect: *They had been bitten all over by mosquitoes/fleas/red ants.* | *They were covered in mosquito bites.* For some insects, however, we use the word **sting**: *He had been stung by an angry wasp/bee/scorpion.* | *His eye was swollen from a particularly bad bee sting.*

■ USAGE **Room** [U] and **place** [C] can both mean free space that can be used for a purpose; but **place** is used for a single particular piece of space, while **room** means space in general: *"Is there (any) room for me to sit down in here?" "Yes, there's a place in the corner."* | *This is the place where we keep the coal.* | *There's no room for any more coal in here.*

■ USAGE **1** The following sentences have a similar meaning, but note how the nouns **blame** and **fault** are used in different ways: *They were not to blame for the accident.* | *The accident was not their fault.* **2** In conversation **fault** is more commonly used than **blame** to say that someone is (or is not) responsible for something bad which has happened: *It's all your fault! I should never have listened to you.* | *Don't blame me! It's not my fault you were late.*

Errors – checking words

When you think a word may be wrong (or when your teacher marks a word without saying what is wrong with it), you can check it in the dictionary.

8 Using your own dictionary, check these underlined words and expressions, and correct them:

1 He didn't give me the <u>informations</u>.
2 Going out in the rain <u>brought up</u> a fever.
3 He is an <u>electric</u> engineer.
4 It is <u>sure</u> that he'll come tomorrow.
5 We enjoy a high standard of <u>life</u>.

VOCABULARY 119

GRAMMAR

This part of the book has five main sections and can be used *at any time and in any order*, both in class – as part of the course – and for self-study. The units are cross-referenced to relevant units in the **Skills** part and the Workbook.

page

NOUNS	122
VERBS	135
PREPOSITIONS	158
SENTENCES	167
PARAGRAPHS	175

NOUNS

REVIEW	page
	122
Articles 1: *the / Ø (zero article)*	123
Articles 2: *a some any*	124
Quantities 1: *a few a little not many not much*	125
Quantities 2: *all most some no none both neither (of the)*	126
Quantities 3: *countables and uncountables*	128
Quantities 4: *a box of a jar of a tube of a tin of a packet of a bunch of a pair of a couple of*	129
Comparative adjectives: *easier (than) the easiest more useful (than) the most useful*	130
Joining nouns: *'s of Ø*	131
Modifying the noun: *a woman (who) I like a man in a suit*	132
REFERENCE: a summary of grammatical forms	134

REVIEW
Before you start this section, these are the items you should have met.

countable and uncountable	Is there **any** fruit?
	    Yes, there **is**.
	Are there **any** apples?
	    No, there **aren't**.
		a few a little
		some a lot of
		many much
			She's got **a few** minutes
			. . . **a little** time.
			He reads **a lot of** books.
			He takes **a lot of** sugar.
			Do they read **many** books?
			I don't take **much** sugar.
			He bought **some** books.
			I'll have **some** sugar.

-er -est more most (comparative and superlative adjectives)	The house is **bigger**, but it's **more expensive**. *Star Wars* was **more successful than** *Gone with the Wind*. Jane is **the busiest** of them all. The Matterhorn is **the most difficult** to climb.	's s' of (possessives)	It's the man**'s** newspaper. the boy**'s** books the boys**'** books the children**'s** books It's the cause **of** the problem.

mine   ours
    yours
his   theirs
    hers
	Is this sweater **mine** or **yours**?
	The bicycle is **his**.
	The car is **hers**.
	The dog is **theirs**.		

someone anyone no-one something anything nothing	There is **someone** at the door. Is there **anyone**? **No-one** is here. He left **something**. He didn't leave **anything**. **Nothing** was left.		

LOOK

Look at **the time**!

Time is money.

NOUNS
Articles 1
the
ø

Put **the food** on that table.
You can live for about 60 days or so without **food**.

1 Why do we use **the** in two sentences and not in the other two?

CHECK 1 Complete these sentences with **the** if necessary. If **the** is not necessary, use ø:

1 When _____ water freezes it turns into _____ ice.
2 _____ rain yesterday was really heavy.
3 Can you clear _____ snow off my path, please?

PRACTICE 2 Complete these sentences with words from the box, and **the** if necessary:

| electricity | industry |
| insurance | protection |

1 You ought to insure your house. Think of _____ which _____ gives you.
2 A good supply of _____ is vital for _____ .

| health | safety | diet | rules |

3 _____ of our workers depends on everyone observing _____ for using each machine.
4 Doctors think that _____ depends to a large extent on _____ .

| confidence | future |
| intelligence | strength |

5 He had _____ of a weightlifter and _____ of a hippopotamus.
6 You must face _____ with _____ .

GRAMMAR
Here are two main ways of using nouns:
1 You make it clear which item you are talking about:
   The time I spent in Wales was delightful.
   This is a specific period of time.

★ **The** is one of a number of words which will make a noun specific. You can also use:
   this   these   my
   that   those   your etc.

2 You are talking in general:
   Time is **money**.
   This is not a specific period of time or amount of money; it refers to any period and amount.

The most common way of talking generally is to use the noun alone, without an article.

★ ø = no article, for example: **the**: the money
                                 ø: money

SEE ALSO: Skills, pages 32–3;
Workbook, page 40;
Teacher's Book.

GRAMMAR **123**

NOUNS
Articles 2

a
some
any

LOOK

He's got **a** book to read.

He's got **some** books to read.
He's got **some** milk.

He hasn't got **a** book to read.

He hasn't got **any** books to read.
He hasn't got **any** milk.

Has he got **a** book to read?

Has he got **any** books to read?
Has he got **any** milk?

1 When are **a**, **some** and **any** used in the sentences above?
   Ask yourself these two questions:
      Is the noun singular, plural or uncountable?
      Is the sentence affirmative, negative or interrogative?

CHECK 1 Now complete these sentences with **some**, **any** or **a**:

1 Is there _____ cheese in the fridge?
2 He hasn't made _____ changes.
3 We don't need _____ doctor.
4 There are _____ children waiting to see the nurse.
5 Nobody here seems to know _____ English.
6 I would like _____ advice, please.

GRAMMAR

	Affirmative	Interrogative	Negative
Singular noun	a book	a book	a book
Plural noun	some books	any books	any books
Uncountable noun	some milk	any milk	any milk

PRACTICE 2 Complete these sentences with words from the boxes, and **a**, **some** or **any**:

| information   radio   newspaper   tomatoes |

1 There weren't _____ left in the fridge.
2 Have you got _____ to listen to?
3 I didn't buy _____ , so I don't know who won the election.
4 Do you have _____ on the new product?

| dentists   sugar   time |

5 It'll take me _____ to do the job.
6 I'm afraid you can't have _____ in your coffee; there's none left.
7 Have you got _____ on your list, or are they all doctors?

3 Make up questions *or* negative statements using these and other phrases, and put **any** or **a(n)** before each one:
Example: *accident*
         Have you ever seen a car accident?

1 princess   2 time   3 house   4 hospitals   5 butter   6 brothers / sisters

SEE ALSO:
Workbook, page 40;
Teacher's Book.

NOUNS
Quantities 1

a few
a little
not many
not much

LOOK We have **a few** sandwiches left, and **a little** milk.

There are**n't many** cakes left, and **not much** sugar.

1 Which words are used when the *items* are countable? uncountable?
2 Which words are used when the *feelings* are positive? negative?

CHECK 1 Complete these sentences with phrases from the box:

| a little | not much |
| a few | not many |

1 _____ people came today; it's hardly worth showing the film.
2 There's _____ sugar left here. Would you like some in your coffee?
3 We've got _____ customers already, so I hope the company will grow.
4 There's _____ difference between the two products. They're almost identical.

GRAMMAR

A few and **not many** are used with plural nouns:
  I have **a few** good friends, and I like seeing them.
  I do**n't** have **many** envelopes; I can't send all the letters.

A little and **not much** are used with uncountable nouns:
  I have **a little** time now; how can I help?
  I haven**'t** got **much** money; I can't afford it.

a few / a little = a small amount but enough.
not many / not much = a small amount and not enough.

PRACTICE 2 Complete each sentence with the appropriate phrase, A, B or C, and complete each one with a phrase from the box:

| much   a little   many   a few |

1 He wrote a lot of poetry, but unfortunately . . .
2 He spoke excellent French, but . . .
3 There wasn't any cheese, but . . .

A . . . he didn't speak _____ English.
B . . . there was _____ ham.
C . . . he didn't write _____ novels.

4 We haven't got any vegetables, but . . .
5 I really don't know much about this, because . . .
6 The hospital was poorly staffed, but . . .

A . . . I haven't paid _____ attention to it.
B . . . there's _____ fruit on the table.
C . . . there were _____ doctors available.

SEE ALSO:
Workbook, pages 41–2;
Teacher's book.

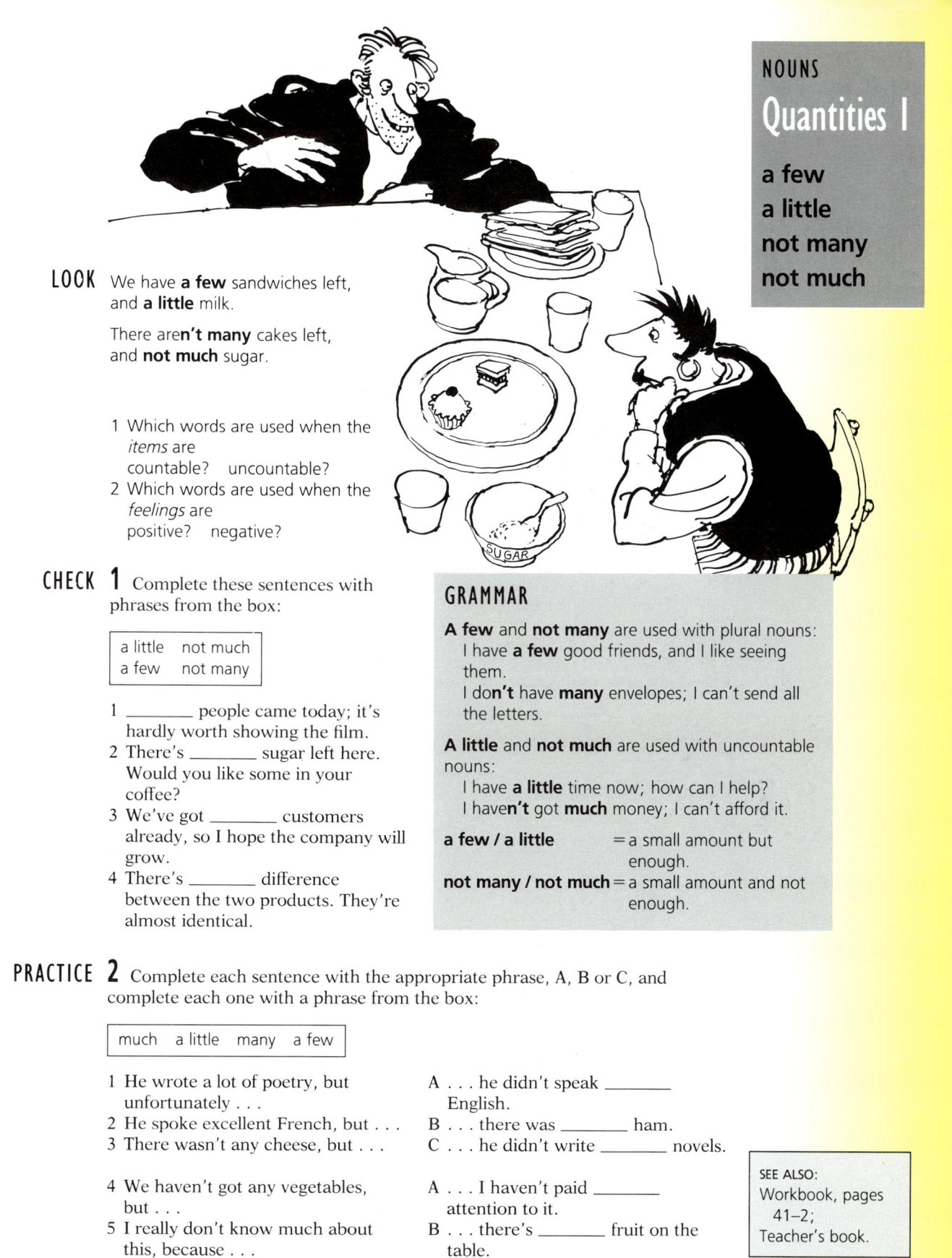

GRAMMAR **125**

NOUNS
Quantities 2

all
most
some
no
none
both
neither
    (of the)

LOOK

1
All babies cry for attention.
Most babies wake up at night.
Some babies sleep more than others.
No babies can walk when they are born.

2
All (of) the programmes were in colour.
Most of the programmes were light entertainment.
Some of them were quite good.
None of them was in black and white.

3
Neither of the two doctors was on duty.
Neither doctor was on duty.
Both (of) the doctors were away for the weekend.
Both doctors were away for the weekend.
Both of them were away for the weekend.

1 What is the difference in meaning between the words in **bold** in set **1**?
2 What is the difference in meaning between set **1** and set **2**?
3 What is the difference between: **all** and **both**?
                                    no / none and **neither**?

CHECK 1 Complete these sentences with **(of) the**, **of the** (or **of them**) *if necessary*:

1 Most _____ cars have four wheels, though a few have three.
2 All _____ books in the library have now been catalogued.
3 Both _____ girls came to work, but unfortunately . . .
4 . . . neither _____ arrived on time.
5 Some _____ third world cities are extremely polluted today.
6 None _____ people I spoke to were interested in attending.
7 All _____ businesses everywhere have the same aim: to make money.
8 Jim spends most _____ day asleep, I think.

GRAMMAR

all	= 100%		**both**	= 100% (of two)
most	= 60–90%	(very approximately)		
some	= 20–60%			
no / none	= 0%		**neither**	= 0% (of two)

Refers to any example of the item
All animals are . . .
Some meals are . . .

Refers to particular examples of the item
Most of our customers are . . .
None of the people are . . .
Both (of the) boys are . . .
Neither (of the) boy(s) is . . .

★ 1 **All of the** and **both of the** are commonly contracted to **all the** and **both the**.
    This is *not* true of the other words.
  2 **No** is general: **No** books . . .
    None is specific: **None** of the books . . .
  3 **Both** and **neither** refer to two items only; they are always specific.

NOUNS
Quantities 2
continued

PRACTICE 2 Complete each sentence with a suitable word or phrase from the box. You can discuss your choices with a partner. The sentences are in three groups, A, B and C. What is the difference between them?

all   most   some   no

A

1 Sorry, _____ dogs are allowed.
2 _____ males in Switzerland must do military service.
3 _____ Europeans are in favour of the Common Market, and a small number are against it.
4 In Great Britain _____ people do their shopping during the week and others prefer to shop on Saturdays.

all (of) the   most of the   some of the   none of the

B
I left London last month for a week, to go on a tour of Paris. There were about 15 of us on the tour. _____ members were women (about 11 altogether), but _____ group were men. _____ men were English, but three of the women were from other countries. There was a fashion show on the Wednesday, but _____ men went to that; they all went for a boat ride on the Seine instead.

both [(of) the]   neither [of the]

C
Jean and Chris Adams had four children, two boys and two girls. _____ girls liked going to the cinema, but _____ boys did; they hated the cinema.

3 Now you can make up your own sentences, and compare them with those written by your partner.

A Think of four *general* statements, which you think are true in *any* circumstances:
Example: *Most young people like dancing, but a few don't.*

1 No _____
2 Some _____
3 Most _____
4 All _____

B Think of six *specific* statements, which you think are true:
Example: *None of the people in my family can play the violin.*

1 None of / my _____
2 Neither of / my _____
3 Some of / my _____
4 Most of / my _____
5 All / my _____
6 Both my _____

SEE ALSO: Skills, pages 36–8; Workbook, pages 41–2; Teacher's Book.

NOUNS
Quantities 3
Countables and uncountables

LOOK

furniture   chair

A: Look, here's **a** Victorian **chair**.
B: Good **furniture** makes all the difference to a room.

music   song

A: I heard **a** lovely **song** on Radio Four yesterday morning.
B: Yes, you hear very good **music** in the mornings.

1 Can you count **chairs**, **furniture**, **songs**, and **music**?

PRACTICE 1 Here are some pairs of words. Put each word in the right place, making it plural if necessary:

1 money   dollar
  A: How much _____ have you got?
  B: I've got a hundred _____ and some travellers' cheques.

2 luggage   suitcase
  C: How much _____ are you taking?
  D: I'm taking two _____ and a handbag.

3 television   programme
  E: What is there on _____ tonight?
  F: There are two _____ about animals which I want to watch.

4 traffic   taxi
  G: Well, let's take a _____ to the airport.
  H: I hope there isn't too much _____ .

5 progress   step forward
  We haven't made any _____ with the problem of traffic for years. If they start talking about it, that's a _____ .

SEE ALSO:
Workbook, page 43;
Teacher's Book.

128   GRAMMAR

NOUNS
Quantities 4

a box of
a jar of
a tube of
a tin of
a packet of
a bunch of
a pair of
a couple of

LOOK

A
a tin of . . .
a jar of . . .
a tube of . . .

B
a box of . . . 
a packet of . . . 

C 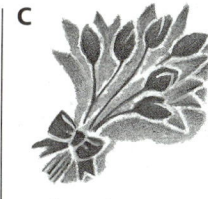 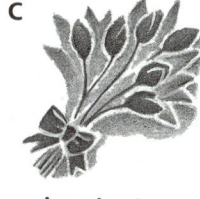
a bunch of . . .

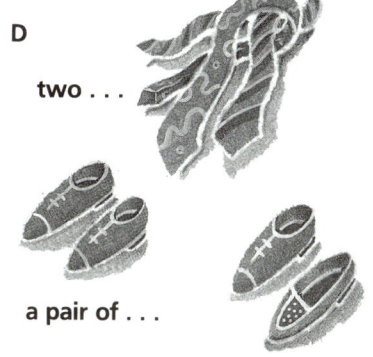

D
two . . .
a pair of . . .
a couple of . . .

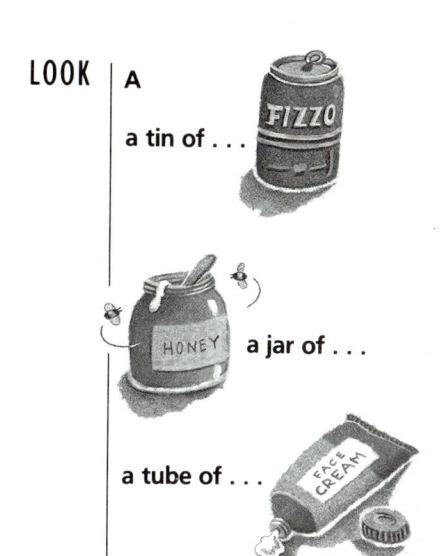

1 Look at **D**. What is the difference between **a pair** and **two**?
2 What is the difference between **a pair** and **a couple**?

SEE ALSO:
Workbook, page 43;
Teacher's Book.

CHECK

1 Complete these with **A**, **B** or **C** from LOOK above:

1 _____ is not a container.
2 _____ are usually for liquids and creams.
3 _____ are usually for solids.

2 Which of these items are pairs, and which are individual items? Make two columns in your notebooks:

trousers shirts pyjamas gloves
hats glasses coats jeans
umbrellas ties shoes blouses
socks skirts belts pants

PRACTICE

3 Put the appropriate form of a word from the box in each space (use each word once):

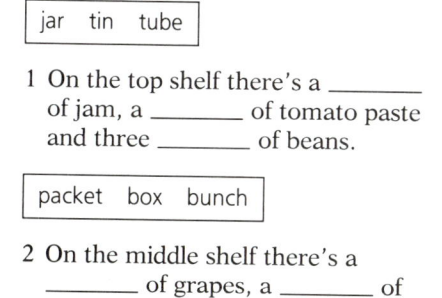

| jar tin tube |

1 On the top shelf there's a _____ of jam, a _____ of tomato paste and three _____ of beans.

| packet box bunch |

2 On the middle shelf there's a _____ of grapes, a _____ of sugar and a _____ of tissues.

GRAMMAR

countable: one book, two books . . .
uncountable: bread sugar tea

a box of
Uncountables can be made countable by using a word like **cup**, **packet**, **tube**, etc.:
  a cup of coffee   a tube of toothpaste

★ **Tin** is normal in British English, **can** in American English. **Can** is commonly used in BrEng and AmEng for liquids:
  a can of coke   a can of soup

a pair of / a couple of
a pair: two items which together form a unit:
  a pair of scissors
  a pair of shoes
a couple: approximately two similar items which are not a pair:
  a couple of shirts
  a couple of shoes (when they are not a pair)

★ **a couple**: also a man and a woman who are connected:
  a married **couple**
  a **couple** dancing together

GRAMMAR 129

NOUNS
Comparative adjectives

easier (than)
the easiest
more useful (than)
the most useful

LOOK

It's **easier** to find what you want in ICB Superstore. They've got one of **the simplest** ways of laying out their goods that I've seen anywhere.

This is a **more modern** version of our 1983 model; it's **the most useful** one we have on the market at the moment . . .

1 Notice that **modern** and **useful** end with consonants, and **easy** and **simple** end with vowels or vowel sounds.

CHECK

1 Now complete this table by putting these adjectives in the right group. Some have been done for you.

easy	careful	clever	early	foolish	famous
helpful	modern	narrow	frequent	funny	gentle
simple	(un)tidy	useful	pretty	shallow	silly

easier / easiest	*more / most modern*
Clever easy _____ _____ gentle	careful modern
shallow _____ _____ _____	_____ _____
_____	_____

PRACTICE

2 Complete each sentence with the comparative or superlative form of one of the adjectives in the boxes:

| helpful   untidy   funny   early |

1 Hello John, it's only 6 o'clock, you're _____ than we expected.
2 The service was good, and the girl in the blue dress was the _____ girl in the shop.
3 Bob Hope is funny, but Charlie Chaplin was a lot _____ .
4 Sue is one of the _____ people I've ever met; she leaves her things lying about all over the place.

| narrow   frequent   gentle |

5 French canals are wide; English canals are _____ than French ones.
6 He seems terribly aggressive, but in fact he is one of the _____ men I have ever met.
7 Trains on Sunday are few and far between; they are _____ during the week.

GRAMMAR

Adjectives of one syllable make comparisons with **-er** and **-est**; adjectives of three syllables with **more** . . . and **most** . . .

Adjectives of two syllables can be of either kind:

-er / -est
Adjectives ending in: -y   -ow
                      -le   -er

more . . . / most . . .
Adjectives ending in: -ful   -ish
                      -ent   -ous
                      -ern

| happy   careful   clever |

8 This boy is always laughing and smiling; he is one of the _____ children I have ever met.
9 Sam, you must be _____ with your things. I found your scarf lying outside on the pavement.
10 He's very intelligent; in fact he's the _____ person I've ever met.

SEE ALSO: Skills, pages 22–3, 26–7, 36–8, 42–5, 54–5, 56–7; Workbook, page 44; Teacher's Book.

130 GRAMMAR

NOUNS
Joining nouns:
's
of
ø

LOOK **A** That <u>man</u>**'s coat** is torn.
B 1 This <u>country</u>**'s population** . . .
2 The **population** of this <u>country</u> . . .
C A <u>week</u>**'s work** . . .
D Here's a <u>coat</u> **hanger** for your jacket.

The nouns underlined are joined to the nouns in **bold** in three different ways: **'s**, **of** or **ø** (nothing). How are they joined:
1 if the underlined noun is a thing?
2 if the underlined noun is a person?
3 if the underlined noun is a period of time?
4 if the underlined noun is a group of people (a city, a company, etc.)?

CHECK 1 Look at these sentences. Are they like **A**, **B** (1 or 2), **C** or **D** above?

1 This took us three months' concentrated effort.
2 This city's streets are reasonably clean.
3 The table leg is wobbly.
4 The children's supper is in the kitchen.
5 The streets of the city are reasonably clean.

GRAMMAR Three ways of joining two nouns together:

		Second noun	Main noun	Second noun
People:	('s)	a man	**'s** coat	
Human groups:	('s / of)	the company	**'s** strength	
		the	strength	**of** the company
Things:	(ø)	the car	industry	
Times:	('s)	a week	**'s** work	

PRACTICE 2 Complete each sentence with a word from the box, and **'s** if necessary:

1 I need a new _____ ribbon; this one is worn out.
2 He bought a _____ bicycle for his daughter.
3 You should buy a _____ frame for that lovely painting.
4 _____ progress in the last fifty years has been incredible.

5 We'll see the results in a _____ time.
6 He's taking _____ lessons.
7 He bought two _____ shirts for himself.
8 The _____ sales record has been excellent.

In two of the above sentences **'s** can be replaced with **of**. Which are they?

picture
girl
Japan
typewriter

company
men
tennis
week

3 Read these sentences, and change the **'s** forms to **of** forms. Two of the sentences cannot be changed. Which are they, and why not?

1 The world is arguing about the Antarctic's natural resources.
2 It should take about an hour's work to get it finished.
3 The United States' attitude is one of growing concern.
4 Today's paper has some exciting news in it.

SEE ALSO: Skills, pages 34–5, 68–9; Workbook, page 45; Teacher's Book.

NOUNS
Modifying the noun

a woman (who) I like
a man in a suit

LOOK

1
A The **girl who / that sat** next to Brian was very nice.
B The **books which / that sell** are not the best.

2
A She is a **woman (who / that) I** like.
B That's **something (which / that) I** shall never forget.

3
You met the daughter.
Do you remember **the woman whose daughter** you met?

1 Which examples in **1**A and **1**B and **2**A and **2**B refer to people and which to things?
2 Look at the subjects in the examples in **1** and **2**. How are **1**A and **1**B different from **2**A and **2**B?
3 Who does **whose** refer to in **3**?

CHECK

1 Which items from the box will fit in each of these sentences? (Usually there is more than one possibility.)

which	that
whose	(no word)
who	

1 Someone _____ is really ill gets treated at once.
2 There are hospitals _____ make you wait for six months for an operation.
3 All those boys _____ parents have already arrived should go into the main hall.
4 I was looking at the sea shells _____ my sister had collected.
5 That's a person _____ I haven't seen for years.

LOOK

I was *looking for* a person.
There's the person **(who / that) I** was *looking for*.

1 Where is the preposition in the second sentence?

PRACTICE

2 Join the sentences together with **that**, **who**, **which**, **whose** or no additional word. How many possibilities are there in each case? Which sentences have prepositions after the verbs?
Example:
They finally got the job. They'd been training for the job.
They finally got the job (which / that) they'd been training for.

1 The young man will be very pleased.
   He gets the job.
2 This is the man.
   His best friend betrayed him.
3 There are many problems.
   I can't go into them today.
4 The team was from Scotland.
   It won the match.
5 The woman didn't know what she was talking about.
   They spoke to her.

3 Now make up similar sentences, using information about yourself and your situation. You can make up sentences like these:

The house (which) I live in . . .
The building which is on the corner of . . . is . . .
The man who owns the . . .
The girl / boy (who) I went out with last . . .
The people who live . . .

NOUNS
Modifying the noun
continued

LOOK

. . . a **man with** black hair
. . . a **woman with** a briefcase

. . . a **woman in** a light suit
. . . a **man in** black

. . . a **man of** six foot
. . . a **woman of** great intelligence

1 Can you say 'a girl in a briefcase'? What would it mean?
2 In these sentences, **with**, **in**, and **of** mean: 'wearing', 'being', 'having / carrying'. Which is which?

PRACTICE 4 Complete these sentences with **with**, **in** or **of**. Are they 'wearing', 'being' or 'having / carrying' sentences?

1 She went to the garden party dressed _____ white.
2 He is a man _____ great intelligence.
3 I'm waiting for a tall man _____ blue eyes.
4 Cars _____ two doors are safer if you have young children.
5 You see that man dressed _____ a red coat? He's my brother.
6 Don't let your feelings _____ insecurity hold you back.
7 This is a gift _____ great value; I hope they appreciate it!
8 That woman _____ the green skirt is looking for you.
9 There's a man over there _____ an umbrella; can you see him?

GRAMMAR There are two main ways of adding a descriptive phrase *after* the noun:
1 *Relative clauses*

	Person	Thing
Subject	The man **who** came . . .	The car **which** crashed . . .
	The man **that** came . . .	The car **that** crashed . . .
Object	The man (**who**) I saw . . .	The car (**which**) I bought . . .
	The man (**that**) I saw . . .	The car (**that**) I bought . . .
Possessive	The man **whose** car I . . .	

2 *Prepositional phrases*
a **man with** a coat — who has / is carrying a coat
a **man in** a coat — who is wearing a coat
a **man of** intelligence — who is intelligent

SEE ALSO: Skills, pages 34–5, 46–7, 48–9, 68–9, 74–5, 76–7; Workbook, pages 46–7; Teacher's Book.

GRAMMAR 133

REFERENCE: a summary of grammatical forms

ARTICLES

	Specific	General Affirmative	General Negative / Interrogative
Singular	**the** book	**a** book	**a** book
Plural	**the** books	**some / 0** books	**any / 0** books
Uncountable	**the** advice	**some / 0** advice	**any / 0** advice

QUANTITIES

	'Positive' meaning	'Negative' meaning
Plural	**a few** sandwiches	**not many** cakes
Uncountable	**a little** milk	**not much** sugar

Specific
all (of) the babies   **all of** it / them
most of the babies   **most of** it / them
some of the babies   **some of** it / them
none of the babies   **none of** it / them

General
all babies
most babies
some babies
no babies

both (of) the doctors   **both of them**
both doctors
neither of the doctors   **neither of them**
neither doctor

	a ...	the ...	two ...	some ...	0 ...
Countable	chair song	chair song	chairs songs	chairs songs	chairs songs
Uncountable	—	furniture music	—	furniture music	furniture music

Common uncountable nouns
advice   knowledge
bread   milk
furniture   money
hair   news
homework   progress
information   music

a tin of soup   **a bunch of** flowers
a jar of honey   **a pair of** shoes
a tube of cream   **a couple of** shirts
a box of matches
a packet of rice

COMPARATIVE ADJECTIVES

ADJECTIVES WITH TWO SYLLABLES

easier / easiest
clever easy silly gentle
shallow early (un)tidy simple
narrow funny (un)happy
    pretty

more / most modern
careful frequent
helpful foolish
useful famous

JOINING NOUNS

People	a man**'s** coat
Human groups	the company**'s** growth / the growth **of** the company
Things	the car industry
Times	a week**'s** work

MODIFYING THE NOUN

RELATIVE CLAUSES

Subject	*Person* The man **who** came ... The man **that** came ...
	Thing The car **which** crashed ... The car **that** crashed ...
Object	*Person* The man **(who)** I saw ... The man **(that)** I saw ...
	Thing The car **(which)** I bought ... The car **(that)** I bought ...
Possessive	The man **whose** car I bought ...

PREPOSITIONAL PHRASES

a **man with** a coat   a **man of** intelligence
a **man in** a coat

134 GRAMMAR

VERBS

REVIEW	page
	135
Tenses 1: present simple present progressive	136
Tenses 2: dynamic and stative verbs: *see / look hear / sound feel smell taste*	137
Tenses 3: past simple past progressive and *used to*	138
Tenses 4: present perfect past perfect	140
Tenses 5: future time	141
Modals 1: probability: *will should could / may / might (well) won't*	142
Modals 2: ability: *could managed to can be able to*	144
Modals 3: deduction: *must be can't have*	146
The passive	147
Multi-part verbs	148
Reporting statements / questions / instructions	150
Modifying the verb 1: adverbs of manner	152
Modifying the verb 2: comparative adverbs	153
Verbs followed by: *to* + infinitive / noun *to* + infinitive / clause (*that*)	154
REFERENCE: a summary of grammatical forms	156

REVIEW

Before you start this section, these are the items you should have met.

drives
is driving
	What **does** Frank **do**?
	   He **drives** a taxi.
	What **is** he **doing**?
	   He**'s driving** to the airport.

was having arrived	I **was having** a shower . . . . . . when Paul **arrived**.
has finished since for ever never been gone	Julia **has finished**. She has worked there **since** 1990 / **for** two years. Have you **ever** seen . . . ? I have **never** seen . . . Have you **been** out? John has **gone** to the shops.
had left	When he got to the station the train **had left**.
is having is going to will	At 12.30 he **is having** lunch with Priscilla. He **is going to invite** her out to the theatre. Perhaps **I'll go** skating.

will won't might	She **will** die one day. She **won't** live for ever. You **might** live until you're 90 years old.
(don't) have to can('t) should(n't) must(n't)	You **(don't) have to** buy a ticket. You **can** dance if you like. You **can't** buy drinks. You **should** smile. You **shouldn't** push. You **must** drive on the left in England. You **mustn't** drive on the right.
If I have . . . If you climbed . . .	**I'll go** tomorrow if I **have** time. You **would be** famous **if** you **climbed** Mount Everest.
is spoken was spoken was painted by	Catalan **is spoken** in Barcelona. Latin **was spoken** in Italy. *Guernica* **was painted by** Picasso.
. . . to go . . . going	Jane **wants to go** to Egypt. Mark **enjoys going** on adventure holidays.

GRAMMAR   135

VERBS
Tenses 1
Present simple

Present progressive

LOOK

1
A Julie **sings** in an opera company.
  She usually **eats** too much.

B I **know** Julie quite well.
  She **loves** opera.

2
A This week she**'s singing** in Milan.
  She**'s eating** less nowadays.

1 What is the difference in *form* between the sentences in **1**A and **2**A?
2 What is the difference in *meaning*?
3 There are no sentences in column **2** for B. Why not?

CHECK **1** Copy these verbs into your notebooks in two columns as shown below:

walk   believe   dance   want   jump   like   work
sell   understand   hear   write see   run   mean
eat   hate   prefer

What you **do**
(*outside you*)

___walk___ _____
_____ _____
_____ _____

What you **think**, **feel**,
experience, **observe**, *etc.*
(*inside you*)

___believe___ _____
_____ _____
_____ _____
_____

PRACTICE **2** Complete these sentences with an appropriate verb from the boxes, in the *present simple* or *present progressive* tense:

| rain   watch   walk   smell   hate |

1 A: Where's Jason?
  B: He and Jim _____ in the park with the dog.
2 Hmmmm! That casserole _____ good!
3 I _____ classical music; it's so boring.
4 C: What _____ you _____ ?
  D: It's a film about animals.
5 Don't forget your umbrella, it _____ every day here.

| like   write   work   understand   want |

6 I _____ (not) _____ this, can you explain it to me?
7 Martin _____ hard at his job. He never takes days off.
8 I _____ you to help me with this – I can't do it.
9 E: _____ you _____ Madonna?
  F: Yes, I think she's great.
10 Can we talk later? I _____ a letter to apply for a job.

SEE ALSO: Skills,
pages 20–1,
26–7, 30–1,
60–1, 62–3,
66–7, 68–9,
72–3;
Workbook, pages
48–9;
Teacher's Book.

3 Now look at the sentences in Practice 2 again, and say whether they are like **1**A, **2**A or **1**B in LOOK above.

GRAMMAR SEE next page.

136 GRAMMAR

VERBS
Tenses 2

Dynamic and stative verbs:
see / look
hear / sound
feel
smell
taste

LOOK 1

1
I **can see** some trees in the distance.
You **can hear** the underground trains.
I **can feel** the vibrations.
Can you **smell** that fish?
I **could taste** garlic in the soup.

2
They **look** beautiful.
They **sound** noisy.
They **feel** funny.
It **smells** bad.
It **tasted** delicious.

1 How are all these verbs connected in meaning?
2 In columns **1** and **2**, three of the verbs are the same and two are different. Which ones are the same?
3 What is the connection between the *object* in column **1** (for example, **trees**) and the *subject* in column **2** (for example, **they**)?

CHECK 1

Complete these sentences with **can(not)** or **could (not)** if possible. If not, do not add anything:

1 I _____ see Ben and Marcia over there, but I _____ see Sarah.
2 These mushrooms _____ taste excellent. Who cooked them?
3 You _____ look cold. What's it like outside?
4 We _____ hear very well because we were sitting at the back.
5 I _____ smell anything; I've got a cold.

PRACTICE 2

Complete these sentences with an appropriate *present tense* form of one of the verbs in the box, and **can** *if necessary*:

see hear smell look sound taste feel

1 That song _____ beautiful.
2 _____ you _____ that noise? There's somebody in the house.
3 This car is a wreck, I _____ all the bumps on the road. It _____ different from travelling in a limousine!
4 This stew is very spicy; I _____ the chilli in it.
5 What are we having for supper? There's something in the kitchen that _____ very good.
6 I _____ your sister; look, she's standing over there. She's wearing a new suit; she _____ very smart.
7 This apple pie _____ delicious. Can I have another piece?

GRAMMAR

Dynamic verbs usually describe actions, temporary or permanent.
If the action is happening now or for a limited period of time, use the present progressive:
   Julian **is looking** well these days.

If the action continues all the time, or there is no time limit on it, use the present simple:
   Julian always **looks** well.

Stative verbs often describe feelings and perceptions.
They do not usually have a time limit, so you only use the present simple:
   I **understand** films in English.

With some statives, especially **see**, **hear**, **feel**, **smell**, **taste** and **understand**, we often use **can**:
   I **can hear**, but I **can't see**.   I **can't understand** that.

Look and **sound** are the dynamic equivalents of **see** and **hear**.

SEE ALSO: Skills, pages 22–3; Workbook, pages 48–9; Teacher's Book.

GRAMMAR 137

VERBS
Tenses 3
Past simple

Past progressive *and* used to

LOOK

1
Yesterday evening I **was writing** a letter.

Everyone **was leaving** when Roy walked in.

2
Yesterday evening I **wrote** a letter.

Everyone **left** when Roy walked in.

1 In what ways are the two sentences in column **1** different from the two sentences in column **2**?

CHECK 1 Look at these sentences, and choose the correct verb form. In one sentence both are correct but have different meanings. Which one?

1 He took / was taking a plane from Stockholm to Oslo and arrived at 6.15.
2 She was walking / walked out of the house when she saw him.
3 I finished / was finishing the work yesterday and handed it in.

PRACTICE 2 Complete the sentences with appropriate forms of the verbs given:

1 What did they do yesterday? They _____ of going to a Greek restaurant, but I don't know whether they _____ to go or not after all. (think   decide)
2 The dog _____ out of the house and _____ the postman. (run   bite)
3 We _____ round the table waiting for the chairman when she _____ in at 10 o'clock precisely. (sit   walk)
4 Years ago the trains always _____ punctually, but that is no longer the case. (arrive)
5 They _____ the hotel when an explosion _____ the building. (enter   shake)

3 Below is a list of the past simple tenses of common irregular verbs. Match them with the correct infinitive:

swung	felt	lent	dug	tore	set	led	chose
shook	let	bit	rang	lay	bent	hid	hung
sank	struck	blew	kept	lit	spread	rose	fed

bend	_____	keep	_____	set	_____
dig	_____	lead	_____	spread	_____
feed	_____	lend	_____	strike	_____
feel	_____	let	_____	swing	_____
hang	_____	light	_____		
bite	_____	lie	_____	shake	_____
blow	_____	ring	_____	sink	_____
choose	_____	rise	_____	tear	_____
hide	_____				

138 GRAMMAR

VERBS
Tenses 3
continued

4 Complete these sentences with the *past tenses* of the verbs given:

| light feed set rise |

1 The sun _____ at 5 a.m. and _____ at 8.55 p.m.
2 The farmer's wife came out and _____ the chickens. Afterwards she _____ a fire in the living room.

| let swing feel lead |

5 The Board _____ him manage the company, but he _____ it into bankruptcy.
6 Kevin _____ cold, so he _____ his arms vigorously to and fro while he waited.

| shake keep blow lend |

3 I _____ her £5, but she didn't pay it back; she _____ it!
4 The wind _____ the door open and _____ the curtains.

| dig ring hang strike |

7 They _____ the bell and waited.
8 He _____ the security guard and knocked him unconscious.
9 They _____ a hole in the earth and buried the evidence.
10 He _____ the big picture on the wall facing the front door.

LOOK **A** Yesterday he **went** to the cinema.

B He often **went** to the cinema.
He often **used to go** to the cinema.

1 Compare **A** and **B**. Do they describe one occasion, or a number of occasions? What tenses are used?

CHECK **5** Put **used to** + verb in these sentences *if possible*:

1 The old man died last week.
2 They played tennis every day.
3 Pat took Julia to the hospital on Friday with appendicitis.
4 The train arrived at six.

In one sentence **used to** + verb would mean the same. In another one **used to** + verb would change the meaning. Which is which?

PRACTICE

6 Complete these sentences in the *past tense*, using a form of the verb given, and **used to** *if possible*:

1 The children _____ Hopscotch when they were young. (play)
2 The lorry _____ into the bus and _____ three people. (crash injure)
3 He _____ a good worker, but I'm afraid he isn't now. (be)
4 Armstrong _____ on the moon on 20th July 1969. (land)
5 Men _____ bowler hats in London, but today it's unusual. (wear)

7 Make sentences up about yourself, your family and friends, like this:

A Things you did, and when you did them:
   Last week I went . . .
B Things you were doing when you were interrupted:
   I was . . . when my brother . . .
C Things you used to do regularly, but don't any longer:
   Years ago, we used to . . .
   Last year I used to . . .

GRAMMAR

Past simple
Used for events in the past, which may be a single event:
   The bridge **collapsed**.
or repeated events:
   She **went** to work every day.

Past progressive
Used for incomplete or interrupted events:
   I **was living** in Paris at that time.
   She **was having** tea when Philip walked in.

used to
Used for repeated events in the past:
   She **used to swim** every day.

SEE ALSO: Skills, pages 26–7, 30–1, 46–7, 62–3, 74–5; Workbook, pages 50–1, 53; Teacher's Book.

VERBS
Tenses 4

Present perfect

Past perfect

LOOK

I (**A**) **have known** Adam for a year and a bit altogether, so when he (**B**) **went** to Uganda two months ago, I (**C**) **had known** him for a year and we were good friends. I (**D**) **have heard** from him twice so far.

1 There are four verbs in **bold**:
Verb ____ started and finished in the past.
Verb ____ started and finished before another event in the past.
Verb ____ started and finished in the past but has a result in the present.
Verb ____ started in the past and continues to the present.

CHECK 1 Complete these sentences with the correct form of the verb in brackets:

1 I _____ not _____ (see) the new Citroen yet.
2 I _____ (see) a similar car in 1986, but it wasn't the same.
3 I _____ not _____ (drive) a car like that until last week, when I drove one for the first time.
4 I _____ (travel) all over Europe for the last six years.

GRAMMAR

'Before past'	Past	Present
I **had left**[1] when he **arrived**.[2]		I **am living**[3] here.
		I **have lived**[4] here for a year.
		I **have read**[5] that - - - >

[1] happened before a past event
[2] happened in the past
[3] is happening in the present
[4] continues to the present
[5] has an effect in the present

PRACTICE 2 Choose the best ending for each sentence:

1 Mary has met the Queen . . .   . . . last week.
  Mary met the Queen . . .   . . . on several occasions in the last two years.

2 What happened . . .   . . . to you last night?
  What has happened . . .   . . . since I went away?

3 John has fallen . . .   . . . down a hole and broke his leg.
  John fell . . .   . . . down a hole and I can't get him out.

4 Prices had risen . . .   . . . every year for five years.
  Prices have risen . . .   . . . before 1988, but more slowly.

5 They bought . . .   . . . their house last year.
  They have bought . . .   . . . a new house; it's lovely!

6 Have you seen . . .   . . . Harrison Ford's latest film? You should go!
  Did you see . . .   . . . the news on TV last night? It was dramatic!

SEE ALSO: Skills, pages 30–1, 46–7; Workbook, pages 48–9, 53; Teacher's Book.

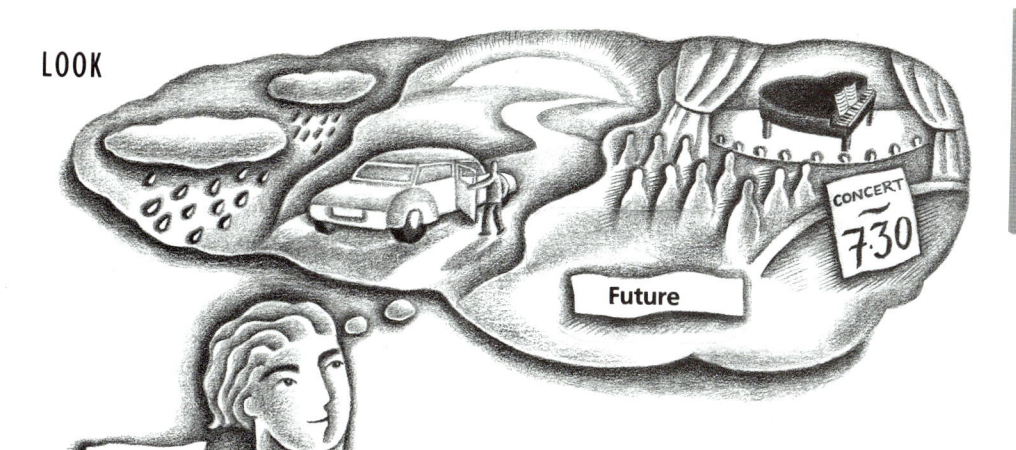

VERBS

Tenses 5

Future time

LOOK

A Look! It**'s going to** rain.
I**'m leaving** early tomorrow.
The concert **starts** at 7.30.

B It **will (might)** rain in July.
We **won't (may not) be** late if the train gets in on time.

1 What tenses are used in **A** and **B**?
2 What is the difference between **will**, **may** and **might**?

CHECK

1 Are these sentences like the sentences in **A** above, or **B**? Discuss and complete (there are usually two or three alternatives):

1 If they use nuclear weapons, they _____ us all. (destroy)
2 What _____ you _____ tonight? (do)
3 I hear you're going to Finland! It _____ cold there. (be)
4 Look out! That car _____ ! (crash)

PRACTICE

2 Look at these sets of sentences, and discuss the differences in meaning:

1 a She'll come tomorrow.
  b She may come tomorrow.
2 a Right, I'll ask Miss Jones to do that.
  b Yes, I'm asking Miss Jones to do that.
3 a He sings.
  b He sings at 6.45 tonight.
  c He's going to sing.
4 a Sarah is playing the piano.
  b Sarah is playing the piano tonight.

GRAMMAR

In this unit we deal with two areas of the future:

1 *The future 'in the present'*
The present is joined to the future. There is a schedule or arrangement, or an intention, or some evidence *now* of what is going to happen:

Schedule	My plane **leaves** (**is leaving**) at 6.55.
Arrangement	He**'s seeing** the manager next week.
Intention	He**'s going to see** the manager next week.
Evidence	The helicopter**'s going to take off**!

2 *The future 'in the future'*
The action is centred in the future. There is a prediction or a reaction, saying what will happen in the future:
   It **will** rain in July.
   I **might** help him if he cooperates.
   That's a good idea, I**'ll** do that.

SEE ALSO: pages 142–3 for **will** / **may** / **might**.

★ The above is a general guide only.

3 Make up sentences of your own of two kinds, and compare them with a partner:

First kind: arrangements, plans and intentions
   Next term begins on . . .
   My brother is moving to a new house on . . .
   I'm going to have lunch today in . . .

Second kind: predictions and reactions
   The next election will be in . . .
   I may (might, will) get a salary raise next year if . . .

SEE ALSO: Skills, pages 26–7; Workbook, page 52; Teacher's Book.

VERBS
Modals 1

Probability:
will
should
could / may /
might (well)
won't

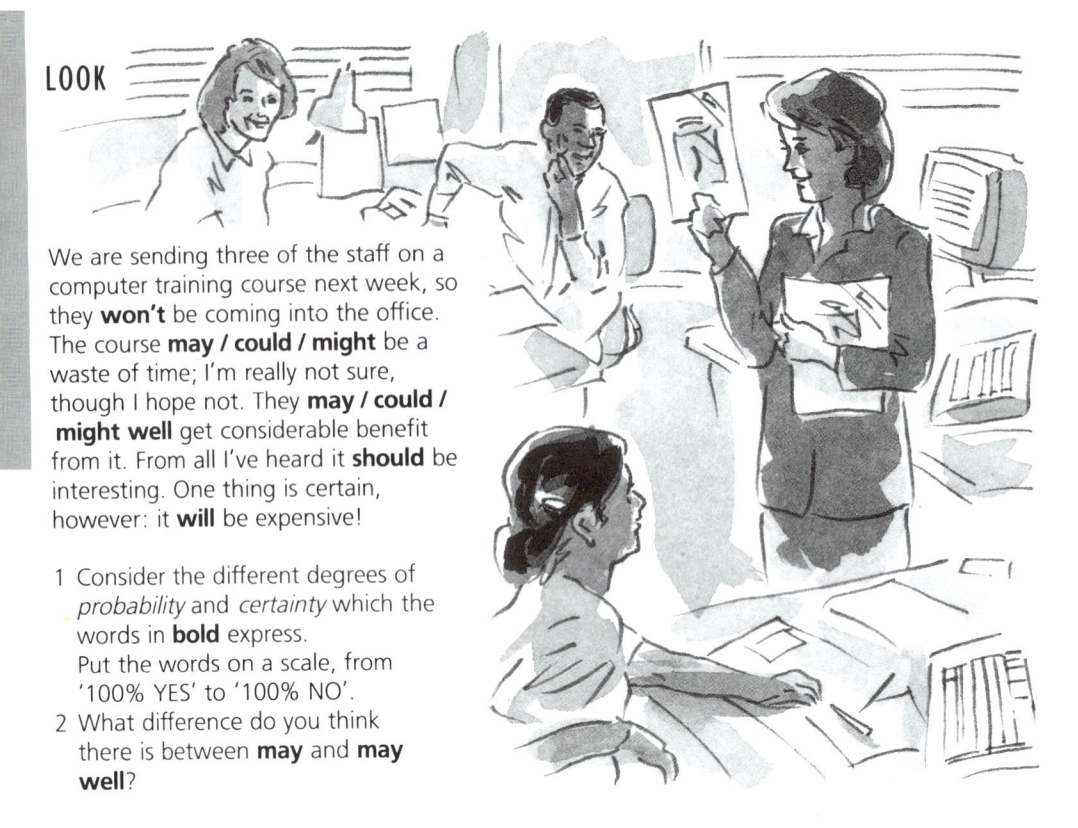

LOOK

We are sending three of the staff on a computer training course next week, so they **won't** be coming into the office. The course **may / could / might** be a waste of time; I'm really not sure, though I hope not. They **may / could / might well** get considerable benefit from it. From all I've heard it **should** be interesting. One thing is certain, however: it **will** be expensive!

1 Consider the different degrees of *probability* and *certainty* which the words in **bold** express.
   Put the words on a scale, from '100% YES' to '100% NO'.
2 What difference do you think there is between **may** and **may well**?

CHECK

1 Complete these sentences with a word from the box and discuss with a partner *why* you chose one word and not another:

| will   won't   may   may well |

1 It's raining. If you go out without a raincoat, you _____ get wet.
2 Stay indoors, then you _____ get wet.
3 It's been raining a lot these days, so it _____ rain again tomorrow.
4 Of course, it _____ rain any day in the year; you never know in this country.

GRAMMAR

These modals indicate various degrees of probability from something which is impossible to something which is certain. This is a way of referring to the future.
(SEE ALSO: Tenses 5, Future time, page 141.)

Indicating degrees of probability

will	It is certain that . . .
should	Something makes me think that . . .
may / could / might (well)	There is a strong possibility that . . .
may / could / might	It is possible that . . .
won't	It is certain that . . . not . . .

★ The modals below also have other meanings:
   should   also advice / command / obligation:
      You **shouldn't** smoke so much.
   may   also formal requests or permission:
      May I come in?
   could   also ability:
      That cat **could** jump six feet in the air.

142 GRAMMAR

PRACTICE 2 Read this:

KAREN'S FUTURE
What can we guess from what we know already?

Karen is 21 years old. She did well at school and got a good degree in economics. Her father, who has a market research company, tried to make her study the piano, but it never interested her although she gets on very well with him. She is an attractive girl, and has a steady boyfriend. She loves children, and is very interested in health and fitness. She goes to an aerobics class regularly, and reads magazines about diet and food. She is thinking about looking for a job, but she's also considering the idea of taking a master's degree. She wants a place to live; fortunately, her brother is an estate agent, and deals mostly with flats.

VERBS
Modals 1
continued

Now complete these sentences with appropriate modals from the box. Discuss with a partner the reasons for your choice. In some sentences there is only one logical possibility; in others it is a matter of opinion:

may / could / might (well)   should   will   won't

1 She _____ be 22 next birthday.
2 She _____ be a great pianist.
3 She _____ get married soon.
4 She _____ be a year older next year!
5 She _____ get a job easily, as economists are in demand.
6 She _____ try for a job in her father's business.
7 She _____ go back to university.
8 She _____ have no trouble finding a flat, because her brother is an estate agent.
9 She _____ study to be an aerobics teacher.
10 She _____ have two or three children.
11 She _____ die one day.
12 She _____ have a happy life; she always seems to enjoy herself.

(One solution is that in these sentences **will** is used three times, **won't** once, **should** three times and **may / might / could well** five times – but your opinion may be different!)

3 Using the words and phrases in the box in Practice 2, make up sentences about what you expect to happen (or not happen) in your own life and the lives of your friends and family, like this:
 My brother Pierre may well fail his next exam; he doesn't study enough.
 I won't go away anywhere this year; I'm too busy.

SEE ALSO: Skills, pages 18–19, 20–1, 24–5, 46–7, 50–1, 68–9, 70–1; Workbook, pages 54–5; Teacher's Book.

VERBS
Modals 2

Ability:
could
managed to
can
be able to

could / managed to

LOOK

Did Lewis do it on that occasion?
Lewis **could** play the piano.

Lewis **could** climb mountains.
(We don't know whether
he did or not.)

Victor did it.
Victor **managed to** pass grade six.

Victor **managed to** get to the top.

(Yes, he did.)

1 What is the difference in meaning between the two columns?

CHECK

1 Now complete these with **could** or **managed to**:

1 When I was five years old I _____ (not) ride a bike, but I _____ swim.
2 I didn't think I _____ walk 20 miles, but I _____ get there.
3 A hundred years ago most people _____ ride a horse.
4 With the money they had saved, the Smiths _____ buy a new car.

GRAMMAR

Could is general, **managed to** is specific.

	General abilities	Specific events
Past	I **could** climb trees.	I **managed to** climb this tree.

PRACTICE

2 Complete these with **could** or **managed to**:

1 Norma studied French for years, and she _____ speak it quite well. Harry's French wasn't very good, but he _____ find his way to the Eiffel Tower.
2 In spite of bad weather, the team _____ complete the Rally.
3 Jill _____ (not) swim very well, but somehow she _____ get across the river.
4 Fred _____ (not) cook as well as his sister, but yesterday he _____ produce a reasonable meal for four people.
5 My Russian is practically non-existent, but I _____ buy two tickets for the Bolshoi Ballet.

3 With a partner, talk about your life. When you were very young, what were the things you could (and couldn't) do?

Now think about the last month or so. You have done a few difficult things. List the difficult things you managed to do.

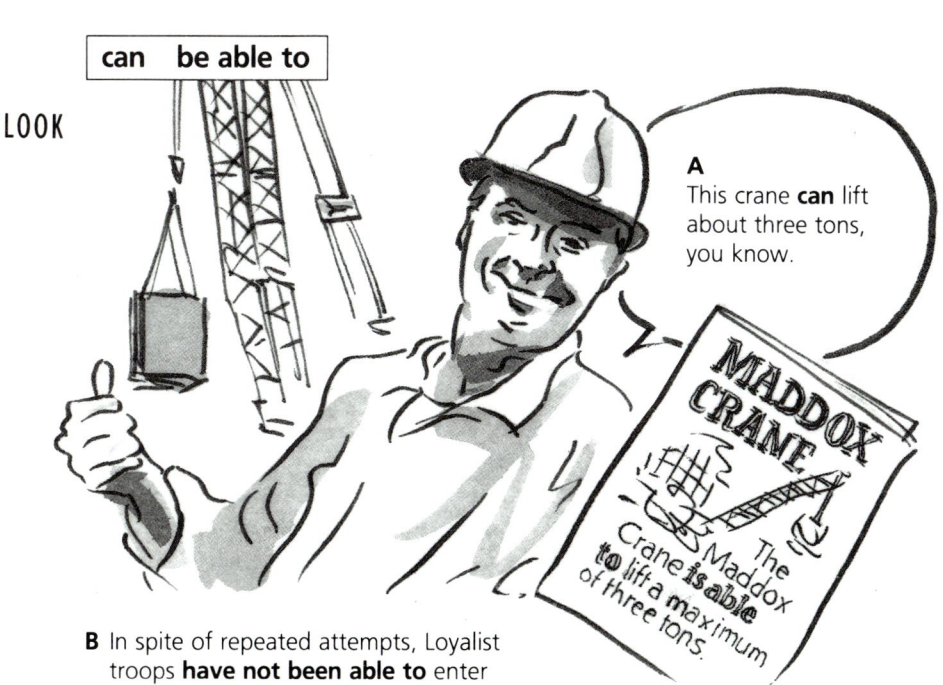

VERBS
Modals 2
continued

LOOK can   be able to

A This crane **can** lift about three tons, you know.

MADDOX CRANE — The Maddox Crane is able to lift a maximum of three tons.

B In spite of repeated attempts, Loyalist troops **have not been able to** enter the capital.

C The troops **will be able to** take the capital soon.

1 What is the difference in formality between the sentence in **A** and the sentence on the document?
2 Can you use **can / could** in **B** and **C**? If not, why not?

GRAMMAR
Apart from **can**, another way to express ability is to use **be able to**:

Present	**can / is able to** (see note below)
Past	**could / was able to**
Present perfect	**have been able to**
Past perfect	**had been able to**
Future	**will be able to**

★ It is common to find **be able to** in more formal sentences:
He **was able to** complete the project as agreed. (formal)
He **managed to** get the job done. (neutral)
Are you **able to** attend the meeting at 6 p.m. Ms Jones? (formal)
Can you come tonight, Sue? (neutral)

SEE ALSO: facing page and Tenses 2, page 137.

CHECK 1 Complete these sentences with forms of **be able to**:

1 Because of heavy rains, the famine relief organisations _____ not yet _____ send adequate supplies to the remote villages.
2 The relief organisations hope that more trucks _____ get through next week.
3 The United Nations _____ usually _____ give help when famine strikes.

PRACTICE 2 Complete these sentences with appropriate forms of **can** or **be able to**. Use **can** if the present tense is needed, unless you think the sentence is formal:

1 Michael _____ (not) _____ get a job yet, although he is trying hard.
2 Jim, I _____ help you if you want me to.
3 Mr Wilberforce, we _____ assist you if required to do so.
4 You _____ walk without crutches in about three weeks' time.
5 My little boy _____ ride a bicycle, and he's only four.
6 I was informed that they _____ get the job finished by noon, but I now see that that is not the case.
7 The Queen _____ attend the reception for 10 minutes only, as she is due to leave for the presidential palace at 6.15.

SEE ALSO: Skills, pages 46–7, 64–5; Workbook, pages 54–5; Teacher's Book.

GRAMMAR 145

VERBS
Modals 3
Deduction: must be can't have

LOOK

(Knock, knock)
A: Who **can** that **be**?
B: It **can't be** Tom; it's too early.
A: I know, it **must be** Fred. He said he might drop by.

Look at this picture. A child **must have drawn** it.
It **can't have been** an adult, surely.

CHECK

1 Complete each sentence with an appropriate phrase from the box:

A: What time do you think it is?
B: About 7 o'clock.
A: What! It _____ 7 o'clock!
B: Well, we got here at 4 o'clock, and we've been here for three hours, so it _____ 7 o'clock.
A: No! we _____ been here for three hours!
B: We have, you know.
A: In that case where's Michael? He _____ got lost.

> must be
> must have
> can't be
> can't have

GRAMMAR

... **must** { **be** / **have** ... -**ed**	You have good reason to believe that something is true.
... **can't** { **be** / **have** ... -**ed**	You have good reason to believe that something is *not* true.
who / what **can** ... **be**?	You have no idea (questions).

PRACTICE

2 Complete these sentences with the phrases in the box:

> must be   can't be   can be
> must have   can't have

1 A: Look at this funny-looking creature! What on earth _____ it _____ ?
  B: It _____ a spider.
  A: No, don't be silly, it _____ a spider. It's only got six legs. Spiders have eight.

2 Both of these stories _____ true; that's impossible. One of them _____ false, surely!

3 R: I can't find that cheque anywhere. I _____ sent it to the bank, but I can't remember.
  C: Oh Richard, you _____ forgotten already!
  R: Well I have. But if I didn't send it to the bank, where _____ it _____ ?

3 Look at this picture, and discuss it. What do you think the items **must be** / **can't be**, and what do you think **must have** / **can't have** happened?

SEE ALSO: Skills, pages 18–19, 20–1, 28–9, 68–9; Workbook, pages 54–5; Teacher's Book.

146 GRAMMAR

VERBS
The passive

LOOK

Speech bubble: They **have treated** more patients here than ever before. To do this, you **must increase** funding and you **should expand** the facilities.

Poster: OUR HOSPITAL facts you should know. More patients **have been treated**. Funding **must be increased** and facilities **should be expanded**.

1 What difference do you notice between the doctor speaking and the written document?

CHECK 1 Change these sentences to the active form starting with **you** or **they**:

1 Next, the potatoes and carrots are cut up and boiled.
2 The bridge was built in 1873.
3 These books can be obtained from the public library.
4 She was asked to speak more quietly.

PRACTICE 2 Rewrite these sentences in *the passive*, using the appropriate tense or modal. The new subject has been underlined:
Example:
You must protect young babies against excessive cold.
Young babies must be protected against excessive cold.

1 They destroyed <u>the original picture</u> years ago.
2 They have never explained <u>the events of that night</u>.
3 You shouldn't store <u>cleaning fluid and soft drinks</u> together.
4 You can buy <u>film for this camera</u> anywhere.
5 They took <u>the stolen goods</u> across the frontier.
6 You will show <u>passes</u> when entering the building.
7 They had told <u>her</u> to make an application.

SEE ALSO: Skills, pages 32–3, 42–5, 46–7, 48–9, 52–3; Workbook, page 56; Teacher's Book.

GRAMMAR

The passive can be used when you don't know who did something:
   The cathedral **was built** in the twelfth century.

It is also used if the person who did something is obvious:
   He **was arrested** last night. (By the police, obviously.)

It is especially used when you want to focus on the person who received the action, not the one who performed it:
   Mary **was hurt** in the accident.

In casual speech it is common to use **you** and **they**:
you = 'you or somebody':
   You can buy stamps at the post office.
they = 'somebody, but not you':
   They built the port in a year.

In more formal speech or writing, the passive is common:
   Stamps **can be bought** at the post office.
   The port **was built** in a year.

GRAMMAR 147

VERBS
Multi-part verbs

LOOK

A: Hello, George, **sit down**. Let me **ask for** *some more tea*. How are you?
G: Fine. **I bumped into** *your mother* yesterday. She looked well.
A: Yes, she is. She went to visit her brother Henry for a month, and she **stayed on**.
G: Henry **looks after** *her* very well, I imagine.
A: Yes, he never **goes out**.

1 There are two different structures in **bold**. In your notebooks put them in two columns headed *Type 1* and *Type 2*. What is the difference between them, and what is the role of the words in italics?

CHECK

1 Complete each sentence with a form of a multi-part verb from the box. Examples are given to help you with the meaning:

> account for (e.g. your actions)   get away (e.g. from prison)
> lie down (e.g. on a bed)   run into (e.g. an old friend)

1 Quick! There goes the thief! Don't let him _____ !
2 I _____ Sammy last night at a party; I haven't seen him for years.
3 If you're not feeling well, why don't you _____ for half an hour or so?
4 You'll have to _____ the money you've spent.

Two of the verbs are type 1 and two are type 2. Which ones?

GRAMMAR

Type 1: *Verb + particle*   These verbs are used intransitively.
   Examples: come in   go out   get on   break off   stand up

Type 2: *Verb + particle + object*
   Examples: account for (the money)   get into (the car)

SEE ALSO: Reference, page 156, for more examples.

PRACTICE

2 Complete each sentence with a form of a verb + particle taken from the boxes:

| ask | come | | up | down |
| stand | fall | | for | from |

1 He caught his foot in the carpet and _____ .
2 Go to the store room and _____ a box of envelopes.
3 A: Where do you _____ ?
  B: Edinburgh, in Scotland.
4 Everybody _____ when the president entered the room.

| die | laugh | | up | down |
| get | come | | at | across |

5 You shouldn't _____ students if they make mistakes.
6 The noise gradually _____ until the room was quiet.
7 I _____ your school notebooks in the attic; I thought you might like to see them.
8 I usually _____ at about 7 a.m. during the week.

Which of these are type 1, and which type 2?

148 GRAMMAR

LOOK

VERBS
Multi-part verbs
continued

A: Let's **switch on** *the television*.
B: OK, you **switch** *the television* **on**, and I'll make the tea.
A: Right, I'll **switch** *it* **on**.

C: I need to **look up** *a word*.
D: Why don't you **look** *this word* **up**?
C: Right, I'll **look** *it* **up** in a minute.

1 In each set, the same verb appears three times, twice with a noun and once with a pronoun. Why does it only appear once with a pronoun?

GRAMMAR

Type 3: *Verb + object + particle*
The object can be a noun or a pronoun:
 Look the word **up**.   **Look** it **up**.

The object and the particle can be changed round *if the object is a noun*. If it is a pronoun, it cannot be changed round (see LOOK above):
 Look up the word.
SEE ALSO: Reference, page 157, for more examples.

CHECK 3 Complete each sentence with a multi-part verb from the box. Some help is given with the meaning:

| throw away (e.g. rubbish) | look up |
| sort out (e.g. documents) | give away |

1 If you don't know the meaning, _____ it _____ in the dictionary.
2 You'd better _____ those old shoes _____ !
3 What a mess! It'll take me the whole day to _____ it _____ .
4 He _____ most of his money _____ before he died.

Can any of these particles and objects be changed round?

PRACTICE 4 Complete these sentences with a verb and a particle taken from the boxes:

| put | cross | up | away |
| fill | turn | out | on |

| take | hand | on | off |
| let | try | back | off |

1 If it's not right, _____ it _____ and start again.
2 _____ the light _____ . It's dark in here.
3 Can you _____ the tank _____ with petrol, please?
4 _____ your toys _____ . It's time for supper.
5 I'd like to _____ this sweater _____ , please.
6 I'll mark your essays tonight and _____ them _____ tomorrow.
7 Hello Mary, come in and _____ your coat _____ .
8 It's the first time he's broken a window. Shall we _____ him _____ ?

The order can be changed in five of these sentences. Decide which ones and change them.

SEE ALSO: Skills, pages 26–7, 58–9;
Key words, pages 106–7;
Workbook, page 57;
Teacher's Book.

VERBS

Reporting statements / questions / instructions

Reporting statements

LOOK

1	2
'I like her.' →	Tony **says (tells me)** he likes her.
'I saw her.' →	Tony **says (tells me)** he saw her.

1 What is the difference in form between **says** and **tells**?
2 Does the tense of the main verb in column **1** change in column **2**?

CHECK 1 Report these statements in the way shown in LOOK:

1 'I haven't seen my sister this week.' ⟶ He tells me _____
2 'I'll repair it today if I have time.' ⟶ He _____
3 'We didn't enjoy the film.' ⟶ They _____ me _____

LOOK

1	2
'I like her.' →	Brian **said (told me)** he liked her.
'I'm leaving.' →	Jack **said (told me)** he was leaving.
'I saw her.' →	Andrew **said (told me)** he saw / had seen her.

1 Discuss the changes in tense in the underlined verbs from column **1** to column **2**.

CHECK 2 Report these sentences in the same way:

1 'I love my job.' ⟶ He told me _____
2 'I'm having a good time.' ⟶ She said _____
3 'I spoke to the manager myself.' ⟶ Charlotte said _____

> **GRAMMAR** When the reporting verb is *present tense* (**says / tells**), the main verb does not change. When the reporting verb is in *past tense* (**said / told**), the main verb can change.
>
> SEE ALSO: Reference, page 157, for a list of changes in reported speech.

PRACTICE 3 Sue has just received a phone call from the Area Manager at Head Office. This is what the Area Manager said. How did Sue report it?
Example:
'I'm coming to see your branch tomorrow.'
He said he was coming to see our branch tomorrow.

1 'We saw your last month's figures.'
2 'We're worried.'
3 'I haven't been to see you for over a year.'
4 'I will be arriving at 8.30 a.m.'
5 'I can't stay for more than an hour.'

4 Now practise reporting your own remarks, in threes, like this:

A: *I don't like jazz.*
B: *What does / did he say?*
C: *He says / said he doesn't / didn't like jazz.*

150 GRAMMAR

VERBS

Reporting statements / questions / instructions
continued

Reporting questions

LOOK

1
A 'Are the boys there?' ⟶
B ⟶
C 'Where are the boys?' ⟶
D ⟶

2
A She **is asking** <u>if</u> the boys <u>are</u> there.
B She **asked** <u>if</u> the boys <u>were</u> there.
C She **is asking** <u>where</u> the boys <u>are</u>.
D She **asked** <u>where</u> the boys <u>were</u>.

1 What is the difference in word order between columns **1** and **2**?
2 What are the differences between A and B and between C and D in column **2**?

CHECK **1** Report these questions by completing the sentences on the right:

1 'What do you want?' ⟶ I am asking Dr Maley _____
⟶ I asked Dr Maley _____
2 'Can I be of any help?' ⟶ The nurse is asking _____
⟶ The nurse asked _____

PRACTICE **2** Report these questions in two different ways, and comment on any changes in meaning:
Example: *'Are you hungry?'*
She's asking if you're hungry.
She asked if you were hungry.

1 'Where did Jane go last night?'
2 'Have you finished your supper?'
3 'Can you see all right?'
4 'How are the twins?'

3 Ask other questions in threes, like this:
A: *What time is it?*
B: *What is he asking / did he ask?*
C: *He is asking / asked what time it is / was.*

Reporting instructions and requests

LOOK

1
A 'Wait a minute!' ⟶
B 'Don't sit down!' ⟶
C 'Can you wait a minute?' ⟶

2
A Rashid **told** her <u>to wait</u> a minute.
B Rashid **told** her <u>not to sit</u> down.
C Rashid **asked** her <u>to wait</u> a minute.

CHECK **1** Report these instructions and requests in the same way as LOOK above:

1 'Will you help me?' ⟶ Liz _____ us _____
2 'Stop that noise!' ⟶ Liz _____ them _____
3 'Can you hold my bag?' ⟶ She _____ me _____
4 'Don't do that!' ⟶ He _____ Penny _____

GRAMMAR Questions: 'What time *is it*?' ⟶ He **is asking** what time *it is*.

★ Note the change of word order in a reported question.

Instructions: 'Stop!' ⟶ He **told me** to stop.
'Don't stop!' ⟶ He **told me** not to stop.

Requests: 'Could you stop?' ⟶ He **asked me** to stop.

SEE ALSO: Skills, pages 36–7, 46–7, 56–7, 62–3; Workbook, pages 58–9; Teacher's Book.

GRAMMAR 151

VERBS
Modifying the verb 1
Adverbs of manner

LOOK

Nick performed **brilliantly** in the 800 metres. In fact he won <u>the race</u> **easily**, because he had practised **hard** and lived **sensibly** for weeks. Adam did **badly**; but then he didn't take <u>the training</u> **seriously** and he smoked **heavily**.

1 Compare the spelling of the adverbs above with their related adjective.
2 How do the words underlined affect the position of the adverb?

GRAMMAR

1 Many adverbs are formed by adding **-ly** to adjectives:
  cheap**ly**   clear**ly**   peaceful**ly**
  Notice spelling:
  gentle ⟶ gent**ly**   easy ⟶ eas**ily**
  frantic ⟶ frantic**ally**
  (but notice: public ⟶ public**ly**)

2 It is common to place adverbs of manner after the object of the verb, or after the verb if there is no object. (However, adverb position may vary according to the meaning of the sentences.)

CHECK 1 Fill each space with an appropriate adverb from the box:

| right   fluently   happily   violently |

1 He speaks Arabic _____ .
2 They laughed and chatted _____ together.
3 The guerrillas burst _____ into the television station.
4 You'll never make money if you don't do your sums _____ .

PRACTICE 2 Put an appropriate form of one of the adverbs from the boxes in the right place in each sentence. The verb each one modifies is in **bold**:

| exact   thin   frank   tight |

1 If the lid doesn't **fit**, then the liquid will run out.
2 You'd better **speak** to her. You can't hide the truth any longer.
3 **Tell** him what it is he has to do, so that he has no doubts in his mind.
4 **Spread** the butter. It's not healthy to eat too much of it.

| effective   patient   bright   graceful |

5 She **danced** across the floor and sank down at his feet.
6 It was a tropical night and the stars **shone**.
7 The old man **stood** in the queue waiting for his chance to buy food.
8 You must **organise** your work if you want to get it done in time.

| hasty   automatic   gentle   public |

9 Toasters are designed to **switch off**, although sometimes they stick.
10 He **put** the Chinese vase **down** on the table.
11 The Prime Minister must **state** what his government intends to do.
12 He got the news at the last minute, so he **packed** and left.

SEE ALSO:
Workbook, page 60;
Teacher's Book.

152 GRAMMAR

VERBS
Modifying the verb 2
Comparative adverbs

LOOK **A** Prices usually rise **faster than** wages. (*comparative*)
The immigrants work **hardest**. (*superlative*)

B I hope you can now see **more clearly** what is happening. (*comparative*)
Owls are **most commonly** seen at night. (*superlative*)

1 What is the difference between the forms in **bold** in **A** and **B**?
2 Two of the adverbs are the same as adjectives. Which ones?

CHECK **1** Join these sentences together, and say which is the comparative adverb:

1 She did better . . .
2 As time was getting short, . . .
3 The concert was a disaster . . .
4 To recover their losses . . .

A they must manage the business more effectively.
B than we expected.
C because she played much worse than usual.
D he began to walk more quickly.

GRAMMAR A few adverbs are the same as adjectives:

a **fast** car	to drive **fast**	a **high** ball	to fly **high**
a **hard** worker	to work **hard**	a **long** stay	to stay **long**
an **early** train	to arrive **early**	a **late** night	to stay **late**

These adverbs form comparatives / superlatives with **-er** and **-est**:
She arrived **earlier** than I did.

Most adverbs use **more** and **most**:
Male lions are **most commonly** seen in the early evening.

Comparative adverbs are much more common than superlatives.

★ As adjectives: good   He was **better**.   She was **best**.
              well   She got **better**.
  As adverb: well   He played **better**.   He played **best**.

PRACTICE **2** Complete each sentence with the correct form of a word from the box, adding **more**, **most** or **than** if necessary:

| high   smoothly   early   cheaply   heavily   comfortably |

Example:
My car runs <u>more smoothly</u> after being serviced.

1 The train arrived _____ expected, and we just caught it.
2 The people who were sitting _____ of all were the Stockwells; they were in first class.
3 We'll be relying _____ on our partners than we did before.
4 We can get there _____ by bus; the train's very expensive.
5 He threw the ball _____ anyone else could.

3 Now make up sentences about *your* family and environment, using phrases like these:

more carefully . . .   more fluently . . .   more quietly . . .
more clearly . . .   more politely . . .   more quickly . . .
more dangerously . . .   more smoothly . . .

Example:
My mother drives more carefully than my father.

SEE ALSO: Skills, pages 36–8, 54–5, 56–7; Workbook, page 60; Teacher's Book.

GRAMMAR 153

VERBS

Verbs followed by:
to + infinitive /
noun to + infinitive /
clause (that)

LOOK

Below are sentences with two verbs. The first verb (the principal one) fixes what comes after it:

	1	2	3
A **plan**	Mike planned **to go**.	_____	_____
arrange	He arranged **to go**.	_____	_____
B **invite**	_____	Mike invited **Sue to go**.	_____
C **think**	_____	_____	Mike thinks (that) **she will go**.

1 Match these headings to columns **1**, **2** and **3**:
   Verbs followed by: to + infinitive
   Verbs followed by: noun to + infinitive
   Verbs followed by: clause (that)

CHECK

1 Complete each sentence with *as many of these phrases as possible*:

1 They invited . . .
2 Peter has arranged . . .
3 I am planning . . .
4 She thought . . .

A . . . me to wait a few minutes.
B . . . (that) he was leaving.
C . . . to leave at once.
D . . . Jim to start work.
E . . . (that) they would go.
F . . . to go next week.
G . . . (that) I would have time.
H . . . the boys to sit down.

LOOK

Here are some more examples:

	1	2	3
D **want**	I want **to go**.	I want **her to go**.	_____
like	I'd like **to go**.	I'd like **her to go**.	_____
E **hope**	I hope **to go**.	_____	I hope (that) **she'll go**.
decide	I decided **to go**.	_____	I decided (that) **she'll go**.

154 GRAMMAR

VERBS

Verbs followed by:
to + infinitive / noun to + infinitive / clause (that)
continued

CHECK 2 Complete each sentence with the right phrase or phrases (both phrases may be correct):

1 He invited | we join him.
              | us to join him.

2 Steven arranged | him to take the last plane.
                  | to take the last plane.

3 I want | them to play in the team.
         | that they play in the team.

4 They thought | he would pass.
               | him to pass.

5 I expect | to leave on Friday.
           | she'll leave on Friday.

PRACTICE 3 Put the verbs in the correct *place* and the correct *form* in each sentence:

1 The doctor _____ her to stay in bed, and for once in her life she _____ to obey him. (decide   tell)

2 Karen _____ Brian to stay for supper with her parents. She _____ he would accept. (invite   hope)

3 I _____ to help you finish this if you _____ me to stay for supper. (ask   promise)

4 David _____ to do a French course next year; his uncle _____ he would pay for it. (plan   promise)

5 I _____ he'll go to Spain this year; he's certainly _____ to go, because he _____ me he was. (plan   think   tell)

4 Now make sentences about your own future, and that of your family and friends, starting each sentence with one of these phrases:

I think _____ (something you will do)
I'm planning _____ (something you will do)
I want _____ (something you will do)
I want _____ (something another person will do)
I hope _____ (something you will do)
I hope _____ (something another person will do)

GRAMMAR Different verbs can be followed by different grammatical forms (infinitive, or noun plus infinitive, or clause, etc.)

Three ways of completing a sentence after a verb (*complementations*) are given here:

1 **to** + infinitive   I want **to go**.

2 noun **to** + infinitive   I want | **Peter to go.**
                                       | **him to go.**

3 (that) clause   He thinks (that) **she'll go.**

Many verbs can have several different complementations; some verbs will only take one.

SEE ALSO: Skills, pages 54–5, 64–5; Workbook, page 61; Teacher's Book.

GRAMMAR 155

REFERENCE: a summary of grammatical forms

TENSES

PRESENT SIMPLE AND PRESENT PROGRESSIVE

Dynamic verbs
Julie **sings** in the opera.
This week she**'s singing** in Milan.

Stative verbs
I **know** Julie quite well.

Common stative verbs
want	see	think	cost
like	hear	believe	own
prefer	smell	know	
hate	taste	understand	
dislike	feel		

PAST SIMPLE AND PAST PROGRESSIVE

Single event
He **went** out.

Repeated event
He often **went** out.
He **used to go** out.

Interrupted event
He **was going** out when . . .

PRESENT PERFECT AND PAST PERFECT

Joining past and present
I **have known** Adam for two years. / since April.

Effect of past on present
She **has learned** the poem (and she can recite it now).

An event before another past event
She **had left** when I **arrived**.

FUTURE TIME

The future 'in the present'
Schedule — My plane **leaves** (is leaving) at 6.55.
Arrangement — He**'s seeing** the manager next week.
Intention — He**'s going to see** the manager next week.
Evidence — The helicopter**'s going to take off**!

The future 'in the future'
Prediction — I **will / might** help him.
Reaction — That's a good idea. I**'ll do** that.

MODAL VERBS (AUXILIARIES)

PROBABILITY

She **will** be there.	100%
She **should** be there.	
She **may / could / might well** be there.	
She **may / could / might** be there.	
She **won't** be there.	0%

ABILITY

Ability		Achievement
can / could	**is / was able to** (formal)	**managed to** (neutral)

DEDUCTION

	Speaker believes so	Speaker believes not
Present	**must be**	**can't be**
Past	**must have** + **-ed**	**can't have** + **-ed**

THE PASSIVE

Form
1 *Present perfect*
  Patients **have been treated** (in / by . . .)
2 *Past perfect*
  The press **had been told** (of / in / by . . .)
3 *Modals*
  Patients **should be kept** (in / by . . .)
  Batteries **can be bought** (in / by . . .)
  Equipment **will be left** (in / by . . .)

Active (informal / neutral / formal)
(they) They **built** the house in 1923.
(you) You **cut up** the potatoes . . .

Passive (often formal)
The house **was built** in 1923.
The potatoes **are cut up** . . .

MULTI-PART VERBS

Type 1 Verb + particle (adverb)
The party **broke up**.

break up down off in out away
come up down on off in out back away
die down out away
drop off in out
fall down off out back
get up down on off in out back away
go up down on off in out back away
lie down back
run out away
settle down in
sit up down
speak up
stand up out back
stay up on in out away

Type 2 Verb + particle (preposition) + object
They **accounted for** the loss.

account for
ask for after
call for
come for across from to
get into
laugh at
live for at
look for after at
plan for
run after into across
see to
stand for
take after
walk into

156 GRAMMAR

Type 3A *Verb + object + particle (adverb)*
    3B *Verb + particle (adverb) + object*
They **brought** the bags **up**.
They **brought up** the bags.

bring up down in
       back
cross off out
cut off out
eat up
fill up in
follow up
give back away
hand in out
let off in out

look up out
put up down on
       off back away
switch on off
take up down off
       in back away
throw away
try on out
turn down on off

* Some Type 1 verbs can also be used as Type 3 verbs.

REPORTING STATEMENTS / QUESTIONS / INSTRUCTIONS

1 *Reporting present tense statements*
Present He **says** ____ he likes her.
         tells me he likes her.
Past   He **said** ____ he likes / liked her.
         told me he likes / liked her.

2 *Reporting past tense statements*
Present He **says** ____ he saw her.
         He **tells** me he saw her.
Past   He **said** ____ he saw / had seen her.
         told me he saw / had seen her.

3 *Reporting modal statements*
Present He **says** he will see her.
         tells me he can see her.
Past   He **said** he could see her.
         told me he would see her.

4 *Reporting present tense questions*
Present
(yes / no) She **is asking** (us) **if** the boys are in.
(wh-)   **where** the boys are.
Past
(yes / no) She **asked** (us) **if** the boys are / were in.
(wh-)   **where** the boys are / were.

5 *Reporting past tense questions*
Present
(yes / no) She **is asking** (us) **if** the boys were in.
(wh-)   **where** the boys were.
Past
(yes / no) She **asked** (us) **if** the boys did / had done it.
(wh-)   **where** the boys were / had been.

6 *Reporting instructions*
She **told** me **to** stop.
She **told** me **not to** stop.

ADVERBS OF MANNER

Adjective cheap gentle easy frantic (public)
Adverb cheaply gently easily frantically (publicly)
Adjective / adverb far fast first hard right wrong

COMPARATIVE ADVERBS

	Comparative	*Superlative*
effectively	more effectively (than)	the most effectively
fast	faster (than)	the fastest
well / badly	better / worse (than)	the best / the worst

VERBS FOLLOWED BY TO + INF. / NOUN TO + INF. / CLAUSE (THAT)

Followed by:	to + inf.	noun to + inf.	clause (that)
	to go	him to go	(that) he'll go
I **planned**	to go		
I **invited**		him to go	
I **think**			(that) he'll go
I **want**	to go	him to go	
I **hope**	to go		(that) he'll go
I **expect**	to go	him to go	(that) he'll go

IRREGULAR VERBS

- In Classes 1 to 4 the past and past participle are the same.
- In Classes 5 and 6 the past and past participle are different.

Infinitive	Past simple	Past participle	Infinitive	Past simple	Past participle
Class 1			*Class 5*		
bend	bent	bent	bite	bit	bitten
build	built	built	break	broke	broken
lend	lent	lent	choose	chose	chosen
pay	paid	paid	draw	drew	drawn
spend	spent	spent	drive	drove	driven
			fall	fell	fallen
Class 2			grow	grew	grown
bring	brought	brought	hide	hid	hidden
buy	bought	bought	ride	rode	ridden
catch	caught	caught	steal	stole	stolen
feel	felt	felt	tear	tore	torn
keep	kept	kept	throw	threw	thrown
lose	lost	lost	wear	wore	worn
sell	sold	sold			
tell	told	told	*Class 6*		
			begin	began	begun
Class 3			ring	rang	rung
cut	cut	cut	run	ran	run
hit	hit	hit	sing	sang	sung
let	let	let	sink	sank	sunk
set	set	set	swim	swam	swum
spread	spread	spread			
Class 4					
dig	dug	dug			
feed	fed	fed			
find	found	found			
hang	hung	hung			
hold	held	held			
lead	led	led			
light	lit	lit			
shine	shone	shone			
stick	stuck	stuck			
strike	struck	struck			
swing	swung	swung			
win	won	won			

PREPOSITIONS

	page
REVIEW	158
Prepositions of place 1: *away from towards over under*	159
Prepositions of place 2: *not far (from) (quite) a long way (from) beside behind beyond along past*	160
Other prepositions: *by for*	162
Fixed expressions	163
REFERENCE: a summary of grammatical forms	166

REVIEW

Before you start this section, these are the prepositions you should have met.

into out of on / onto off	Edith is getting **into** the car. Kenneth is getting **out of** the car. At Dover you drive straight **onto** the ferry. And at Calais you drive straight **off** again.	behind next to between near in front of	Peter is **behind** Sue. He is **next to** me. I'm **between** him and Tim. Jane is on the grass **near** Tim. That's Sam lying down **in front of** everyone.
above below	There's a clock **above** the fireplace. There's a table **below** the window.	at on in from . . . to . . . for	. . . **at** 4 o'clock / midnight . . . **on** Wednesday / Christmas Day / Friday morning . . . **in** the morning / the summer / 1992 . . . **from** March **to** September / 6 p.m. to 8 p.m. . . . **for** an hour / six months / a year
past along through across	She walked **past** the house . . . . . . and **along** the street. The dog ran **through** the bushes . . . and **across** the garden.	since until	She's been here **since** 9 o'clock, ... and she won't have a break **until** lunchtime.

PREPOSITIONS
Prepositions of place I

away from
towards
over
under

---

away from   towards

LOOK **A** The Prime Minister is moving **towards** the centre in politics. He is moving **away from** his party.

B To get **away from** the man, she moved **towards** the door.

1 Are **A** and **B** both about physical movements?

CHECK 1 Complete these sentences with **towards** or **away from**:

1 Most societies are trying to progress _____ racial equality and _____ discrimination.
2 Europe is moving _____ conflict and _____ integration.

(For mixed practice see page 162.)

---

over   under

LOOK **A** The man on the left weighs **over** 100 kilos.
The man on the right weighs **under** 45 kilos.

B If somebody faints, put a blanket **over** them.
They sat **under** a tree and talked.

1 What is the difference in the meaning of the words in **bold** in **A** and **B**?

CHECK 1 Complete these sentences with **over** or **under**:

1 In the UK young persons _____ 17 years of age may not drive a motor vehicle.
2 Let's throw that Indian blanket _____ the sofa.
3 Women _____ 60 years old receive the old age pension.
4 There were market stalls _____ the arches in the town square.

Look at the sentences again. Two of them are like **A** above, and two are like **B**. Which ones?

(For mixed practice see page 162.)

GRAMMAR **Towards** and **away from** indicate direction to and from, but without arriving at the destination:

towards   * | *   away from
——————→   ——————→

Here we use **over** and **under** in two ways:
over = more than   **over** = covering or crossing
under = less than   **under** = below (and covered by)

SEE ALSO:
Workbook, page 62;
Teacher's Book.

GRAMMAR 159

PREPOSITIONS
Prepositions of place 2

not far (from)

(quite) a long way (from)

beside

behind

beyond

along

past

LOOK

[Map of York showing various landmarks including Bootham School, Bootham Bar, Art Gallery, Minster Library, Treasurer's House, The Minster, St William's College, St Cuthbert's, Borthwick Institute of Historical Research, National Railway Museum, Station, Viking Centre, Wax Museum, Clifford's Tower, Castle Museum, Fishergate Bar, Mecca Conference Centre, with the River Ouse and River Foss. 'You are here' marker is shown near the Minster.]

A: Could you tell me the way to St William's College?
B: Yes, it's **not far from** here. It's **behind** the Minster.

C: Could you tell me the way to Castle Museum?
D: It's **quite a long way from** here. It's **beside** the river Foss.

E: Could you tell me the way to Melbourne Street?
F: Oh, it's **a long way from** here. It's **beyond** Fishergate Bar, opposite Blue Bridge Lane.

1 How far away are the three places? Do the expressions show that one is further than another?
2 Discuss the meanings of **behind**, **beside** and **beyond**. Draw diagrams in your notebooks to show the differences.

CHECK 1 Using the map, complete these sentences with the expressions in the box:

Can you tell me the way to . . .
1 The Treasurer's House?
   Yes, it's _____ here. It's _____ the Minster.
2 The Mecca Conference Centre?
   Yes, it's _____ here. It's _____ Fishergate Bar.
3 St Cuthbert's?
   Yes, it's _____ here. It's _____ the Borthwick Institute.

behind
beyond
beside
not far from
quite a long way from
a long way from

160 GRAMMAR

PREPOSITIONS
Prepositions of place 2
continued

along   past   (*also* turn left into   on the left   until you get to)

LOOK

A: Can you tell me how to get there?
B: Yes, walk **along** this street to the corner, then **turn left into** Blake Street. Keep going **along** Blake Street, which becomes Davygate, **until you get to** the end, then **turn left and right into** Parliament Street. Walk **along** Parliament Street **until you get to** the crossroads, and **turn right into** Coppergate. Go **past** the Viking Centre to the end of the street, and you should see it **on the left**.

1 Look at the map on the facing page and say which place speaker A is referring to by the word **there**.

GRAMMAR

1 **not far from** = a short distance
quite a long way from = a medium distance
a long way from = a long distance
★ 'Distance' is a matter of personal opinion!

2 beyond / behind / beside / along / past

3 Two useful expressions for giving directions:
turn left (right) into . . .
on the left (right) . . .

4 **until** + clause can be used for space or time:
Space: **until** you get to Brick Street
Time: **until** John arrives

CHECK

1 Read and complete these directions, using the map:

A: Can you tell me how to get to St William's College?
B: Yes, go _____ Duncombe Place to the end, then _____ Minster Yard and walk _____ the Minster. You'll see the college _____ .

PRACTICE

2 Complete these sentences by looking at the map and using expressions from the box:

until you get to	to the end
turn left (into)	on the left
turn right (into)	on the right
	along

Directions to:
1 Bootham School
Walk along to the corner, and _____ St Leonard's. Walk _____ there _____ Bootham Bar, then _____ . Walk _____ that road for about 200 metres and you'll see the school _____ .

2 Coney Street
Walk along to the corner, and _____ Blake Street. Go _____ Blake Street _____ a crossroads, then _____ . When you get _____ , _____ ; that's Coney Street.

3 Using the map, say how far away these places are, where they are, and how to get there from where you are:

National Railway Museum   Castle Museum   Railway Station
Borthwick Institute   Wax Museum   Dundas Street
Mecca Conference Centre   Art Gallery   New Street
Viking Centre

4 Now think of three places *you* know. *How far away are they?* What are they **behind / beside / beyond**? *Without naming the places, describe them to your partner, and see if they can guess which places you are describing.*

Begin: *I can think of a place that's not far from here. It's beyond . . . and beside . . .*

SEE ALSO:
Workbook, page 62;
Teacher's Book.

GRAMMAR 161

PREPOSITIONS
Other prepositions
by
for

LOOK

The book is **by** Dickens.
He got a prize **for** his work.
They left **by** plane **for** Hong Kong.

CHECK

1 Complete these sentences with **by** or **for**:

1 I'll make lunch _____ you.
2 He entered _____ the back door.
3 They took sandwiches _____ the journey.
4 They sent the letter _____ post.

PRACTICE

2 Complete these sentences with prepositions from the box:

| by | over | towards |
| for | under | away from |

1 The glacier is moving slowly down the valley _____ the sea.
2 The dog is asleep _____ the chair.
3 It's a big store; there must be _____ 100 people working there.
4 He'll do anything _____ money.
5 Africa and South America, which were once touching, are moving _____ each other at the rate of about two centimetres a year.
6 She went to America _____ ship, then to California _____ road.
7 The boys climbed _____ the wall and ran away.
8 This sponge is _____ washing dishes.
9 I usually keep my shoes _____ the bed.
10 I think you are moving _____ a great discovery, but don't get too far _____ the facts.

GRAMMAR

by:
  A symphony **by** Mozart.
  He came **by** car.

for:
  This room is **for** private study.
  They set out **for** Florence.
  The brush is **for** clean**ing** your shoes.
  He charged £50 **for** the work.

3 Look at the picture, and complete with words from the box:

past	along	behind
across	beside	beyond
not far from	a long way from

As it is _____ Buckingham Palace to Trafalgar Square, he decided to go on foot. He walked _____ The Mall, _____ St James's Park, and arrived in Trafalgar Square. _____ the square he could see the National Gallery, and _____ it the Sainsbury Wing. _____ the Gallery is the National Portrait Gallery, and _____ that he could see the top of a tall building called Centrepoint. But he didn't walk to Centrepoint, because it is quite _____ Trafalgar Square.

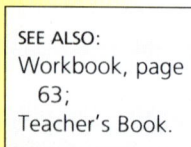

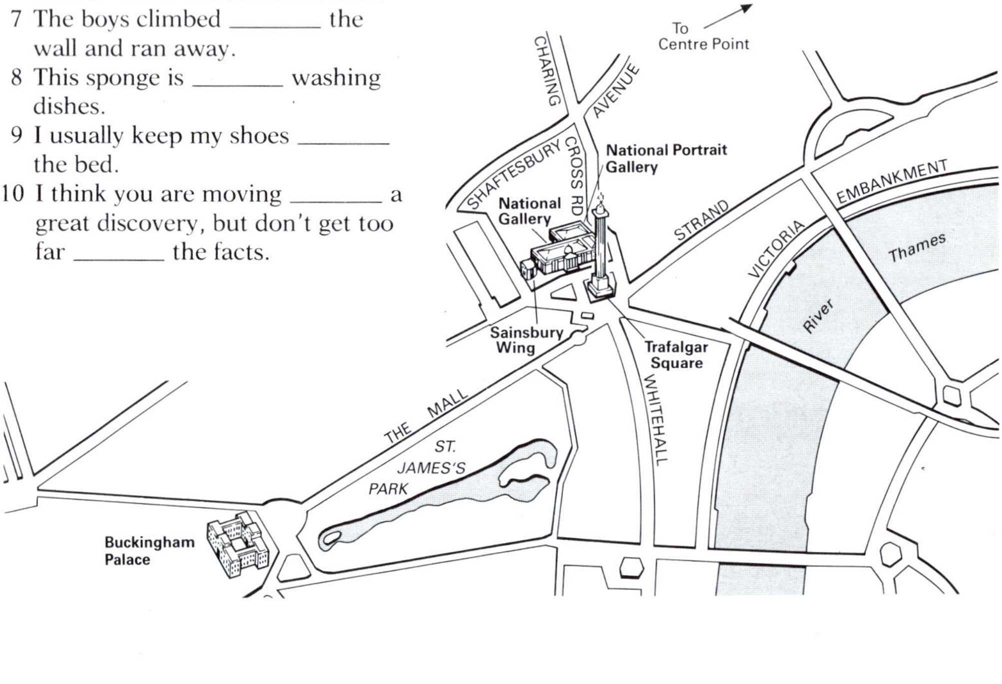

SEE ALSO:
Workbook, page 63;
Teacher's Book.

PREPOSITIONS
Fixed expressions

LOOK Here are two groups of words / phrases which go with certain prepositions:

at first   last   short notice   once   present   that time
by mail   hand   phone   fax   messenger

1 Here are two drawings which give an approximate idea what the words in each group are about. Which is which?

Time   Communications

CHECK 1 Complete these sentences with **at** or **by**, and say which of the two groups in LOOK each one is in:

1 She didn't see me _____ first.
2 Send the invitations _____ mail.
3 _____ that time they were young.
4 Send the letter _____ fax.
5 The parcels go _____ messenger.
6 I'll let you know _____ phone.
7 Sit down _____ once!
8 I'll deliver it _____ hand.
9 You're here _____ last!
10 I haven't time _____ present.

PRACTICE 2 Complete these paragraphs with appropriate phrases taken from the boxes:

| at that time   by telephone   at the present time   by mail   at first   by hand |

The Swift Messenger Service has been operating since 1846.
_____ , when they were quite small, all messages were sent _____ . There was no postal system _____ . But by about 1850, people started to do business _____ , and _____ many people conduct their affairs _____ .

| at last   by fax   at once   by messenger   at short notice |

But if you want to send a package or document _____ , the best way is still _____ .

The SMS is now modernising its services, and _____ we are able to send documents for our customers _____ . This means the documents reach their destination _____ .

GRAMMAR The groups in LOOK consist of fixed phrases, in which the preposition and noun always go together. The same prepositions are used in other ways:

At is also used for place: **at** the crossroads
By is also used for transport: **by** car, **by** road
  (passive) for agents: **by** Beethoven

PREPOSITIONS
Fixed expressions
continued

LOOK

Here are three groups of words / phrases which go with certain prepositions:

by accident chance mistake good fortune surprise
on business duty holiday
in difficulty danger debt

1 Here are three drawings which give an approximate idea what the words in each group are about. Which is which?

CHECK

3 Complete these sentences with **by**, **on** or **in**, and say which of the three groups in LOOK each one is in:

1 He posted it _____ mistake.
2 In the war he was _____ danger.
3 The soldiers were _____ duty.
4 We were _____ holiday in Greece.
5 We met in a café _____ chance.
6 He was there _____ business.
7 He hit you _____ accident.
8 She was _____ difficulty.
9 If you're _____ debt, pay up!
10 She caught me _____ surprise.

PRACTICE

4 Complete these paragraphs using appropriate phrases taken from the ones below:

on holiday   in danger   by mistake
in difficulty   by good fortune

on duty   by chance   on business
by accident

When we were _____ in Devon last summer, we had quite a scare one afternoon, because we found ourselves _____ . We went for a walk along the cliffs overlooking the sea, but it started to rain so we turned back, but we took the wrong turning _____ , and got too close to the edge. We soon found ourselves _____ and, with the sea roaring 150 metres below us and the way back looking slippery and treacherous in the rain, we stared at each other in horror. _____ a policeman came by and saw us and helped us back up to the path.

After thanking him profusely, I asked him: 'Are you _____ here?' 'Oh, no,' he said, 'I came along _____ . I was actually on my way home to supper.'
    'Are you in Devon _____ ?' he asked me. 'No,' I said, 'this is a holiday. We only came up on these cliffs _____ .' 'Lucky for you it didn't turn into a real accident!' he said.

GRAMMAR

The groups in LOOK consist of fixed phrases, in which the preposition and noun always go together. The same prepositions are used in other ways:

On is also used for place: **on** the table, **on** the top
In is also used for place: **in** the room, **in** Budapest
SEE ALSO: Grammar box opposite.

PREPOSITIONS
Fixed expressions
continued

LOOK Here are two groups of words / phrases which go with certain prepositions:

in order control stock (the right) place time
out of order control stock place date

1 Here are two drawings which give an approximate idea what the words in each group are about. Which is which?

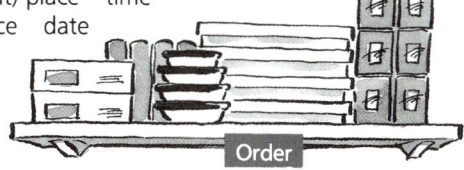

Order

Chaos

CHECK 5 Complete these sentences with **in** or **out of**, and say which of the two groups in LOOK each one is in:

1 A: Is everything _____ order?
   B: Yes, we're ready.
2 He arrived _____ good time for the meeting.
3 The rocket went _____ control and crashed.
4 We still have 15 hairdryers _____ stock.
5 She looked very smart; there wasn't a hair _____ place.
6 The manager is _____ complete control of his company.
7 This licence is no good. It's _____ date.
8 There is a sign on the drinks machine that says ' _____ Order'.
9 *Gone with the Wind* is _____ stock; you'd better order some more copies.
10 Try to put things away _____ the right place.

PRACTICE 6 Complete this paragraph using appropriate phrases taken from the ones below:

out of order   in control   in time   in order   out of control

As Kate drove quickly round the curve, hoping to be _____ for the meeting, the car went _____ and crashed into a tree at the side of the road. She wasn't hurt but she was terribly late, and she wasn't really _____ of herself. Her briefcase had fallen open so her papers were _____ , and her boss really liked everything to be _____ !

out of date   in . . . place   in stock   out of stock

In our local supermarket the manager tries to keep a complete range of items _____ , and makes sure that the perishable items aren't left on the shelves when they are _____ . It's also vital that he keeps all the goods _____ their right _____ , because if he doesn't, there's a danger of thinking that an item is _____ when it is simply _____ the wrong _____ .

GRAMMAR The groups in LOOK consist of fixed phrases, in which the preposition and noun always go together. The same prepositions are used in other ways:

In is also used for place: **in** the room, **in** Budapest
Out of is also used for movement: He got **out of** bed.

SEE ALSO:
Workbook, page 63;
Teacher's Book.

REFERENCE: a summary of grammatical forms

PREPOSITIONS OF PLACE

AWAY FROM   TOWARDS

away from   towards

OVER   UNDER

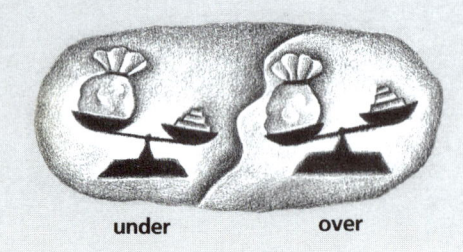

under   over

BEHIND   BEYOND   BESIDE

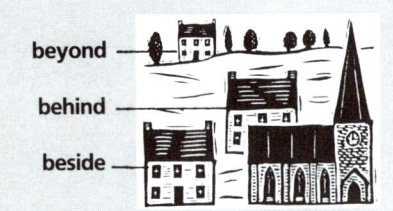

beyond
behind
beside

ALONG   PAST

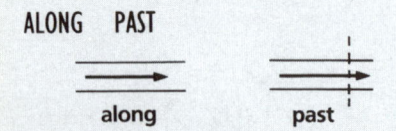

along   past

OTHER EXPRESSIONS RELATED TO DIRECTIONS

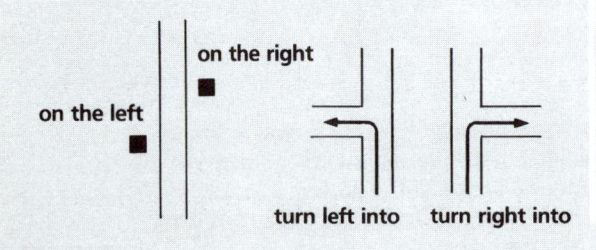

on the left   on the right

turn left into   turn right into

NOT FAR (from)   (QUITE) A LONG WAY (from)

a short distance
It's **not far from** . . .
X is **not far** (away).

a medium distance
It's **quite a long way from** . . .
X is **quite a long way** (away).

a long distance
It's **a long way from** . . .
X is **a long way** (away).

OTHER PREPOSITIONS

BY   FOR

by	the agent:	a symphony **by** Mozart
	the means:	He came **by** car.
for	the purpose:	This room is **for** private study.
		The brush is **for** cleaning your shoes.
	the reason:	He charged £50 **for** the work.
	the aim:	They set out **for** Florence.

FIXED EXPRESSIONS

A selection of fixed prepositional expressions in groups by meaning:

Related to *time*:
at first   **at** once   **at** present
at last   **at** short notice   **at** that time

Related to *messages*:
by hand   **by** mail   **by** phone
by messenger   **by** fax

Related to *chance*:
by chance   **by** good fortune   **by** surprise
by accident   **by** good luck   **by** mistake

Related to *activities*:
on business   **on** holiday
on duty

Related to *problems*:
in difficulties   **in** debt
in danger

Related to *systems*:
in order   **out of** order
in control   **out of** control
                      out of date

166 GRAMMAR

SENTENCES

REVIEW	page 167
Conditionals: if I were . . . if I had been . . . unless even if no matter whether . . . or not	168
Linkers: if because although so that	170
Questions and answers 1: tag questions	171
Questions and answers 2: short answers	172
Infinitives and gerunds: it . . . to run -ing	173
REFERENCE: a summary of grammatical forms	174

REVIEW

Before you start this section here are the items you should have met.

so because	He was thirsty, **so** he drank the water. He drank the water **because** he was thirsty.	I am she does (short answers)	Yes, **I am**. Yes, **she does**. Yes, **you can**, but **Fred can't**. **I am**. **John did**.
and / as well so / therefore but / however	The company is making money. It is expanding **as well**. It is expanding. It **therefore** needs new premises. There is a site. **However**, it will be expensive.	what . . . ? which . . . ?	**What size** do you want? **Which colour** would you like?
		which . . . ? which one(s)? . . . the one(s)	**Which** picture do you like? **Which one(s)** do you like? I like **the** big **one(s)**.
first then before after	**First** you wash the clothes, **then** you iron them. You wash the clothes **before** you iron them. You iron the clothes **after** you wash them.	loudly quietly (adverbs)	She played the music **loudly**. The car runs **quietly**.
who that (relative clauses)	The man **who** knew too much . . . It was my car **that** broke down. The girl (**who / that**) Ted is going to marry is . . . The book (**that**) I'm reading is about . . .	sometimes never (position of adverbs)	He **sometimes** has a shower in the evening. I have **never** seen a kangaroo.
who . . . ?	**Who** likes Mary? **Who** does Mary like?	word order	She is . . . ⟶ Is she . . . ? He lives . . . ⟶ Does he live . . . ? a lovely grey farmhouse a beautiful Venetian palace

GRAMMMAR 167

SENTENCES
Conditionals

if I were . . .
if I had been . . .
unless
even if
no matter
whether (or not)

if I were . . .   if I had been . . .

LOOK

A **If we moved** further west, **we would get** a bigger house.
B **If she hadn't become** a doctor, **she might have started** her own business.
C **If they had seen** the danger, **they would have left** the building.
D **I would wait** for a little while **if I were you**.

1 All these sentences are about imaginary situations, but they are of two different kinds:
   They refer to the present or the future.
   They refer to the past.
Which kind is each sentence?

CHECK

1 Join these pairs of sentences together:

1 If she knew what she wanted to do,   A she wouldn't have got the job.
2 If she had known it was so cold,   B she would do it.
3 If she hadn't made such an effort,   C she wouldn't wear high heels.
4 If Jane were as tall as Sally,   D she would have worn gloves.

GRAMMAR

The two types of conditional sentences given here are imaginary.

1 The imaginary (improbable) present or future:
   If + past | would
   If I had time | **I would** wait.

★ When the verb **be** is used, the past tense is usually **were**:
   If I **were** you . . .   If he **were** here . . .

2 The imaginary (impossible) past:
   If + past perfect | would have
   If I had had the time | **I would have** waited.

PRACTICE

2 Put an appropriate form of a verb from the box in each space:

| speak   cost   be   find |

The imaginary present
1 If the men left the village, they _____ it difficult to get work.
2 I would be surprised if that coat _____ less than £50.
3 If you _____ to him politely, he might agree to move to the next seat.
4 If we booked seats now, we _____ sure of getting in.

| take   make   ask   phone |

The imaginary past
5 If anybody _____ me, I could have told them.
6 I _____ more photographs if I had realised how important the event was.
7 If I had thought the baby was seriously ill, I _____ the doctor at once.
8 If the lawyer _____ a better closing speech, he might have won the case.

SENTENCES
Conditionals
continued

3 Use your imagination!
With a partner, think about your own lives today. Imagine some changes you could make, which would make your life different. Here are some ideas:
   You could change your appearance:
   clothes   weight   make-up   hairstyle

   You could study / work at something new or different:
   apply for a job   take evening classes

Example: *If I ate less, I would lose weight.*

Now think about your lives in the past. Imagine some changes you could have made (but didn't). Here are some ideas:
   You could have moved to a different room / house / flat.
   You could have changed your eating and sleeping times.
   You could have changed your job / your appearance.

Example: *If I had gone to bed earlier last night, I wouldn't have got up so late.*

| **unless   even if   no matter   whether (or not)** |

LOOK

People will complain
- **unless** salaries improve.
- **even if** salaries improve 100 per cent.
- **no matter** how much you increase salaries.
- **whether** you increase salaries **or not**.

CHECK 1 Complete this sentence in four different ways, using **unless, even if, no matter,** or **whether . . . or not**:

We'll have a picnic
- _____ it pours with rain.
- _____ you don't want to.
- _____ what the weather is like.
- _____ it rains _____ .

GRAMMAR

unless: (if not)   You'll be late **unless** you go now.
                                        (if you do *not* go now.)

even if: (emphatic 'if')   You'll be late **even if** you fly there.

whether . . . or not: ('if' + alternative)   You'll be late **whether** you fly **or not**.

no matter: ('whatever')   She'll be angry **no matter** what you do.
                                        (whatever you do.)

PRACTICE 2 Complete with **unless, even if, no matter** or **whether . . . or not**:
1. _____ you like it _____ , Steven is going to get the job.
2. I think we should go, _____ you really hate the idea.
3. I'll do it _____ I end up in prison.
4. _____ what he does, the police will catch him.
5. _____ you've tried it, you can't imagine what fun it is.
6. _____ how you look at it, neutrality in this case is wrong.
7. I would have married her _____ she had been penniless.

SEE ALSO: Skills, pages 46–7, 50–1, 62–3; Workbook, pages 64–5; Teacher's Book.

SENTENCES
Linkers

- if
- because
- although
- so that

LOOK

Let me know **if**
I'm very pleased **because**
I'll explain carefully **so that**
You're not doing it properly **although**

} you understand what you've got to do.

1 The words in **bold** express *contrast*, *cause and effect*, *action and result*, and *condition*. Say which is which.

GRAMMAR

In the example sentences below:

if is a condition:
 I'll buy it **if** you want me to.

because is cause and effect:
 He fell asleep **because** he was tired.
 [effect] ← [cause]

so that is action for a purpose:
 He went to bed **so that** he could sleep.
 [action] → [desired result]

although is contrast:
 He got the job **although** he wasn't well qualified.
 [fact] → [contrast]

SEE ALSO: Conditionals, pages 168–9.

CHECK

1 Complete this sentence four times with a suitable word from the box:

| if | because | so that | although |

Mrs Evans will buy canneloni for supper

_____ her family love it.
_____ her daughter doesn't like it.
_____ her children get used to eating Italian food.
_____ there is any in the shops.

PRACTICE

2 Complete these sentences with suitable words from the box:

| if | although | because | so that |

1 _____ he was rude to me I couldn't feel angry with him, _____ I liked him too much.
2 We always took hats _____ it was hot, _____ we wouldn't get sun stroke.

3 Complete these pairs of sentences in two different ways, using the words in the boxes:

1 I didn't enjoy his company _____ he was often rude to me.
  I couldn't feel angry with him _____

| although |
| because |

2 _____ it was raining we usually stayed indoors.
  _____ we stayed indoors.

| if |
| because |

3 They arranged things _____ they could meet in the afternoons.
  They were pleased _____

| so that |
| if |

4 She arranges every minute of his day _____ he doesn't have time to go out.
  He loves the cinema _____

| although |
| so that |

4 Make up sentences of your own using **if**, **because**, **although** or **so that**:
Examples:
She'll get the job if . . . (condition)
I got home late because . . . (cause and effect)
I bought a sweater so that . . . (action and result)
She accepted my invitation although . . . (contrast)

SEE ALSO: Skills, pages 40–1, 46–7, 60–1, 70–1; Workbook, page 66; Teacher's Book.

SENTENCES
Questions and answers 1
Tag questions

LOOK
A: **The Plumbs are** a nice family, **aren't they**?
B: **You haven't seen** the photo, **have you**?
A: **George looks** good, **doesn't he**?
B: **You never met** Susan, **did you**?

1 Compare the phrase in **bold** at the beginning of each sentence with the phrase in **bold** at the end. In what ways are they similar or different?

CHECK 1 Put in the correct auxiliary verb (+ **n't** if necessary):
1 It isn't raining, _____ it?
2 You like football, _____ you?
3 Brian didn't like the show much, _____ he?
4 It gets too hot, _____ it?

GRAMMAR *Form*
Notice these features of tag questions:

- same verb tense:
- affirmative ⟶ negative: } He **is** ready, **isn't he**?
- same subject (pronouns only in tag):

- negative ⟶ affirmative: John **isn't** ready, **is he**?

- auxiliary verbs only in tag: John **went** home, **didn't** he?
  you **will** do it, **won't** you?

Use
The question tag shows that you expect the person to agree with you, or to confirm what you said.

PRACTICE 2 Complete these sentences with tag questions:

Having a nice meal
1 You will open the wine, _____ ?
2 I can sit here, _____ ?
3 Our host cooks very well, _____ ?
4 This meat isn't bad, _____ ?
5 They didn't make this cake themselves, _____ ?
6 You haven't finished already, _____ ?

Getting ready for a journey
7 You've got the passports, _____ ?
8 We won't leave for an hour, _____ ?
9 Peter packed his bag, _____ ?
10 We should have travel insurance, _____ ?
11 We don't need birth certificates, _____ ?
12 We're ready to go, _____ ?

3 Prepare four tag questions, two negative and two positive, *which you think your partner will confirm*. Use different auxiliary verbs in each question tag. Possible themes:
the weather   one of your colleagues   a recent film   travelling in your area

Example: *It's warm today, isn't it?*

SEE ALSO: Skills, pages 62–3; Workbook, page 67; Teacher's Book.

SENTENCES
Questions and answers 2
Short answers

LOOK

Jim wants more time.
So does Susan.

He won't be able to finish.
Neither will Susan.

1 Compare the verbs in the statements and the answers. How are they similar and different?

CHECK 1 Here are four statements and four answers. Which answer goes with which statement?

1 She couldn't understand the question.
2 They want to leave now.
3 I've finished what I had to do.
4 John doesn't like my hat.

A Neither does Sue.
B So have I.
C So do the boys.
D Neither could I.

GRAMMAR *Form*

So answers
- keep the same tense:
- use any subject:
- agree with an affirmative:

He**'ll wait** for you.   So will I.

Neither answers
- keep the same tense:
- use any subject:
- agree with a negative:

He **won't** wait.   Neither will Jim.

★ The short answer **Me too!** is also commonly used in informal situations.

Use
Normal answers are short in most situations:
Did you like the film?   Yes (I did).   So did I.
                          No (I didn't). Neither did I.

PRACTICE 2 Give a short reply to these statements, agreeing in each case with the speaker:
Example: *I can't understand a word of this.   Neither can I.*

1 Peter can speak French.   _____ John.
2 William didn't bring a typewriter.   _____ I.
3 Shirley won't like this young man.   _____ Jill.
4 I usually play bridge on Fridays.   _____ I.
5 I haven't been to Rome before.   _____ I.
6 Mike and Jill went to Spain last year.   _____ I.
7 They've been to Spain three times.   _____ I.

SEE ALSO:
Workbook, page 67;
Teacher's Book.

172   GRAMMAR

SENTENCES
Infinitives and gerunds

it . . . to run
-ing

LOOK It took us a month **to get** here.

Speech bubble: It's expensive **to run** a car.

1 **It** in these sentences refers to something later in the sentence. What does it refer to?

CHECK 1 Complete these sentences with **It** and one of the phrases below:

is sure   surprised   is expensive   takes

1 _____ me to hear him say that.
2 _____ to be fine tomorrow.
3 _____ to send your children to a private school.
4 _____ several weeks to do the journey.

LOOK **Swimming** regularly is healthy.
Seeing you with your books is a nice change.

1 Change the sentences in this LOOK, so that they are similar to the sentences in the first LOOK. Discuss the changes you make with a partner.

GRAMMAR
Smok**ing**, climb**ing**, walk**ing**, etc. are regularly used as nouns. When the subject of the sentence is a verb, you can say it in one of two ways:
   Playing football is fun. OR
   It's fun **to play** football.

When the subject is a clause, you must use the impersonal **it**:
   It's obvious **that he is ready**.

CHECK 2 Complete each sentence with an appropriate form of one of the verbs given:

begin   dance   train   behave

1 _____ badly at work will only bring trouble.
2 _____ the staff is an investment for the company's future.
3 _____ a project is easier than finishing it.
4 _____ is not allowed in this restaurant.

PRACTICE 3 Complete these sentences appropriately, using the phrases given:
Example: *It's a good idea* to open a bank account; your money is safer.

easy   lucky   a pity   healthy   obvious

1 _____ he's angry; look at his red face!
2 _____ you weren't here; we had a lovely time.
3 _____ to remember this; it's very short.
4 _____ he's so tall; he can reach the top shelf for us.
5 _____ to go for a walk every day.

Look at the sentences again; two can be changed to sentences starting with a verb + ing. Which ones? Change them.

4 Make up sentences about *your* family and environment, using these and other phrases:

   It's nice to . . .
   It's not very nice to have to . . .
   It was a good idea to . . .
   Studying . . .
   Working . . .
   Playing football, etc. . . .

Example:
It's not very nice to have to make your bed in the morning.

SEE ALSO: Skills, pages 50–1; Workbook, page 68; Teacher's Book.

REFERENCE: a summary of grammatical forms

CONDITIONALS

If I **were** . . .   If I **had been** . . .
Imaginary present or *improbable*:
Conditional | Past
I **would wait** | if | I **were** you.
If I **were** you, | I **would wait**.

Imaginary past or *impossible*
Conditional perfect | Past perfect
They **would have left** | if | they **had seen** her.
If they **had seen** her, | they **would have left**.

Conditional linkers
Clause | Clause
People will complain **unless** | salaries improve.
People will complain **even if** |
People will complain **no matter (what)** | we do.
                        (how much) | salaries improve.
People will complain **whether** | salaries improve
                                 | **or not**.

LINKERS

Condition: Let me know **if** you're coming.
Cause and effect: He fell asleep **because** he was tired.
Purpose: He went to bed **so that** he could sleep.
Contrast: He went to bed **although** he wasn't tired.

TAG QUESTIONS

Chris was here, **wasn't he**?   He wasn't here, **was he**?
She came, **didn't she**?   Jane didn't come, **did she**?

SHORT ANSWERS

So (*agree with affirmative*) | **Neither** (*agree with negative*)
So do I. | **Neither** do I.
So can they. | **Neither** can they.
etc. | etc.

INFINITIVES AND GERUNDS

-ing | It . . . to . . .
Swimming is fun. | It's fun **to swim**.
Travelling is expensive. | It's expensive **to travel**.

                              | It . . . that . . .
                              | It's true **that** it rains in July.
                              | It's a pity **(that)** you weren't here.

174 GRAMMAR

PARAGRAPHS

	page
INTRODUCTION	175
Linking ideas with phrases	176
Linking ideas by reference	178
Linking ideas with general words	180

INTRODUCTION

All the items of grammar that appear in the earlier sections of this part have been items which appear **in sentences**: nouns, verbs, adjectives, modals, prepositions and so on. However, sentences do not appear in isolation, and it is important to see the way they are joined together.

In this section we deal with three ways of joining sentences.

1 *Phrases*   These may be adverbial phrases, like **in spite of that**, **on the other hand**, **in addition**, **in that case**, etc., or words like **and**, **then** and **but** which also appear inside sentences.

2 *Reference*   A word in a second sentence may join the two sentences together by referring to a word or phrase in a previous sentence. Pronouns like **she** and **they** can do this, and words like **the** and **this**, or **then** and **there**. Some words are *only* used for this purpose, like **previous** or **the former**.

3 *General words*   You can often use a more general word to refer to a number of words in the previous sentence:

> In the sixteenth century, *most people thought that the world was flat*. **This belief** was seriously challenged in 1540 by the ideas of Copernicus.

The simpler ways of joining sentences together are constantly used in both speaking and writing. However, many of the more complex ways are only used in writing or formal speech. This section is intended to help you *recognise* the ways sentences are joined together, especially so that you can *read and write* better.

PARAGRAPHS
Linking ideas with phrases

LOOK

A Treating boys as if they were responsible adults brings out the best in them; **in the same way / similarly**, if you treat them as criminals that is how they will behave.

B We can catch the train at 6.35. **Alternatively**, there's a bus at 7 o'clock.

1 The sentences in **A** and **B** are linked together in two different ways:
 suggesting another possibility
 saying how two things are really the same.
Which is which?

CHECK 1 Link these sentences together, using the most appropriate word from those in the box:

1 If you are nice to your children they will be nice to you.
 If you are rude to them they will probably be rude back.
2 There's a nice Greek restaurant round the corner.
 We could go to the Italian across the road.

| Alternatively |
| Similarly |

LOOK **A** He was very uncomfortable.
However,
Nevertheless, he fell asleep.
Despite this,

B He didn't look pleased when he heard the news.
Instead,
On the contrary, he looked more and more depressed.

1 The sentences in **A** and **B** are linked together in different ways:
 The second sentence agrees with the negative in the first.
 The second sentence disagrees with the first.
Which is which?

CHECK 2 Link these sentences together, using a phrase from the box:

| Instead / On the contrary   However / Nevertheless / Despite this |

1 Fred felt most disheartened.
 He was not going to let himself be beaten.
2 The sales figures were not improving at all.
 They were getting worse and worse.

PARAGRAPHS
Linking ideas with phrases
continued

LOOK **A** The company has lost its market in Spain.
Otherwise / Apart from this it is doing very well in Europe.

B The rain looked as if it had come to stay.
For this reason / Consequently they decided to give up the picnic and go back home.

1 In one of the pairs of sentences, the *second* sentence is the reason, and in the other the *first* sentence is an exception. Which is which?

CHECK 3 Join these sentences together, using the most appropriate phrase from those in the box:

For this reason / Consequently   Otherwise / Apart from this

1 The musicians were disappointed by their reception in Hampton.
The whole tour was very successful.

2 The cost of living has been rising steadily.
They decided not to go on holiday this year.

LOOK **A** John Major was Chancellor for a few months. **Afterwards / Later** he became Prime Minister.

B They now live in Cambridge. **Previously / Before that** they lived in Oxford.

1 Is the second event *before* or *after* the first in each case?

CHECK 4 Join these sentences together, using a word or phrase from the box:

1 The minister said he was against the new tax.
He had taken a different attitude.

| Afterwards / Later |
| Previously / Before that |

2 The boys played football all the afternoon.
They went home and had a bath.

PRACTICE 5 Join these sentences with *any* of the words or phrases presented on this double page. There are sometimes alternatives to discuss:

1 The wedding was held in St Michael's Church.
There was a reception at his father-in-law's house.
2 She was certainly not getting fatter.
She was losing weight by the minute.
3 Employees will usually be loyal if they are well-treated.
They will react badly if they are not looked after.
4 You can wait here for me.
You can go home and wait there.
5 The shops are terribly crowded at this time of the year.
We have got to buy presents for the children.
6 Working conditions are considerably better at Macy's.
They decided to accept the job offer.
7 He is now working in a construction company.
He travelled abroad extensively.
8 The photocopier needs some maintenance.
The office is working quite well.

6 With a partner, think of pairs of sentences which you can link together with the words and phrases presented on these two pages.

SEE ALSO: Skills, pages 22–3, 24–5, 28–9, 40–1, 76–7; Workbook, pages 69–71; Teacher's Book.

GRAMMAR 177

PARAGRAPHS
Linking ideas by reference

LOOK

A Jamieson closed **his** office door and walked away. Then **he** realised **he** hadn't locked **it**. **He** went back, locked **it**, and then walked to **his** car.

B We stayed with a very nice family in Poitiers. There were two children in **the** family. **The** girl was nine and **the** boy was four.

1 What do **he**, **his** and **it** refer to in **A**?
2 What does each **the** refer to in **B**?

CHECK 1 Which words in the two sentences link them together?

1 There was a note from Rose. She just said, 'I won't be there on Friday'.

2 He threw open the door of his bedroom. It was empty.

LOOK

A Last year we took our holiday in Spain. **That** holiday turned out to be the best we had ever had.

B John thought Sue was a really nice girl. Sadly, **this** turned out to be a mistake.

1 Does the word in **bold** refer back to one word or more than one?

CHECK 2 Which words in the two sentences link them together?

1 'I'll think about it.'
   That statement was the end of our conversation.

2 Make sure you make a list of what you want to buy. Anything you really need should go on this list.

LOOK

A Douglas Hurd and John Major both offered themselves as leader of the party. **The former** was Foreign Secretary at that time, and **the latter** was Chancellor.

B I went to Stuttgart in 1987. I soon found a job **there**.

C Many centuries ago people believed that myths were really true. Of course things were different **then**.

1 To what do each of the words in **bold** refer?
2 In **A**, **B** and **C**, which is about *order*, which about *time* and which about *place*?

CHECK 3 Which words in the two sentences link them together?

1 This subject requires a full chapter or just a brief mention. Unfortunately space forbids the former alternative.

2 I ran quickly into my study. There was no-one there.

178 GRAMMAR

PARAGRAPHS

Linking ideas by reference

continued

PRACTICE 4 Find the references which include the three kinds presented on this double page:

1 The pianist is so dreadful, my husband and I are leaving. We have heard quite enough of his playing.

2 'There was a peculiar half-Chinese woman sitting there,' she said contemptuously. That was me.

3 Moving goods in the seventeenth century was a slow process. Of course there was no motor transport then.

4 Smile while you're waiting. It makes a good impression.

5 He had played football and tennis at school, and he had been a prefect. All that counted in his favour when he applied for a job.

6 Can you lend Jane a sweater? Hers has got lost.

7 Great pine trees fill the entire valley. Many of these are more than a thousand years old.

8 John Smith and Neil MacDonald were both British. The latter, however, was from Scotland, which he made a great point of.

9 He decided to walk home. But that turned out to be a bad idea.

GRAMMAR **He, my, theirs**, etc. refer to someone known or mentioned earlier.

This / that   refers back to things:
   That was the answer.
   That gave me a clue.

This / that   refers back to a person only when followed by **be**:
   That was me.   **That** ~~told~~ me.

Then   refers back to a time.
There   refers back to a place.

The former / the latter   refer back to one of two items.

PRACTICE 5 The references below are sometimes ambiguous. With a partner, discuss how you can rewrite them to make the reference clear. You may think of more than one way of solving the problem:

1 John and Brian spent a week together. The trouble was, he didn't like him.

2 I looked into the cafeteria and the library. I found him there.

3 My first memories from childhood are of a big farm with cows. Years later I went back to visit the place. My father was still alive then.

4 Both the children and their parents were at fault in this case. They were always rushing about the place and they didn't pay enough attention to what they needed, so of course they didn't like it and they got upset.

SEE ALSO: Skills, pages 28–9, 34–5, 40–1, 42–5, 50–1, 52–3, 74–5, 76–7; Workbook, pages 72–3; Teacher's Book.

PARAGRAPHS
Linking ideas with general words

LOOK

A Look at <u>Brian</u> climbing that tree. **The idiot** is going to fall if he's not careful.

B Peter has bought <u>a new Jaguar</u>. He sits in **the car** all day admiring it.

1 What is the link between the underlined words and the words in **bold**?

CHECK 1 Which words in the second sentence refer to the underlined part of the first sentence?

1 I went to see <u>my grandmother</u>. The poor old lady is getting very forgetful these days.

2 I've just received the architect's <u>proposal</u>. The whole thing is very well thought out.

3 <u>Brian</u> is behaving rather strangely these days. I think you ought to have a talk with the boy.

LOOK The washing machine broke and the dryer stopped working. This was **a disaster** for Jenny and Mike.

1 How is the reference in this LOOK different from the sentences in the first LOOK?

CHECK 2 Which words in the second sentence refer to the underlined part of the first sentence?

1 Mrs Mayer thought <u>her daughter was foolish</u>. It was a pity she had this opinion.

2 When the police found the drugs in the man's suitcase, they decided <u>he was responsible</u>. However, they were mistaken in their conclusion.

3 In the sixteenth century people thought that <u>the earth was flat</u>. This belief was shattered by Copernicus and Galileo.

GRAMMAR Sentences are linked together in a number of ways. One way is to have different words in different sentences referring to the same thing.

This may be a pair of noun phrases:
Sam wants to swim the English Channel.
We must persuade the fool not to try.

The fool in the second sentence is identified by referring back to the previous sentence; it must be **Sam**.

Or it may be a noun phrase which refers back to a whole clause:
Sam wants to swim the English Channel.
The idea is completely mad.

The idea in the second sentence is identified by referring back to the previous sentence; it must be **Sam wants to swim the English Channel**.

PRACTICE 3 Complete each of the following sentences with a word from the box, and write out the part of the previous sentence that each word refers to:

1 What shall I do with all this crockery? Leave the _____ here; we can pick it up later.

2 Can you tell me where to stay in London? I've never been to the _____ in my life.

3 Didn't everyone expect the Director to resign? Yes they did, but it didn't seem to have any effect on the _____ .

```
place
man
stuff
```

4 Three of the students insisted on talking about the number of hours they had to attend class each week. But this _____ was not one that the Professor wanted to discuss.

5 There was a slight chance that the murderer would be identified. However, the police did not want to rely on this _____ .

6 Steve spent a month driving a taxi round London. As a result of this _____ he changed his attitude to driving.

7 Inflation was rising, unemployment was widespread, and the army was restless. This _____ filled the President with concern.

8 The Princess slipped and fell as she walked up the steps. Although she was not hurt, the _____ was widely reported in the press.

```
state of affairs
incident
topic
experience
possibility
```

9 The Government has finally managed to eliminate inflation. This _____ is the admiration of many other countries.

10 One way of reducing inflation is to put large numbers of people out of work. But this is not really a good _____ to the problem.

11 The first man went over Niagara Falls in a barrel at the beginning of the century. This extraordinary _____ has now been repeated several times.

12 The Minister was found by reporters in a night club with a young woman who was not his wife. This was a _____ which he could not easily get out of.

13 Thirty-five people were killed in the rail crash. This _____ would not have occurred if it had not been for the carelessness of one of the staff.

```
exploit
predicament
achievement
tragedy
solution
```

PARAGRAPHS
Linking ideas with general words
continued

SEE ALSO: Skills, pages 28–9, 34–5, 60–1, 76–7; Workbook, pages 72–3; Teacher's Book.

SELF-CHECK KEY

STARTING OUT

What will you be doing? (page 9)
1 1 E 2 A 3 D 4 B 5 C
2 1 page 30 2 pages 84–5 3 exercises 1–4 in Unit 3 4 pages 136, 138–9, 140, 123, 147, 131, 132–3, 178–81
3 1 C 2 D 3 A 4 B

Talking about words and grammar (pages 12–13)
Words
1 It can be any of the four items mentioned.
2 First picture: noun/object Second picture: noun/person Third picture: verb
3 (*The obvious solution*) *Noun* picture flower *Verb* go *Adjective* green *Preposition/adverb* up away
4 **Upped** is used as a verb. **Go** is used as a noun. **Flowering** is used as a verb. **Picture** is used as a verb. **Greens** is used as a noun. **Away** is used as an adjective.
5 It is common to make verbs/nouns from other words. It is less common to make adjectives from other words. It is impossible (?) to make prepositions from other words. It is impossible (?) to make pronouns from other words. It is impossible (?) to make linkers, etc. from other words.
6 1 noun 2 verb 3 verb 4 noun
Grammar
1 A adverb B past perfect C modal verb D multi-part verb (also called phrasal verb) E linker F article
2 A reported speech B relative clause C comparative/superlative D tag question E conditional F passive
3 1 L 2 F 3 E 4 I 5 B 6 D 7 J 8 K 9 H 10 G 11 A 12 C

The right language for the right situation! (page 14)
1 1 B 2 D 3 C 4 A
2 Dialogue 1 Formal Asking about prices Dialogue 2 Informal Persuading someone to wait Dialogue 3 Formal Persuading someone to wait Dialogue 4 Informal Asking about prices

SKILLS

UNIT 1: WRITING

Books and writers (pages 18–19)
3 2 *Sample answer*: B C G D A E F
5 1 Newspaper articles. (Other possible sources: personal experience friends' experiences observation of strangers history books) 2 The first chapter, so that she is not tempted to write all the most interesting parts first. 3 At least twice. (Changes may include: adding, deleting or substituting punctuation marks, words, phrases, sentences or paragraphs, or moving text around.)

Choosing something to read (pages 20–1)
2 A an adventure story B a ghost story C a murder / detective story D science fiction E a romantic novel
3 1 B C D 2 A B D
4 look / bookshops / think / surprise / blurb / surprises / didn't / unless / economics
6 Can you recommend anything? What sort of book is it? What's it about then? . . . do they succeed?

Descriptions (pages 22–3)
2 1 Not true: stunningly attractive isolated cool drinks and local snacks are always available free umbrellas emerald-green sea tall mountains rise dramatically
3 D A C B *Sample answer*: This is perhaps considered the order of importance to tourists, and the order in which they would be experienced by new visitors. The hotel is certainly the main point of interest in the photograph, despite its size in relation to the the beach. The present simple.
3 *Sample answer*: The hotel is a building standing alone in a bay. In front of the hotel is a beach, where drinks and snacks are always available. You can relax in the sun or under the umbrellas, while your children play in the sea. Behind the hotel, mountains rise towards the sky.
5 *Sample answers*: 1 The waves sounded like rolls of thunder. 2 The museum smelt like a public toilet. 3 The soup tasted like washing-up liquid. 4 The hat looked like a bowl of fruit.
6 *Sample answers*: 1 The underground station reminded me of a bomb shelter. 2 The shopping centre reminded me of a prison. 3 The mountains reminded me of the Alps. 4 The sitting-room reminded me of a dentist's waiting-room.
7 *Sample answers*: loathed/hated/detested liked/admired/adored

UNIT 2: PRIVATE LIVES

Romance and friendship (pages 24–5)
2 1 Important: warmth honesty intelligence Unimportant: physical appearance 2 Something you allow to happen; a flash of lightning from above. 3 A lifestyle which fits in with your own and does not stop you doing things that have become important to you.
3 1 D 2 A 3 B 4 C
4 They are stressed to signal the nature of the point that follows, or – in the case of 'first of all' – the overall structure of what is to come.
6 *Sample answers:* Male 1: female A or B Male 2: female C (if he is a graduate) Male 3: female B (if they do not mind the age difference. It is possible that none would be suitable – he may not be a graduate, and he may not be seen as a 'professional'. It might be difficult for a professional woman to work from a farm.)

Parents and children (pages 26–7)
2 1 *Bill and Anthea*: They have had very close relationships with their parents, living in the same house or nearby and helping each other. *Jill and Stephen*: As adults, they have had very little contact with their parents. They are not as close to them physically or emotionally, and they seem to feel little sense of responsibility towards them. 2 *Anthea*: She appears to have been a full-time mother with little child-care help from her husband. She and her children remained close, and lived together even for a period after the children's marriages. *Jill*: She stayed at home until the children were ready to start school, and then went out to work. Her children now live a long way away and rarely visit.
3 1 *Sample answer*: He is about 11; young enough to have a relatively early bed-time, and to accept his father's authority if persuasion fails. The biggest clue to his age is of course his voice. 2 His father wants him to go to bed at the usual time. No, he doesn't. 3 The boy wants to stay up late to watch a comedy programme. Yes, he does.
4 1 A son B son C son D father E father 2 He means that he (reluctantly!) accepts his son's arguments and promise, and that he will allow his son to do what he wants.

Family matters (pages 28–9)
1 *Sample answer*: The writer is a teenager who enjoys discos more than sight-seeing, classical music or ballet, and has a rather difficult relationship with his parents. Instead of making the most of a situation which is less than ideal, he gets bored and miserable.
2 1 how glad I am to be home in prison no fun no excitement boring tedious so-called places of interest awkward conversation silly and dull absolute misery counting the days 2 tedious dull 3 absolute misery *Sample answers*: 4 He was tied to his parents and unable to do what he enjoyed. 5 Pop music. 6 A stay at a holiday resort where entertainment specifically for young people is provided by the hotel or available locally.

UNIT 3: FEAR

Is fear good for you? (pages 30–1)
1 1 fear of water (drowning) fear of loneliness fear of falling fear of flying
2 1 Stage fright. 2 Yes, very common.
3 1 B D F 2 No, on the whole it goes away as it becomes converted into the energy an actor needs to perform – although it does not disappear completely until the end of the performance. 3 Relieved and relaxed.
4 1 They practise the lines they are going to say, or talk to other people. 2 She prefers to be quiet, and not to speak to anyone. She gets changed and made-up immediately before going on stage. 3 It helps to concentrate your mind and energy on your performance.
5 1 E 2 C 3 A 4 F 5 B 6 D
6 1 His brother, not his sister. 2 Don't turn left; turn right. 3 Jane's father, not Sara's father. 4 I wanted three, not four. 5 It arrives at 11.15, not 10.15. 6 I need his new address, not his old one. 7 It's the director I want to speak to, not his assistant.

Overcoming fears (pages 32–3)
5 1 Fear of flying is very common. 2 Dr Yaffe's courses help people overcome their fear of flying. 3 Most people can successfully overcome their fears.
6 *Sample answers:* Paragraph 2: He explains the principles and physical effects of flying, and ways of overcoming fear. Paragraph 3: About 80 per cent of Yaffe's clients fly again.
7 1 A 2 D 3 E 4 C and F 6 B

Describing fear (pages 34–5)
3 *Sample answer*: *Feelings*: the need to escape a small white circle of terror he knew he was going to fall *Movement*: his chair toppled sideways the pencil fell on to the floor a single step he pressed backwards his hands stretching sideways *Breathing*: like poison gas to smother him to snatch his breath away *Space*: to envelop the room was too small a single step was enough to bring him against the wall *Taste*: his mouth was dry *Sound*: the crash a roaring sound

UNIT 4: SPORT

Women and sport (pages 36–8)
2 1 C 2 D 3 B 4 E 5 A She continued playing football because she enjoyed it and was good at it. At school, she played with boys in the playground, but she was not allowed to join their school team.
3 1 Scandinavian countries Italy Germany 2 The crowds are bigger and noisier. 3 B C D G
4 A athletics B gymnastics C motor racing D boxing E hockey F synchronised swimming G archery H basketball I skating J horse racing
8 horse racing cricket tennis badminton croquet riding hunting cycling golf hockey swimming
9 1 C E 2 A woman (see last sentence). 3 The last sentence gives her opinion. The rest of the article gives information.

Sport and violence (page 39)
2 1 He finds it difficult to understand why normal, nice people behave so badly at football matches. **2a** His neighbours are usually nice, friendly, warm and affectionate. **b** After a football match, they are drunk, aggressive, noisy, and sometimes violent. 3 According to the speaker, Brazilians go to football matches to enjoy themselves; they are not aggressive or violent. 4 At Wimbledon, everyone is there to watch tennis, and they watch in silence. (NB It is implied that everyone there also has a seat.)

Sport and politics (pages 40–1)
1 *B*
2 1 A disagree B disagree C agree D disagree E disagree 2 In my opinion I feel strongly *Other ways*: I believe I think I am absolutely convinced that 3 However.

UNIT 5: DISCIPLINE

Children and discipline (pages 42–5)
1 1 B 2 E 3 A 4 F 5 D 6 C *Other ways*: beating stopping pocket money refusing to allow children to go out
3 1 Being sent to his room and told to stay there. This makes him think about what he's done. 2 He remains stubborn. 3 He feels angry.
4 1 You're feeling ill? ↓ 2 I have to change at Oxford? ↑
6 1 The main topic divides into *rewards* and *punishments*. *Rewards:* Giving attention Praise Special treats Special privileges Bribery *Punishments:* Smacking Shouting Removing attention Loss of privileges Telling off 2 *In schools*: *Rewards*: Giving attention – teacher spends time with a pupil Praise – children are praised for good work and behaviour Special privileges – being given more responsibility and e.g. a special common room Bribery – prizes for good work *Punishments*: Shouting – teacher shouts at child Removing attention – teacher ignores child Loss of privileges – child not allowed to go out at break time Telling off – child spoken to and warned for not doing homework
7 1 Telling off (in list) 2 Reasoning, and trying to make the child think (not in list) 3 Smacking and threatening loss of privileges (in list)
8 1 *Sample answers:* **a** How many times have I told you not to eat with your fingers? **b** How many times have I told you not to come home late? **c** How many times have I told you not to play with matches? 2 *Sample answers*: **b** If you ever do this again, I won't let you go out at all! **c** If you ever do this again, I'm going to smack you!

Discipline in society (pages 46–7)
1 1 A hard manual work in prison B community service C being hit or beaten D training / education
2 *Sample answers*: 1 In my opinion, people who drive dangerously should lose their driving licence. 2 I think people who take drugs should be given help so that they can stop taking them. 3 I feel strongly that young people who damage property should be made to pay for it so they realise what it costs other people. 4 I believe that people who steal and use violence should be sent to prison because they must be prevented from doing it again. 5 I have no doubt at all that anyone who paints graffiti on trains should be forced to clean it and then made to do community service. Then they might think twice before they do it again.

182 KEY

UNIT 6: PEOPLE ON THE MOVE

A way of life (pages 48–9)
2 Text A: Councillors and other people wanting information about gypsies. To give information. Text B: Readers of a local newspaper. To present an argument, supported by information.
3 1 Both 2 A 3 Both 4 B 5 A 6 Both 7 A
4 (See tapescript, page 188.)

Living away from home (pages 50–1)
2 1 Vietnam. 2 No, he is not. He lives with his family. 3 Two years ago. 4 No, probably not.
3 1 False – they have learned little English, are poor and homesick, and find some Britons unfriendly. 2 False – they have Vietnamese friends in Britain. 3 False – they would like to visit Vietnam, but may want to continue living in Britain.
4 a little frightened   shocked   surprised   homesick
5 Sample answer: She speaks English well, and has obviously known British people in the past. She seems to have had few serious problems adapting to Britain, and so her life-style in Mexico was probably fairly similar.
6 1 Bad weather and inefficient public transport. 2 Making friends. 3 The way people do not know how to deal with their emotions; the relationship between people and their elderly relatives. 4 Sample answer: In Mexico the weather may be better. Mexicans probably use more private transport; make friends more easily, although friendships are not so deep; show their emotions more; may be closer, physically and emotionally, to their elderly relatives.

Journeys (pages 52–3)
1 1 At the entrance to an underground station. 2 The Underground/Tube (the London underground railway system). 3 Possible answer: You would probably find another route if you had planned to travel to Holborn. You might decide to take a bus or taxi instead.
2/3 1E Railway station (platform). 2A Motorway; radio announcement (M25 junction 19). 3D Airport (checked in). 4C Coach station (Bay 6). 5B Ferry port (sailing   disembark).
4 Most formal: C (NB very formal)   To someone you do not know well: B or C   To a friend: A
6 B   A   C
7 Sample answers: 1 I am writing to ask about …   2 I am writing to complain about …   3 I am writing to congratulate you on …
8 Sample answers: 1 I am writing to apologise for arriving late yesterday/my late arrival yesterday.   2 I am writing to apologise for forgetting about last week's meeting.   3 I am writing to apologise for not meeting you last Friday.   4 I am writing to apologise for behaving so badly at your party/my bad behaviour at your party.
9 Sample answers: 1 Unfortunately, I was involved in a car accident the day before, and have been in hospital ever since. 2 Unfortunately, I had a broken leg at the time. I had hoped to have the plaster off before the wedding but, since this was not possible, I decided that it would be too difficult to travel.   3 Unfortunately, my son woke up feeling ill that day. As my wife was at a conference, I had to stay at home with him.

UNIT 7: HEALTH

Staying healthy (pages 54–5)
2 GP: General Practitioner; a doctor who is trained in general medicine and who treats patients living in a particular area.   NHS: National Health Service; the British system of medical treatment, paid for by taxes.   prescription: an order for one or more medicines, written by a doctor for a patient to take to a chemist.   arthritis: a serious disease which causes pain and swelling in the joints between your bones.   massage: a treatment which involves someone rubbing your body with their hands, usually to take away pain or stress.
3 1 Unlike 'conventional' medicine, 'alternative' medicine treats the whole body, bearing in mind a patient's feelings, and (it is implied) does not use chemical drugs. GPs have a more limited time to spend with each patient, and treatment is free.   2 The 'alternative' doctor believes that chemical drugs can be extremely useful, alone or with 'alternative' therapy, in the treatment of very serious illnesses. The GP feels that the two kinds of treatment are not as different as many assume, and agrees that ideally patients' feelings should be taken into account.
4 1 A person's body, mind, emotions, and spirit.   2 A patient with arthritis who also had emotional problems.   3 Yes, she does; she mentions severe pain and serious illnesses. 4 Not just their physical condition, but also people's feelings about their illness and treatment.   5 A GP has a limited amount of time to spend with each patient.
5 Sample answers: 1 An 'alternative' doctor can spend as much time as her patients can afford, whereas a 'conventional' doctor has a limited amount of time with each patient. 2 'Conventional' medicine is free, whereas 'alternative' medicine must be paid for. 3 'Alternative' medicine involves the whole body, whereas 'conventional' doctors are only able to treat the illness itself.
7 Sample answer: Doctors should give us advice about healthy living, but then leave us to make our own decisions about what we do or do not do.
8 1 For the writer 'doctor-speak' means the language typically used by doctors to forbid people to do things and to make people feel guilty if they then do them.   2 By telling us to stop doing things that we enjoy, and reminding us that it is often our own fault if we become ill.

Getting enough sleep? (pages 56–7)
1 Sample answers: The man with the moustache can't sleep because his wife is snoring. Loud noises next door are keeping the elderly lady awake. The little girl is too excited to sleep because it is her birthday the next day. The schoolboy is worried about his exams. The young woman is worried about making a speech the next day.
2 1 Problems that she cannot find solutions to, and the worry that she will not sleep. 2 By day she is very tired and unhappy. She cannot concentrate at work. She is worried and easily annoyed.
5 Sample answers: that he is sleeping badly more than two weeks   he is worried about anything   is only worried about not being able to sleep   take regular exercise   see the doctor again.
7 Sample answers: In general, children sleep more than adults. On the whole, young and middle-aged adults only sleep at night. Generally speaking, people between 11 and 50 are not eager to get up in the morning. Compared with most adults, babies sleep a lot.   In contrast to older children, small babies seem to be unhappy when they wake up. Children read themselves to sleep just as adults do.   Young adults have about the same amount of sleep as elderly people.   One- to five-year-olds sleep at similar times to elderly people.

A healthy body (pages 58–9)
1 H   C   G   I   D   E   B   F   A   J
3 A waist   B thighs (and to improve posture)   C –   D back, chest and arms   E –   F upper arms   G thighs (and to improve posture)   H legs   I back, chest and arms   J waist
6 Sample answers: 1 A doctor is speaking to a patient in a surgery or the patient's home. 2 A teacher is testing young pupils orally, or in writing on the blackboard. The sum could also be found in a school textbook or examination paper.   3 This is from a recipe, to be followed by someone cooking (bread, for example). It might be in a recipe book or a women's magazine.   4 A dentist is speaking to a patient whose teeth he or she is examining. 5 A written or printed notice has been placed near or attached to a machine by someone in authority. It is addressed to anyone who might use the machine.   6 This instruction is written or printed on the outside of an envelope by the person sending the photographs. It is addressed to post office workers and anyone else who might handle the envelope.   7 An official or unofficial instructor is talking to someone learning to drive. They are both in a moving vehicle.   8 This written instruction was attached to a house plant by a supplier, so that the person buying the plant knows how to care for it.   9 A man, probably an older man, is speaking to a boy over whom he has authority. The man might be an old-fashioned schoolmaster and the boy a pupil who is not paying attention in class.   10 Someone is speaking to an older or weaker person, perhaps an elderly parent.

UNIT 8: BUSINESS

The right job? (pages 60–1)
1 1A a writer   B a lorry/truck driver   C a teacher   D a factory manager/supervisor   E a shopkeeper
3 'People' skills: persuasion   winning the trust of clients   motivating employees   Special knowledge: legal knowledge relating to buying and selling property and to restrictions on advertising   knowledge of financial matters, such as where house buyers can borrow money   and how to keep accounts   Organisational skills: predicting how many staff members will be needed at any time, and therefore employing the right number and arranging suitable holiday times
4 1 about   2 confidence   3 encourage   4 financial records   5 are likely to
7 There are a number of possibilities, but the best choice for each may be: 1 B   2 G   3 H

Applying for a job (pages 62–3)
1 1 marketing assistant   2 nightclub manager 3 office cleaner and probably nightclub manager   4 marketing assistant   5 sales consultant   office cleaner
2 Sample answers: 1 What does the Marketing Assistant do on overseas trips? How many weeks holiday would I have?   If I had to work at weekends, would I have other days free?   What is the salary for the post? 2 Do you know anything about marketing? What kind of company were you working for in London?   Do you speak any foreign languages other than French?   Why did you leave university after a year?
3 1 C   B   A   2 Sample answers: C Past simple: Why did you decide to leave? B Present simple: Do you get on well with your colleagues?   A Type 2 conditional: If I got the job, what would my hours be exactly?
3 … are there any questions you would like to ask about the job?

Dealing with companies (pages 64–5)
2 1 Mr Daley is already on the phone to someone else.   2 Sample answers: He is in a meeting / not in the office / on holiday / away on a business trip / at lunch.
6 paragraph 1: reason for writing   paragraph 2: the problem   paragraph 3: request for action

UNIT 9: POWER

Power in conversation (pages 66–7)
2 1 They keep talking. They pause in the middle of a sentence, so it is clear that they have not finished (and polite listeners will wait for them to continue).   2 Women more often express their views as opinions. Men tend to express their views as facts. Men therefore sound more knowledgeable and confident. Women often finish a sentence by asking for their listeners' agreement, indicating that they might be persuaded to change their opinion.
3 Generally polite: A   B   D   G   H   4 1 unfinished   2 unfinished   3 finished   4 finished   5 unfinished   The voice rises to show that a point has not yet been completed, and falls at the end of the point.

The power of the way you look (pages 68–9)
1 Answers that most British people would give are: 1 B (or E)   2 C   3 E (or D)   4 A   5 D   6 F
2 clothes (conventional or striking)   things people carry   the way they stand or walk   height (men)   hair (men)   young appearance   the way people speak   body language (e.g. the use of arms and hands)
3 1 The speaker thinks that it is sad that women make themselves look more like men by wearing suits.   2 Props are objects used on the stage in a play. Here, props are things people carry/wear to make an impression. 3 The survey shows that there is a relationship between height and success within companies.
6 2a A They must be related, or very close friends.   B One man is showing dominance over the other.   C One man is aggressive; the other is defensive.   D The man is expressing dominance over the woman.   E They must be related, or very good friends; or one woman (the one who moved so close) is trying to dominate the other.

The power of advertisements (pages 70–1)
2 1 C   2 E   3 A   4 D   5 B   6 F
3 Sample answers: Hago 1, 5, 6   Le Jardin 1, 2, 3, 4   Nissan car 2, 3, 4
4 Sample answer and original text from advertisement:

> Sometimes a few pence can make someone feel like a million dollars.
> Although friends and loved ones may be a whole new world away, it's easy to show they're still part of your world with a letter.
> It can bring news of favourite places or photographs of loved faces. Not just once, but every time it's re-read.
> What else costs so little and yet means so much?
> Royal Mail International

UNIT 10: HUMOUR

The cartoonist (pages 72–3)
4 1 **a** mail   **b** oracles   **c** studio   **d** reluctantly   **e** grapple with something 2 **a** verb; shake with horror   **b** indefinite article + adjective + noun; a new way of dealing with something   **c** noun; untidy confusion of things   **d** verb (present participle); hiding and waiting   **e** noun; an agreement with a bank or building society to borrow money, and then make monthly interest payments
5 1 Present simple; describing routines. 2 Examples: … shave a small portion of my face   … in the same way that one acquires a mortgage and grey hairs.
6 1 A and E   2 He is correcting himself, finding a better word to express what he wants to say.
8 1 A man is sitting in a restaurant, looking at a menu, and talking to the waiter. The writing (caption) says: 'Can I have the spaghetti without the siege?'   2 Because he changed a phrase that everyone knows to refer to a situation that everyone has heard about; it is familiar and at the same time surprising.   3 In order not to shock or offend people by joking about something terrible while it was happening.

Jokes (pages 74–5)
3 1 One is from Texas, USA; the other is English.   2 The Texan's farm is much larger than the Englishman's.   3 He says that it takes a day to drive around it.
4 1 His voice rises slightly on 'trees' and 'stream', showing that he has not finished the point he is making; at the end of the

KEY 183

sentence, his voice falls. 2 '*Man*,' he said, 'in *my* spread back in *Texas*, in *my* car it takes me a *whole day* just to drive *around* it.' 'Man' is stressed because he is expressing great surprise. The other words are stressed because he wants to contrast the size of his farm with the Englishman's.

Telling stories (pages 76–7)
2 2 background information events the amusing part

VOCABULARY

WORD GROUPS

Writing (pages 80–1)
1 A (F) science fiction B (F) a ghost story C (F) a romantic novel D (NF) an educational children's book E (F) a historical novel F (NF) a textbook; a book on economics G (F) a collection of short stories H (F) a play I (F) a collection of detective stories
2 1 dull boring 2 funny humorous (ridiculous) 3 exciting thrilling 4 extraordinary interesting 5 moving sad 6 terrifying frightening 7 dramatic (exciting) (thrilling)
3 characters murder romance plot/ (narrative) climax dialogue narrative/ (description)
4 1 front cover 2 biographical details 3 blurb 4 bibliography 5 index 6 contents page

Pronunciation
1 The letters in bold are not normally pronounced in these words.
2 interesting frightening different

Private lives (pages 82–3)
1 1 patient 2 open/honest 3 sincere/ honest/open
2 warm affectionate loving friendly
3 strong generous (kind) sincere/honest tidy
4 film – cinema brush – painting gymnastics – sports passport – travel orchestra – music wings – flying shoes – walking actor – theatre building – architecture program – computers plate – pottery bricks – building poem – literature model – fashion car – driving
6 1 young people and adults 2 *Under 18*: children teenagers babies toddlers young people *Finished working*: pensioners retired people
7 (*Youngest*) babies toddlers teenagers middle-aged people pensioners (*Oldest*)
8 1 Mrs 2 Dad Mum 3 Mum 4 Sir Madam 5 Ms Madam

Pronunciation
1 The /n/ sound changes to /m/.
2 The /n/ sound changes to /ŋ/.

Fear (pages 84–5)
2 (*Weakest*) uneasy worried anxious/ nervous frightened terrified petrified hysterical (*Strongest*)
3 *Sample answers*: 1 Flying makes me nervous. 2 I am terrified of rats. 3 Most people become nervous when they speak in public. 4 I feel uneasy when I see a spider. 5 Some people are petrified just thinking about ghosts.
6 1 *Physical closeness*: hug cuddle *Words*: advise recommend *Either*: calm reassure comfort support **2a** reassuring **b** showing understanding **c** advising

Pronunciation
1**a** The bags are in the car. **b** She can come tomorrow. **c** I've got some dollars. **d** He was so naughty!
2 **a** The man has been sent to prison.
b There are some large birds in the garden.
c Children have an advantage if they come from happy family backgrounds.

Sport (pages 86–7)
1 1 tennis hockey rugby football squash 2 *Teams*: hockey rugby ice hockey football *Individuals*: tennis athletics gymnastics badminton swimming squash
3 1 field 2 pitch/court 3 rink 4 track
4 1 court 2 rink 3 pools 4 stadium 5 pitches tracks 6 field
5 1 Squash is an individual sport that is played on a court. 2 Tennis is an individual sport that is played on a court. 3 Ice hockey is a team sport that is played on a rink. 4 Rugby is a team sport that is played on a rugby pitch.
6 *Ice-hockey player*: A helmet B stick C puck *Badminton player*: A shuttlecock B net C shirt D shorts E racquet F socks G shoes *Cricketer*: A cap B bat C ball D trousers E boots F pads
7 1 throwing 2 running 3 serving 4 jumping 5 kicking 6 saving 7 tackling 8 passing 9 hitting 10 catching

Pronunciation
1 enough – stuff through – two cough – off though – low
2 tough sounds like stuff although sounds like low rough sounds like stuff
3 *Sample answers*: dough (low) trough (off)

Discipline (pages 88–9)
1 1 self– 2 lack of 3 well– 4 badly–
2 *Sample answers*: *How can you punish children?* beat them stop their pocket money stop them going out with friends *How can you reward children?* let them stay up late give them extra responsibility allow them to stay out late
3 1 C 2 E 3 B 4 A 5 D
4 1 defendant 2 jury 3 witness 4 sentenced 5 charged 6 verdict 7 prosecuted
5 *Sample answers*: **prison sentence** – being sent to jail **community service** – working to help the community (e.g. with old people, mentally handicapped people) **probation** – having to report to a 'probation officer' regularly, who tries to help a criminal to stay out of trouble **the death penalty** – being put to death for a crime **warning** – being told not to offend again or there will be trouble **theft** – stealing from someone **vandalism** – destroying property for no reason **assault** – hurting someone physically **murder** – killing someone with intention **smuggling** – bringing goods into a country without showing them to customs officials **arson** – burning a building **fraud** – cheating someone and obtaining money from them by lies and deceit **burglary** – breaking into a building and stealing from it

Pronunciation
1 In the first sentence, **convict** is a verb. In the second, **convict** is a noun.
2 The general rule about word stress on these words is that when the word is a verb, the stress falls on the *last* syllable; when it is a noun, the stress falls on the *first* syllable.

People on the move (pages 90–1)
1 1 hotel guest house youth hostel (official) campsite rented flat 2 night shelter; tent (if you had one, but not at an official campsite) friend's house the open air
2 1 frightened scared 2 lonely isolated alone 3 homesick depressed down miserable
3 *Sample answers*: How about trying to get a job? Have you thought about ringing your family? Wouldn't it be a good idea to move into a flat with other people?
4 1 by train on a train on foot by car in a car by boat on a boat by plane in/ on a plane 2 I'm going by rail. I'm going to walk. I'm going by road. I'm going by sea. I'm going by air.
5 *General words*: delays hold-ups *Specific reasons*: crowds traffic jams breakdowns accidents cancellations
6 *Sample answers*: Travelling by train is frustrating because there are so many cancellations. In these icy conditions there are a lot of accidents on the roads, so I think I'll leave the car at home today. If you're going by plane, expect delays while the snow is cleared from the runways.
7 *Sample answers*: People move as a result of divorce. People move because they want to be near better schools. People move as a result of unpleasant neighbours. People move because they want to live in a better climate. *Other reasons for moving*: Because you are going to have another child. As a result of an argument with your flat-mate.

Pronunciation
1 *Rule*: The first part of each of these compounds carries the main stress.
3 black board: any board which is black blackboard: a black board on the wall that a teacher writes on under ground: below ground level Underground: a railway system that runs below ground level The compound is the second expression in each pair.

Health (pages 92–3)
1 1 prescribe 2 examine treat cure 3 treat cure diagnose
2 1 spots: small, raised, round marks on your skin swelling: a place on your body which is larger than its usual size deep cut: an opening in your skin, from which a lot of blood is flowing infection: you can sometimes see this; for example, if a cut has become infected, the skin around it is red and a yellow liquid may be coming out of the cut 2 'Pain' and 'ache' refer only to what you feel. 'Pain' is stronger.
3 1 have 2 taking 3 have 4 Apply 5 take
5 A She is stretching her arms. B He is turning his head. C She is raising her right leg. D She is lowering her right leg. E He is bending his left arm. F He is straightening his left arm.
6 *Similar*: turn/rotate *Opposite*: raise/ lower tense/relax bend/straighten
7 1 sleepy exhausted drowsy 2 irritable short-tempered 3 unsociable 4 wide awake refreshed alert (happy)

Business (pages 94–5)
1 1 makes cars (goods) 2 sells petrol (goods) 3 provides courses (services) 4 produces books (goods) 5 provides cleaning (services) 6 sells food, etc. (goods) 7 repairs computers (services) 8 provides financial protection (services)
2 *Sample answers*: 1 prepare budgets collect debts prepare accounts deal with petty cash 2 interview and select staff arrange staff holidays train staff draw up staff contracts 3 contact customers prepare brochures advertise goods and services attend exhibitions 4 the Personnel Department 5 the Finance Department 6 the Marketing Department
3 *Sample answer*: They can all be positive – and often are. However, in an informal company being *formal* could be negative; we can also imagine someone saying, 'She's too tolerant' or 'He's too sensitive', and these comments are meant in a negative sense.
4 unintelligent unimaginative intolerant insensitive impatient unpunctual disloyal impractical informal
5 1 make a call hear the engaged signal pick up the receiver put down the receiver listen for the ringing tone dial ring hold the line 2 take a call pick up the receiver put down the receiver hold the line 3 take a call pick up the receiver put down the receiver connect someone put someone through dial
6 pick up the receiver dial listen for the ringing tone hear the engaged signal put down the receiver

Pronunciation
1 unintelligent unimaginative intolerant unpunctual disloyal unenthusiastic insensitive impatient impractical informal
The general rule is that prefixes *un- in- im- dis-* do not carry the main stress. However, note the exception when the prefix is being contrasted.

Power (pages 96–7)
1 1 explain (e.g. By . . ., I mean . . .) 2 add (e.g. Secondly, . . .) 3 inform (e.g. Let me tell you about . . .) 4 promise (e.g. I swear I'll . . .) 5 correct (e.g. You don't mean . . .; you mean . . .) 6 advise (e.g. If I were you, I'd . . .) 7 disagree (e.g. I can't agree with you about that.) 8 request (e.g. I wonder if you could . . . for me.) 9 insist (e.g. She really did say that.)
2 1 to have an argument 2 to make a promise 3 to give an explanation 4 to make a request 5 to give information
3 *Sample answers*: argue: to express strong and often angry disagreement interrupt: to say something while someone else is in the middle of speaking dominate: to have power over another person
4 *Sample answers*: A He is insisting that he is right, or that something should be done. B They are arguing about something. C She is explaining what the graph shows.
5 *Sample answers*: The man: balding cheerful overweight friendly *The woman*: slim attractive smart confident decisive

Pronunciation
2 explanation information domination addition interruption correction insistence disagreement **a** In each case, the main stress falls on the last-but-one (penultimate) syllable. **b** In the first group, the main stress shifts between the nouns and the verbs. In the second group, the stress is on the same syllable in the nouns and in the verbs.

Humour (pages 98–9)
1 1 national stereotypes 2 sex 3 religion
3 1 pun 2 punch line 3 suspense
4 1 laugh chuckle giggle clap snigger titter 2 giggle titter 3 smirk snigger 4 clap
5 1 hilarious amusing 2 tragic shocking 3 boring 4 shocking terrifying 5 exciting
6 1 amused 2 excited 3 shocked 4 interested 5 sad
7 1B clowning playing the fool 2A mimicking impersonating taking someone off 3E making fun of someone teasing 4C playing a practical joke on someone 5D pulling someone's leg teasing

Pronunciation
1 'id' (/ɪd/) endings – excited waited landed tasted 'd' endings – amused begged amazed 't' endings – shocked embarrassed promised
2 Rule: If the final consonant before the 'ed' ending is a 't' or a 'd', the sound is 'id'; if it is a 'voiced' consonant sound (e.g. spelt with the letter 'b' or 'g'), the sound is 'd'; if it is an 'unvoiced' consonant sound (e.g. spelt with the letter 'k' or 'p'), the sound is 't'.

KEYWORDS

see look at watch hear listen to (page 100)
1 1 C 2 A 3 E 4 B 5 D
2 1 (good sentence) 2 'listened to' should be 'heard' 3 'heard' should be 'listened to' 4 (good sentence) 5 'saw' should be 'watched'
4 heard listened to saw watched looked at

become (an architect) go (deaf) get (cold) turn (brown) (page 101)
1 1 go/turn going/turning 2 gets getting 3 became becoming 4 going going
2 1 going 2 getting 3 turned 4 getting 5 became 6 go 7 turned 8 became 9 getting

have take give (page 102)
1 1 take 2 have 3 give 4 give 5 take

184 KEY

6 have (take)
2 1 took 2 give 3 gave 4 have 5 had
6 take 7 gave 8 had 9 took
3 1 gave a short interview 2 have a rest
3 give 10 lectures 4 took power
5 have faith 6 took a decision

make let force allow (page 103)
1 1 A and D 2 B and C
2 1 The company allowed her to have . . .
2 The nurses forced me to take . . .
3 made allowed let made forced let
4 *Sample answers*: 1 The manager lets me take time off if my son is ill. 2 The company forces us to have a medical examination every year. 3 We are allowed to take our holidays when we want them. 4 My boss makes me deal with customer complaints.

rob steal burgle swindle thief pickpocket burglar crook theft burglary fraud (page 104)
1 1 burglar burgled burglary 2 crook swindled fraud 3 pickpocket steals theft 4 thief steals theft
2 1 burglar 2 crooks frauds swindling
3 Burglaries burgled 4 pickpocket
3 1 robbed thieves stole 2 stolen
3 robbed

expect look forward to hope (for) wait (for) (page 105)
1 1 looking forward to hoping for
2 expecting looking forward to waiting for 3 looking forward to 4 waiting for
2 1 waiting for 2 looking forward to
3 is expecting/expects 4 hopes/'s hoping
3 1 hope/expect 2 are looking forward to
3 are waiting/expect/are expecting/hope/are hoping 4 expect/hope 5 is waiting for
4 've been looking forward to expect/hope 'm waiting for

on off in out (page 106)
1 *Starting* turn on *Stopping* cut off called off broke off *Continuing* carried on stay on *Encouraging* Come on! Go on!
2 1 left/taken/kept 2 fits 3 KEEP 4 join
5 took 6 get

up down away back (page 107)
1 1 away 2 down 3 up 4 back
2 1 put down 2 get away 3 sit back
4 fill up 5 give back 6 throw away
7 stay up 8 settle down 9 go back
10 look up
3 4 fill up the petrol tank 5 give back this pen 10 look up the word (Number 6 cannot be rewritten, as object is pronoun.)

travel flight drive tour journey voyage expedition (page 108)
1 *Words that can be nouns and verbs*: travel drive tour (journey) *Nouns only*: flight voyage expedition *Never used as a singular noun*: travel *Key words that tell you how the movement takes place*: flight – by air/plane drive – by road/car or bus voyage – by sea/boat
2 1 voyage/journey 2 travelling 3 drive
4 tour 5 flight/journey 6 expedition
7 journey
3 *Sample answers*: a drive a voyage a flight a tour an expedition a trip a cruise a trek a safari a hike a ride

road street track path way route (page 109)
1 1 path 2 road 3 street 4 track
5 route (way) 6 way (route)
2 1 way 2 track 3 route 4 street
5 road 6 path 7 Road 8 Street
3 1 way (road) 2 path/road 3 track
4 way 5 streets 6 track 7 road 8 way

pay income salary wages fee (page 110)
1 1 wages 2 salary 3 fee(s) 4 income
5 pay
2 1 fee 2 salary 3 income 4 Wages
5 pay 6 salary 7 fees 8 income
9 wages 10 pay

3 *Sample answers*: He has an income of £75,000 p.a. His fee per filling is £7.50. His wages are £6 per hour.

work job career vocation profession (page 111)
1 1 work 2 a job
2 1 job 2 work 3 Work 4 job
3 1 vocation 2 career 3 profession
4 1 career 2 vocation 3 profession
4 career 5 vocation 6 career

customer client patient guest tenant (page 112)
1 1 customer 2 guest 3 someone who stays at your house at your invitation a person who pays to stay at a guesthouse or hotel 4 client (also patient with a private doctor) 5 tenant 6a customer b tenant c client patient (private doctor) guest (in a hotel) 7 patient
2 *customer* – shops – buys goods – the shopkeeper *client* – offices – receives advice or some other service – lawyer, accountant *patient* – surgery, clinic, hospital – receives medical attention – the doctor (if private) *guest* – home, hotel – stays with friends or at a hotel – nobody, or owner of guesthouse *tenant* – house, flat – renting somewhere to live – landlord or landlady
3 1 guests 2 tenant 3 clients
4 customer 5 patients

talk speech lecture meeting conference (page 113)
1 1 conference 2 meeting 3 lecture
4 speech 5 talk
2 1 conference 2 meeting 3 lectures
4 talk 5 lectures/talks 6 speech 7 talk
8 conference 9 speech 10 meeting

cloth clothes material garment dress clothing (page 114)
1 1 dress (to put your clothes on, or to put clothes on someone else) 2 clothes clothing garments (clothes) 3 cloth material 4 garment dress 5 *Sample answers*: metre piece length strip roll
2 cloth clothes dress garment
3 A cloth material B clothes clothing garments C a dress a garment an item of clothing
4 cloth/material garments/clothes/clothing garment/clothing/clothes clothing dresses clothes

next previous last the last latest (page 115)
1 1 Next – because the sentence refers to the future 2 latest – because 'last' cannot be used with the present perfect to mean 'most recent' 3 previous – because it does not refer to the final effort, but the one before that
4 Last – because 'the last' refers to the last thing in a series, which may or may not be past.
2 1 17 April 2 20 April 3 5 April
4 24 April 5 3 April 6 1 April
3 last next previous Last latest
4 D C F A G E B

very fairly quite really extremely terribly awfully pretty reasonably absolutely totally completely (pages 116–7)
1 *Stronger*: really extremely terribly awfully *Weaker*: quite pretty reasonably
2 *Sample answers*: I get very tired towards the end of the week. The weather during the first week of the holidays was quite pleasant. She's fairly old now – about 72 I think. I didn't enjoy the film – it was terribly serious, didn't you think? He's awfully thin. I wonder if he's sick? The meeting's really important. You should try and be there. We had a pretty boring weekend. It is extremely dangerous for children to play near railway lines. My job is reasonably interesting.
3 1 yes 2 no 3 yes sometimes (*see Word Study box*) 4 no 5 yes
4 1 D 2 A 3 E 4 C 5 B

5 *Sample answers*: 1 No. It's pretty awful, isn't it? 2 Well, she's quite nice. 3 Quite good? I thought it was absolutely wonderful! 4 Yes, it's extremely loud, isn't it?

The Dictionary – extending its use (pages 118–19)
1 1 sensitive 3 sensitivity 3 sensible
4 sensitive 4 5 sensitive 1
3 1 over 2 for 3 out 4 behind
5 1 [+ obj + adj/v-ed] 2 [+ that]
3 [obj + to-v] 4 [+ v-ing] 5 [+ to-v]
6 A [+ to-v] B [+ obj + to-v]
C [+ obj + adj/v-ed] D [+ v-ing] E [+ to-v]
F [+ obj + to-v] G [+ that]
7 1 fault blame 2 stings bitten
3 place room
8 1 information 2 brought on 3 electrical
4 certain 5 living

GRAMMAR

NOUNS

Articles 1 (page 123)
1 1 — — 2 The 3 the
2 1 the protection insurance 2 electricity industry 3 The safety the rules 4 health diet 5 the strength the intelligence 6 the future confidence

Articles 2 (page 124)
1 1 any 2 any 3 a 4 some 5 any 6 some
2 1 any tomatoes 2 a radio
3 a newspaper 4 any information
5 some time 6 any sugar 7 any dentists
3 *Sample answers*: 1 I've never seen a princess. 2 Have they got any spare time?
3 Has she bought a house yet? 4 There aren't any hospitals nearby. 5 There's some butter in the dish. 6 Have you any brothers or sisters?

Quantities 1 (page 125)
1 1 Not many 2 a little 3 a few 4 not much
2 1 C many 2 A much 3 B a little
4 B a little 5 A much 6 C a few

Quantities 2 (pages 126–7)
1 1 — 2 (of) the 3 (of) the/—
4 of them 5 — 6 of the 7 — 8 of the
2 A 1 no 2 All 3 Most 4 some
B Most of the some of the All (of) the none of the
C Both [(of) the] neither of the
3 *Sample answers*: A1 No trees grow in the Antarctic. 2 Some people like ice cream and some don't. 3 Most actors like to show off.
4 All cases of typhoid fever must be reported at once.
B1 None of the boys in my family like studying. 2 Most of my parents can speak English. 3 Some of the secretaries in my office are bilingual. 4 Most of the employees in my company work hard. 5 All the patients in my ward are well looked after. 6 Both my parents can speak (Italian).

Quantities 3 (page 128)
1 1 money dollars 2 luggage suitcases
3 television programmes 4 taxi traffic
5 progress step forward

Quantities 4 (page 129)
1 1 C 2 A 3 B
2 *Pairs*: trousers pyjamas gloves glasses jeans shoes socks pants
Items: shirts hats coats umbrellas ties blouses skirts belts
3 1 jar 2 tube 3 bunch packet box

Comparative adjectives (page 130)
1 *easier/easiest*
clever easy early gentle
shallow funny pretty simple
narrow silly (un)tidy
more/most modern
careful foolish helpful useful
frequent modern famous

2 1 earlier 2 most helpful 3 funnier
4 untidiest 5 narrower 6 gentlest 7 more frequent 8 happiest 9 more careful
10 cleverest

Joining nouns: 's of ø (page 131)
1 1 C 2 B1 3 D 4 A 5 B2
2 1 typewriter 2 girl's 3 picture
4 Japan's 5 week's 6 tennis 7 men's
8 company's In sentences 4 and 8 's can be replaced with *of*.
3 1 . . . the natural resources of the Antarctic
3 The attitude of the United States . . . Nos 2 and 4 cannot be changed because they refer to time.

Modifying the noun (page 132)
1 1 who/that 2 that/which 3 whose
4 that/which/— 5 who/that/—
2 1 The young man who/that gets the job will be very pleased. 2 This is the man whose best friend betrayed him. 3 There are many problems that/which I can't go into today.
4 The team that/which won the match was from Scotland. 5 The woman (who/that) they spoke to didn't know what she was talking about.
4 1 in 2 of 3 with 4 with 5 in 6 of
7 of 8 in 9 with

VERBS

Tenses 1 (page 136)
1 (*outside you*) walk dance jump work sell write eat run
(*inside you*) believe want like understand hear see mean hate prefer
2 1 are walking 2 smells 3 hate
4 are watching 5 rains
6 don't understand 7 works 8 want
9 Do like 10 'm writing
3 1A: 5 7 2A: 1 4 10 1B: 2 3 6 8 9

Tenses 2 (page 137)
1 1 can can't 2 — 3 — 4 couldn't
5 can't
2 1 sounds 2 Can (you) hear 3 can feel feels 4 can taste 5 smells 6 can see looks 7 tastes

Tenses 3 (pages 138–9)
1 1 took 2 was walking/walked 3 finished
2 1 were thinking decided 2 ran bit
3 were sitting walked 4 arrived
5 were entering shook
3 bend bent let let
dig dug light lit
feed fed lie lay
feel felt ring rang
hang hung rise rose
bite bit set set
blow blew spread spread
choose chose strike struck
hide hid swing swung
keep kept shake shook
lead led sink sank
lend lent tear tore

4 1 rose set 2 fed lit 3 lent kept
4 blew shook 5 let led 6 felt swung
7 rang 8 struck 9 dug 10 hung
5 1 — 2 used to play 3 —
4 used to arrive No. 2 would mean the same; no. 4 would have a different meaning.
6 1 used to play 2 crashed injured
3 used to be 4 landed 5 used to wear

KEY 185

Tenses 4 (page 140)
1 1 have seen 2 saw 3 had driven 4 have travelled
2 1 Mary has met the Queen on several occasions in the last two years. Mary met the Queen last week. 2 What happened to you last night? What has happened since I went away? 3 John has fallen down a hole and I can't get him out. John fell down a hole and broke his leg. 4 Prices had risen before 1988, but more slowly. Prices have risen every year for five years. 5 They bought their house last year. They have bought a new house; it's lovely. 6 Have you seen Harrison Ford's latest film? You should go! Did you see the news on TV last night? It was dramatic!

Tenses 5 (page 141)
1 1 will/may destroy 2 are (you) doing/are (you) going to do 3 will be 4 is going to crash

Modals 1 (pages 142–3)
1 1 will 2 won't 3 may well 4 may
2 1 will 2 won't 3 may/could/might (well) 4 will 5 should 6 may/could/might (well) 7 may/could/might (well) 8 should 9 may/could/might (well) 10 may/could/might (well) 11 will 12 should

Modals 2 (pages 144–5)
could managed to
1 1 couldn't could 2 could managed to 3 could 4 managed to
2 1 could managed to 2 managed to 3 couldn't managed to 4 couldn't managed to 5 managed to

can be able to
1 1 have (not yet) been able to 2 will be able to 3 is (usually) able to (has usually been able to)
2 1 has not been able to 2 can 3 are able to (will be able to) 4 will be able to 5 can 6 would be able to 7 will be able to (can)

Modals 3 (page 146)
1 A: can't be B: must be A: can't have A: must have
2 1 A: can (it) be B: must be A: can't be 2 can't be must be 3 R: must have C: can't have R: can (it) be
3 *Sample answers*: (Student points) That can't be a washing machine, it's too small. It must be a toaster.

The passive (page 147)
1 1 Next, you cut up the potatoes and carrots and boil them. 2 They built the bridge in 1873. 3 You can obtain these books from the public library. 4 They asked her to speak more quietly.
2 1 The original picture was destroyed years ago. 2 The events of that night have never been explained. 3 Cleaning fluid and soft drinks shouldn't be stored together. 4 Film for this camera can be bought anywhere. 5 The stolen goods were taken across the frontier. 6 Passes will be shown when entering the building. 7 She had been told to make an application.

Multi-part verbs (pages 148–9)
1 1 get away 2 ran into 3 lie down 4 account for
Type 1: get away lie down *Type 2*: run into account for
2 1 fell down 2 ask for 3 come from 4 stood up 5 laugh at 6 died down 7 came across 8 get up
Type 1: fall down stand up die down get up *Type 2*: ask for come from laugh at come across
3 1 look up 2 throw away 3 sort out 4 gave away Yes; nos 2 and 4
4 1 cross out 2 Turn on 3 fill up 4 Put away 5 try on 6 hand back 7 take off 8 let off You can change the order in nos 2, 3, 4, 5 and 7.

Reporting statements (page 150)
1 1 ... he hasn't seen his sister this week. 2 ... says he'll repair it today if he has time. 3 ... tell me they didn't enjoy the film.
2 1 ... he loved his job. 2 ... she was having a good time. 3 ... she spoke/had spoken to the manager herself.
3 1 He said they saw/had seen our last month's figures. 2 He said they were worried. 3 He said he hadn't been to see us for over a year. 4 He said he would be arriving at 8.30 a.m. 5 He said he couldn't/wouldn't be able to stay for more than an hour.

Reporting questions (page 151)
1 1 ... what he wants. ... what he wanted. 2 ... if she can be of any help. ... if she could be of any help.
2 1 She's asking where Jane went last night. She asked where Jane went/had gone last night. 2 She's asking if you have finished your supper. She asked if you had finished your supper. 3 She's asking if you can see all right. She asked if you could see all right. 4 She is asking how the twins are. She asked how the twins were.

Reporting instructions and requests (page 151)
1 1 Liz asked us to help her. 2 Liz told them to stop that noise. 3 She asked me to hold her bag. 4 He told Penny not to do that.

Modifying the verb 1 (page 152)
1 1 fluently 2 happily 3 violently 4 right
2 1 ... doesn't fit tightly ... 2 ... speak frankly to her ... / ... speak to her frankly ... 3 Tell him exactly what ... 4 Spread the butter thinly ... 5 She danced gracefully ... / She danced across the floor gracefully ... 6 ... the stars shone brightly. 7 The old man stood patiently ... / ... The old man stood in the queue patiently ... 8 You must organise your work effectively ... 9 Toasters are designed to switch off automatically ... 10 He put the Chinese vase down gently ... 11 The Prime Minister must state publicly ... 12 ... so he packed hastily and left.

Modifying the verb 2 (page 153)
1 1 B better 2 D more quickly 3 C worse 4 A more effectively
2 1 earlier than 2 most comfortably 3 more heavily 4 more cheaply 5 higher than
3 *Sample answer*: My father's car runs more smoothly than mine.

Verbs followed by: *to* + infinitive / noun *to* + infinitive / clause (that) (pages 154–5)
1 1 ADH 2 CF 3 CF 4 BEG
2 1 ... us to join him. 2 ... to take the last plane. 3 ... them to play in the team. 4 ... he would pass. 5 ... to leave on Friday. / she'll leave on Friday.
3 1 told decided 2 invited hoped 3 promise ask 4 is planning promised 5 think planning told

PREPOSITIONS

Prepositions of place 1 (page 159)
away from towards
1 1 towards away from 2 away from towards

over under
1 1 under 2 over 3 over 4 under Nos 1 and 3 are like A.

Prepositions of place 2 (page 160)
not far (from) (quite) a long way (from) beside behind beyond
1 1 not far from behind 2 a long way from beyond 3 (quite) a long way from beside (behind/beyond)

along past (*also* turn left into on the left until you get to) (page 161)
1 1 along turn right into past on the left
2 1 turn right into along until you get to turn left along on the right 2 turn left into along until you get to turn right to the end turn left

Other prepositions (page 162)
1 1 for 2 by 3 for 4 by
2 1 towards 2 under 3 over 4 for 5 away from 6 by by 7 over 8 for 9 under 10 towards away from
3 not far from along past Across beside Behind beyond a long way from

Fixed expressions (pages 163–5)
1 1 at (Time) 2 by (Communications) 3 At (Time) 4 by (Communications) 5 by (Communications) 6 by (Communications) 7 at (Time) 8 by (Communications) 9 at (Time) 10 at (Time)
2 At first by hand at that time by mail at the present time by telephone at short notice by messenger at last by fax at once
3 1 by (Surprises) 2 in (Problems) 3 on (Activities) 4 on (Activities) 5 by (Surprises) 6 on (Activities) 7 by (Surprises) 8 in (Problems) 9 in (Problems) 10 by (Surprises)
4 on holiday in danger (difficulty) by mistake in difficulty (danger) By good fortune on duty by chance on business by accident
5 1 in (Order) 2 in (Order) 3 out of (Chaos) 4 in (Order) 5 out of (Chaos) 6 in (Order) 7 out of (Chaos) 8 Out of (Chaos) 9 out of (Chaos) 10 in (Order)
6 in time out of control in control out of order in order in stock out of date in (their right) place out of stock in (the wrong) place

SENTENCES

Conditionals: (pages 168–9)
if I were ... if I had been ...
1 1 B 2 D 3 A 4 C
2 1 would find 2 cost 3 spoke (speak) 4 would be 5 had asked 6 would have taken 7 would have phoned 8 had made

unless even if no matter whether (or not)
1 even if it pours with rain unless you don't want to no matter what the weather is like whether it rains or not
2 1 Whether or not 2 unless 3 even if 4 No matter 5 Unless 6 No matter 7 even if

Linkers (page 170)
1 because her family love it. although her daughter doesn't like it. so that her children get used to eating Italian food. if there is any in the shops.
2 1 Although because 2 if so that
3 1 I didn't enjoy his company because he was often rude to me. I couldn't feel angry with him although he was often rude to me. 2 If it was raining we usually stayed indoors. Because it was raining we stayed indoors. 3 They arranged things so that they could meet in the afternoons. They were pleased if they could meet in the afternoons. 4 She arranges every minute of his day so that he doesn't have time to go out. He loves the cinema although he doesn't have time to go out.

Questions and answers 1 (page 171)
1 1 is 2 don't 3 did 4 doesn't
2 1 won't you 2 can't I 3 doesn't he 4 is it 5 did they 6 have you 7 haven't you 8 will we 9 didn't he 10 shouldn't we 11 do we 12 aren't we

Questions and answers 2 (page 172)
1 1 D 2 C 3 B 4 A
2 1 So can John 2 Neither did I 3 Neither will Jill 4 So do I 5 Neither have I 6 So did I 7 So have I

Infinitives and gerunds (page 173)
1 1 It surprised 2 It is sure 3 It is expensive 4 It takes
2 1 Behaving 2 Training 3 Beginning 4 Dancing
3 1 It's obvious 2 It's a pity 3 It's easy 4 It's lucky 5 It's healthy *Two sentences can be changed*: 3 Remembering this is easy ... 5 Going for a walk every day is healthy.

PARAGRAPHS

Linking ideas with phrases (pages 176–7)
1 1 Similarly 2 Alternatively
2 1 However/Nevertheless (Despite this) 2 On the contrary (instead)
3 1 Otherwise/Apart from this 2 For this reason/Consequently
4 1 Previously/Before that 2 Afterwards/Later
5 1 Later (Afterwards) 2 On the contrary (Instead) 3 Similarly/In the same way 4 Alternatively 5 However/Nevertheless 6 For this reason/Consequently 7 Previously/Before that 8 Otherwise/Apart from this

Linking ideas by reference (pages 178–9)
1 1 She I→Rose 2 It→bedroom
2 1 That statement→'I'll think about it.' 2 this list→a list of what you want to buy
3 1 the former→a full chapter 2 there→my study
4 1 We→my husband and I his→the pianist 2 That→a peculiar half-Chinese woman 3 then→the seventeenth century 4 It→Smile 5 All that→(the fact that) he had played football and tennis at school, and he had been a prefect 6 Hers→Jane/sweater 7 these→Great pine trees 8 The latter→Neil MacDonald 9 that→(the fact that) he decided to walk home
5 1 ... The trouble was, John didn't like Brian./Brian didn't like John. (*'The former' and 'the latter' sound too formal here.*) 2 ... I found him in the cafeteria/library. 3 *Make* 'My father was still alive then' *the second sentence, or* Years later I went back to visit the place while my father was still alive. 4 ... The parents were always rushing about the place and they didn't pay enough attention to what the children needed, so of course the children didn't like it and they got upset. *or* ... The children were always rushing about the place and the parents didn't pay enough attention to what they needed, so of course the children/the parents got upset.

Linking ideas with general words (pages 180–1)
1 1 The poor old lady 2 The whole thing 3 the boy
2 1 this opinion 2 their conclusion 3 This belief
3 1 stuff (this crockery) 2 place (London) 3 man (the director) 4 topic (the number of hours they had to attend class each week) 5 possibility (a slight chance that the murderer would be identified) 6 experience (Steve spent a month driving a taxi round London) 7 state of affairs (Inflation was rising, unemployment was widespread, and the army was restless) 8 incident (The princess slipped and fell as she walked up the steps) 9 achievement (The government has finally managed to eliminate inflation) 10 solution (to put large numbers of people out of work) 11 exploit (The first man over Niagara Falls in a barrel) 12 predicament (The Minister was found by reporters in a night club with a young woman who was not his wife) 13 tragedy (Thirty-five people were killed in a rail crash)

186 KEY

ized, and that's almost something very

TAPESCRIPTS

CASSETTE 1

SKILLS

UNIT 1 WRITING

Books and writers

EXERCISES 4 and 5 (page 19)

You are going to hear part of an interview with the author, Anne Melville, in which she talks about *the process* of writing a book.

I = Interviewer   AM = Anne Melville

I: How do you go about the writing process, then? Where do you start with a book?
AM: Very often the best ideas start with something quite simple like a paragraph in a newspaper. You could read, for example, about a man who runs away and his wife says she doesn't know where he is, and you can start asking yourself questions: 'Where's he gone? Why has he gone? Does she really not know? What has led up to this? Erm, what will happen later on?' And then you try and get yourself under the skin of complete strangers, and suddenly you find you've got a plot and all the characters ready made.
I: And after that first stage, which gave you the ideas, the plot, the characters – what comes next?
AM: Oh, a little hard slog. Reading up about a possible background, sketching out a possible plot. Trying to get quite a lot worked out before the real writing starts.
I: And do you start on chapter one and then work through to the end?
AM: I do now. When I was younger, I rather tended to take the plums out first. I used to write some favourite chapter, but I found it was so dull having to work up to it that now I do try and write it absolutely consecutively.
I: How many times do you write it, do you think?
AM: Well, there's certainly a first draft and a second draft. And then I usually give it to my husband to read for me, and how many drafts after that depends on how critical he is.
I: And what stage do you write the title?
AM: Usually before I begin the book. The title is very important – I write a book *to* a title. Occasionally I have to alter the title afterwards, and that can mean a lot of rewriting.

Choosing something to read

EXERCISE 3 (page 20)

A group of people are talking about their reading habits – what they read, how much they read, and so on. At this point in the discussion, one person, Victoria, is telling her friends how she chooses a book to read.

V: But when I look in bookshops, I really – I think I look for surprise elements on, when I read the blurb on the back of the books. I look for something that's sort of, erm ... that surprises me, that I didn't know much about before, unless of course it's about, you know, economics or something ... I probably wouldn't, wouldn't go for one of those – but, erm, I like books that seem to promise interesting relationships between people, erm ... look as though they might have good dialogue and perhaps ... erm, unusual events ...
   When I'm browsing, I sometimes come across a book and I think oh, I've heard of that, I don't know how, maybe somebody mentioned it, maybe I've read a review ...
B: Yes, but I wouldn't actually read a review and then go out and buy the book ...
V: No, I rarely do that ...
B: ... That would be far too organised ...
V: No, I'd be much more likely to buy a book, er, if I'd read a book by that same author before or, er ... you know, if I read the blurb on the back.

EXERCISE 5 (page 21)

Listen to this part of the conversation again.

V: But when I look in bookshops, I really – I think I look for surprise elements on, when I read the blurb on the back of the books. I look for something that's sort of, erm ... that surprises me, that I didn't know much about before, unless of course it's about, you know, economics or something.

EXERCISE 6 (page 21)

Listen to a conversation in which the woman is recommending a book to her friend.

A: I don't know what to read. Can you recommend anything?
B: Erm ... Have you read a book by John Wyndham called *Web*? I've just finished it.
A: No, I haven't. What sort of book is it?
B: Well, you know John Wyndham writes science fiction stories ... This one's a novel set on a Pacific island.
A: What's it about then?
B: Well, the main characters are a man and a woman who join a group of people hoping to start the perfect society.
A: I see, and do they succeed?
B: No, and that's where the science fiction comes in. It turns out that the island they go to is full of huge spiders. They're determined to destroy everything there, including any people who come ... but I won't tell you what happens next or you won't want to read it. I liked it because it was just so ridiculous.
A: All right. I'll give it a try. Thanks.

UNIT 2 PRIVATE LIVES

Romance and friendship

EXERCISES 2 and 4 (page 24)

You are going to hear a woman talking about what attracts her to a partner, or boyfriend.

I = Interviewer   W = Woman

I: When you look for a partner, how important is physical appearance, for example?
W: Well, first of all, I don't *look* for a partner. I just *meet* partners – erm ... but physical appearance ... no ... it's really not very important. I mean, there are other qualities that are so much *more* important. Erm ... first of all, I would say, warmth – a person's warmth is very important. And, erm ... honesty, certainly, erm ... and then ... yes, intelligence ... erm ... it may sound strange but I think – I want to respect a partner and I want to respect them as having greater intelligence, in fact more of quite a lot of qualities than I have.
I: And what about more practical things – like money?
W: Well, it's easy to say that money is not important at all, but that wouldn't be entirely true ... erm, I mean I'm not 17 and ... when you're younger I think it's much easier for you both to struggle together erm, than when you are – let's face it – becoming middle-aged ... and you're used to a bit more comfort. It's difficult to return to poverty!
I: So your choice of a partner at this stage in your life wouldn't be based entirely on love?
W: Well, at this stage in my life I think that love is actually something you allow to happen rather than ... erm ... a flash of lightning from above ... and ... you allow it to happen with someone who is compatible – who leads a compatible lifestyle, and not somebody who's going to be completely unsuitable in important ways.

Parents and children

EXERCISE 3 (page 27)

A father and son are trying to resolve a situation in which each of them wants something different.

FATHER: Come on. It's 9 o'clock – time for bed.
SON: Oh Dad ... can't I stay up a bit longer?
F: No, you've got school tomorrow.
S: Yes, I know, but there's a good programme on TV.
F: What is it?
S: A comedy. All my friends at school are allowed to stay up and see it.
F: Oh. How long is it?
S: Only half an hour!
F: Oh, all right, you can watch the first half of it – but then straight to bed, OK?
S: Oh, can't I watch all of it? I'll go to bed early for the rest of the week. Promise!
F: Oh, all right, but go and put your pyjamas on before it starts.
S: Thanks Dad!

EXERCISE 4 (page 27)

Listen to these sounds. They are lines from the dialogue in exercise 3, but without the actual words. Are they said by the father or the son?

EXERCISE 6 (page 27)

A
MUM: Have a good time, Barry, but you must be home by 10.00. Do you hear me?
SON: Oh, Mum! Can't I stay out longer than that? The party will have hardly started.
MUM: No, you're too young to be walking home alone late at night. I want you home at 10.00.
SON: But Tim's got a car – he'll bring me home. I promise I'll be back by midnight!
MUM: Oh, all right – if Tim brings you. But not a minute after midnight!
SON: Thanks, Mum.

B
DAD: I thought we could all go to France this year.
DAUGHTER: Oh, Dad ... I'm 18 now. I'm too old for family holidays.
DAD: Nonsense. We'll have a lovely time. What would you do here, anyway? You can't stay alone in the house ...
DAUGHTER: I could go and stay with Susie. Her parents won't mind. Please let me.
DAD: We can't just ring Susie's parents and ask them to let you stay for two weeks!
DAUGHTER: Look, I'll ask them nicely. Leave it to me. Will that be all right then?
DAD: Oh, I suppose so, if I can't change your mind about coming with us.

UNIT 3 FEAR

Is fear good for you?

EXERCISES 2 and 3 (page 30)

You are going to hear some extracts from an interview with Angela Phillips, a professional actress.

AP = Angela Phillips   I = Interviewer

Part 1
First, the interviewer asked Angela whether she ever felt any fear before going on stage to perform a play.

AP: I do, yes, I have what they call stage fright, which is, em, something that I think most actors feel actually ... Stage fright is a, a fear of failing I think, something like that, and it's ... er ... it manifests itself in different ways with different people, and a lot of people feel sick, physically sick, people feel ... er ... they want to go to the loo all the time, they ... er ... sweat, their mouths go dry. It's a very frightening feeling, actually.
I: And does it go away when you're actually on stage?
AP: Yes. It does. It's a sort of ... anxiety that ... It's an anxiety that becomes an energy, and the energy concentrates your mind, so when you go on stage ... er ... as soon as you step on stage, actually, the feeling has gone, and then when you come off stage ... er ... you feel a ... just sense of relief that you've got through the first scene or whatever, but ... and it ... but it doesn't actually really leave you until the end of the performance, and then you feel an enormous sense of relief and relaxation ...

EXERCISE 4 (page 31)

Part 2
In the first part of the interview, Angela talked about what it feels like to have stage fright. In this next part, the interviewer asked her how actors deal with these fears before the start of a play.

AP: Again, people deal with stage fright in a lot of different ways. They ... a lot of people go through their lines – endlessly, before going on stage. Other people feel it necessary to talk all the time to other people in the dressing room. Some people have their script by the side of them and just endlessly look through their lines all the time. I personally find it ... I prefer to be quiet. I like to actually ... I don't want to speak to anybody when I'm ... we have what is known as the *half* – which is half an hour before the performance ... you have to be in the theatre half an hour before the performance – and during that, what we know as the half, I actually prefer not to speak to people ... I prefer to try and concentrate my mind on what I'm about to do ... em ... so that's ... and also a lot of people get changed and made up and all that a long time before – some people even before the half. I don't like doing that. I find that for me, it helps to ... relax me if I only get changed and made up immediately before I have to go on stage so there's no time before going on stage, and I get dressed, I go out into the wings and I go on stage. For me, that's how I cope with it.
I: So would it be fair to say that in some ways the fear that you feel before you go on stage is a positive thing?
AP: Yes, I think it definitely is a positive thing. I mean, I think if one doesn't have any fear of what one's going to do then it is ... em ...

187

the mind doesn't concentrate properly ... it's, you know, the energy is kind of dissipated and not being used in the right way, whereas if you are frightened, then your energy is used in the right way in that you can ... gather it together and actually concentrate it on the things you want to do whereas if you haven't got any fright then you're just too relaxed and just too kind of laid back and the performance is not going to be as good – it's definitely not going to be as good, I don't think.

EXERCISE 7 (page 31)

1 His *brother*, not his *sister*.
2 Don't turn *left*; turn *right*.
3 *Jane's* father, not *Sara's* father.
4 I wanted *three*, not *four*.
5 It arrives at *11*.15, not *10*.15.
6 I need his *new* address, not his *old one*.
7 It's the *director* I want to speak to, not his *assistant*.

Overcoming fears

EXERCISE 3 (page 32)

A
A: Hey, Joe. Is there something wrong?
J: Yes, I've got to give a speech at next week's conference and I'm absolutely terrified. I mean, I haven't done anything like this before. I'm sure it'll be a disaster.
A: Of course it won't. Everything'll be fine. Have you finished writing the speech?
J: Yes, but I'll miss a page or forget what I'm saying ...
A: Look, calm down. Everybody gets nervous about something like this. I know you'll be fine on the day.

B
A: Hello. Are you all right?
B: I don't know what to do. My uncle was supposed to meet me, but he hasn't come and it's been two hours now. I don't know what to do ...
A: Don't you know his address?
B: No.
A: Well, why don't you look in the phone book? I'll help you, and you can give him a ring. Don't worry; I'm sure everything will be OK.

UNIT 4 SPORT

Women and sport

EXERCISE 2 (page 36)

You are going to hear an interview with Marieanne Spacey, who plays for the England women's football team. The interview is divided into two parts.

MS = Marieanne Spacey I = Interviewer

Part 1
Marieanne has been playing for England since the age of 18. The interviewer asked her how she began playing football.

MS: Erm, it all started when I was very very small when my uncle, brother and dad all used to play out on the green in front of the house and I just took an interest from there, and I was always playing it and, er, even at school I never used to play with the girls, I used to play with the boys ... playing football in the playground and everything ... it just started like that. It was just something that I felt I was good at or I enjoyed playing and I thought I was good at so I just wanted to keep playing it.
I: How old were you when you first started playing in teams?
MS: In teams, I was about ... I was very, I was about 10 when I started playing five-a-side level, then about 13 when I started to play 11-a-side but, like I was saying, I mean I've always wanted to play and, er, I used ... I wanted to play in the school team when I was nine but the school teacher said that I wasn't allowed to play – it was against the law, against the rules, and that ... erm ... we'd get in trouble with the FA if I played for the boys team. And yet he didn't mind me playing in the blokes' cricket team, which I thought was a bit off.
I: Which clubs have you played for?
MS: The clubs I've played ... I started off with the youth club called Oakway which was basically a five-a-side football club, football team, and then I joined BOC Malden who were based locally. And they folded when I was about four- ... 13, 14, and I've been playing for Friends of Fulham ever since.

EXERCISE 3 (page 37)

Part 2
The interviewer asked Marieanne whether attitudes to women's football in Britain were similar to those in other countries.

MS: The attitudes are very different in other countries. In countries – Scandinavian countries, in Italy, in Germany, you tend to find that it's a way of life. Women are very ... the women's game is very accepted.
When we play in Germany you're getting crowds of 10,000, 11,000, and you come back to England and you try to say to them – yeah, but it's just as good in England and you're sort of getting crowds of maybe 2,500. And very quiet crowds, you know, whereas in Germany they tend to make a lot of noise. And the same in Scandinavian countries – a way of life again. People sort of ... their jobs are, are centred around their football ...
I: Is the women's game at all different from the men's game?
MS: It's different in a lot of aspects. The speed of the game is a lot slower. With men's football it tends to be – get the ball down and move it quickly, whereas in women's football you do the same but it's at such a slower pace that you can see the moves building up from the back. Also physically – I mean, everyone in women's football admits that we're not as strong as men, so we don't play a physical game. We just play a skilful game. We don't dive about the place, hoping to get free kicks and penalties, and we don't, we tend to be ... I think it's ... not fairer but a little bit more sporting, because it's not our job, you know – we are amateur ... but saying that we are very committed and sort of winning the league and winning the cup is sort of the goal at the end of the season.

Sport and violence

EXERCISE 2 (page 39)

You are going to hear three short extracts from a conversation between a group of friends. They are talking about football supporters.

Part 1
M: I have neighbours who, who are very nice, friendly, warm, affectionate people, and I live near a football ground, Tottenham, and on Saturday I avoid them, because they come back from the match about 6 o'clock, 7 o'clock drunk, aggressive – they scream, they shout, and ... After the World Cup Fi-, after the World Cup when England got knocked out, I was in my local pub and they came in and they started pushing people around and smashing glasses, and I was really frightened and I walked out, and I don't understand, I really don't understand what it is about a football match that can turn ordinary, friendly people into monsters.

Part 2
JE: But do you think that's so of a lot of football fans? I mean, I've heard other people say they've gone to football matches and there's been absolutely no trouble in the terraces at all, and people have been ... sat there, you know, quite happily, opposing teams next to each other.
J: Oh but it obviously does happen a lot. I mean, you see it on the news. What happens when British fans go to Europe? There's always trouble, isn't there?
M: Well, but it's, it's not ... it's ... In Brazil, for example, where I've also been to football matches, people go to enjoy themselves, and there's no aggression or violence, or ... there's nothing like that. It seems peculiarly, it seems particular to England and a few other countries that football provides people with the opportunity to show their most violent, aggressive natures.

Part 3
A: But perhaps it's just a function of people getting together in crowds, large groups of people getting into enclosed spaces together.
J: But large crowds go to other kinds of matches – go to rugby matches, go to Wimbledon to watch tennis ...
M: Go to pop concerts ...
J: If they go to Wimbledon to watch tennis, they sit there silently throughout.
A: Yes, but it's interesting that one of the solutions that the police have, think might work is to have all-seater matches, for example, where everybody's seated ...

UNIT 5 DISCIPLINE

Children and discipline

EXERCISES 3 and 4 (page 43)

You are going to hear a child talking about the way parents punish children. The interviewer asked him about being smacked by his parents. Did being smacked stop him doing something a second time?

I = Interviewer T = Thomas

T: It depends, 'cos maybe you think what you did was right and you didn't think it was fair that she should ... em ... you should be punished. But if that happened I'd just be stubborn ... I wouldn't think about that at all.
I: What's the ... what do you think is the best way of punishing you to make you think – to make you change what you've done? What's the fairest way, do you think?
T: Well, I think the best way of making you think about what you've done is sending you up to your room, up to your room and not letting you out, because then – you, you can't really find anything to do, so you just think about what you've done.
I: So that's better than being smacked?
T: Well yeah, 'cos if you get smacked, it's kind of ... you get angry when you're smacked and so you don't really think about it as much.

EXERCISE 5 (page 43)

The speaker is expecting the answer to be *yes* to this question. His voice goes *down* at the end. Listen:

So you enjoy playing football?

Now listen to this sentence. The speaker doesn't know what answer to expect. His voice goes *up* at the end.

You can come to the party tonight?

Listen:

1 You're feeling ill?
2 I have to change at Oxford?

EXERCISE 7 (page 45)

You are going to hear three different parents dealing with children who have behaved badly.

1
PARENT: You did what? You naughty boy. Why don't you ever think? Well, now you'll just have to go next door and apologise. You can use your pocket money to pay for the damage – and next time you want to play football, for goodness sake go to the park.
2
PARENT: Oh, no! Do you really think it was a good idea to kick a ball around in the street? ... OK, so what are you going to do now? ... And what are you going to say to them? ... Uh-huh – and what about the window? ... All right. Off you go then.
3
PARENT: How many times have I told you not to play near other people's houses? I've had quite enough of your cheek. When you've got your ball back, I'm keeping it – yes, for a month. And if you *ever* do this again, you'll come straight home after school and stay in every evening. Do you hear me?

EXERCISE 10 (page 45)

MOTHER: How many times have I told you not to hitch-hike? What's wrong with you? Why don't you listen to me? I warned you last time that I was going to punish you if it ever happened again!
GIRL: But I missed the last bus! What was I supposed to do?
MOTHER: You could have called us. But no – you enjoy disobeying us, don't you?
FATHER: Wait a second ... calm down. Look, love, you must try to understand. It's dangerous for a girl to hitch-hike, especially at night. We are your parents. We're terrified that something will happen to you. You know people are sometimes attacked late at night. Please, promise us you won't do it again.
MOTHER: She's promised before. Listen, my girl – if you ever do this again, you're going to be in big trouble!

UNIT 6 PEOPLE ON THE MOVE

A way of life

EXERCISE 4 (page 49)

You are going to hear parts of a song written and sung by a gypsy.

GYPSY:
I was born a travelling feller
And I took me a travelling wife,
For all of our people were needies
And followed the travelling life.
Such ways, they's hard but they's happy,
For there's plenty of fun on the way;
You don't have to think of tomorrow,
Just think of the living today.
So give us a honk on your horn, bruv,
When you're passing by day or by night,
For no more shall we be a-travelling;
We're stuck on a permanent site ...
... If one day you went a bit hungry,
The next there'd be plenty to eat;
If sometimes you're down when you're travelling
You're soon back up on your feet ...
Now these sites, they seem just like prisons –
And the life here is terrible hard.
Not as free as the side of the road, lads,
Or stopping in some farmer's yard.
Though there's 'lectric and plenty of water,
There's all these rules to obey.
If I only 'ad some place to pull to,
I'd 'itch on and leave 'ere today.
So give us a toot on your hooter
And maybe a flash of your lights,
And if you want to live long and happy,
Stay off these permanent sites.

Living away from home

EXERCISES 5 and 6 (page 51)

Marisol is a Mexican woman who has come to live in Britain. Listen to what she says about how easy it has been to adapt to her new life. The interviewer asked her what kind of physical difficulties she experienced.

M = Marisol I = Interviewer

M: Physical difficulties, well, the weather you could call a physical difficulty. Public transport, which doesn't seem to be so efficient these days. England seems to be at a, at a stage where everything is geared to you using public as opposed to private means of transport, but public transport is yet not good enough, so I find it very tiring.
I: Do you find it difficult to become, to make friends, if you like, with English people?
M: I don't, I personally don't find it's difficult. Er ... however, I see the difference. In a Latin country everybody is prepared to make friends almost immediately, which I think is a much more superficial relationship. I feel that if I make friends with an English person, although it might take a lot longer, that will be a real friendship.

Next the interviewer asked her whether she thought British people were generally less emotional.

M: I used to admire, perhaps because I was younger – I used to admire the way English people were. Why? Because of this absolute, what seemed to me then, an absolute control of your emotions. Now I disagree that it's an absolute control – it's a way of not handling them at all.

And did she think there was a problem of isolation in Britain?

M: Oh yes, absolutely. Er ... when you see it in older people ... er ... whose children have left home, I think they are very lonely. In a way they are, I admire their stoicism and their wanting to live on their own. On the other hand, I think there's something, er, very sad, especially because younger generations never seem to have the opportunity very much of talking to their grandparents' generation – I think that's definitely a limitation.

Journeys

EXERCISE 3 (page 52)

You are going to hear five public announcements. Where would you expect to hear them?

1 This is an announcement for passengers on platform 2 who are waiting for the delayed 6.30 service to London Paddington. This service has now been cancelled. Passengers should catch the 6.50 to Reading, leaving shortly from platform 1, and change at Reading.
2 The police warn of long delays on the M25 as a result of an accident at junction 19.
3 Passengers are warned that unaccompanied luggage found in the building will be taken away and destroyed. Please remain with your luggage at all times until it has been checked in.
4 This is a passenger announcement. Services to Heathrow leave every 15 minutes from Bay 6. Please buy your tickets directly from the driver.
5 Ladies and gentlemen, we shall be leaving in five minutes. If there is anyone on board who is not sailing with us, would they please disembark immediately.

UNIT 7 HEALTH

Staying healthy

EXERCISES 3 and 4 (page 54)

You are going to hear two doctors talking. The first is an 'alternative' doctor, in other words one who is not qualified to work within the National Health Service in Britain, but who offers a rather different kind of treatment. Listen to what she says about 'alternative' medicine.

CLARE: I think that where complementary medicine or alternative therapies are coming from is very much a point of considering the whole person, the whole being, and that's body, mind, emotions and spirit – all those four things. And certainly, in my experience, they all affect each other so that you could treat just the body but you in my opinion also need to have an awareness of what's going on in the person's mind, erm, emotions, spirit. For example, I've just worked with someone recently who has arthritis and ... has a flare-up – it's a long story, but in her, one of her knees. Now I could have just gone and treated the pain in the knee, but it did transpire that ... erm ... there was something at the emotional level that had cropped up because of this pain ...
I – again – believe that there is a place, a wonderful place, for some of the chemical drugs that are around, and I think they're used tremendously sensitively and carefully, for people who are dying of cancer and in a lot of pain. Also I do know that massage and aromatherapy ... erm ... and spiritual healing are used in conjunction with the use of drugs for people who are either, have AIDS or have cancer ...

Now listen to a 'conventional' doctor, who works as a GP for the National Health Service.

BARBARA: The main problem with being a conventional, so-called GP is the time factor, and if you're going to try and treat people in a whole sense, then ... erm, you have to take in their feelings about their illness, their feelings about their treatment, and it's very, very difficult to do that when you have only a very limited amount of time that you can give to any one person, via the NHS, and the only way that people have access to that time factor where you can discuss feelings is often through a private system, and that is effectively what they are paying for when they pay for alternative medicine – as well as the drug side of things. But ... I think to draw a distinction between conventional medicine being, 'Here is a prescription, there is the door – go away and take it!' and the alternative forms which are all herbal and wonderful and people discussing their feelings and taking into account the whole of their diet, their life-style etc. etc. is a very false division ...

EXERCISE 5 (page 54)

Listen to these two sentences. Notice particularly which words are stressed.

1 The 'conventional' doctor works for the National Health Service, whereas the 'alternative' doctor works privately.
2 The 'conventional' doctor works in a surgery, whereas the 'alternative' doctor works at home.

Getting enough sleep?

EXERCISE 4 (page 56)

Listen to the conversation that Mrs M had with her friend.

MRS M: Oh, I feel dreadful! I just can't seem to get to sleep at night!
FRIEND: Oh, I know. It's terrible when you can't get to sleep. What do you think the problem is?
MRS M: Well, I can't seem to stop worrying.
FRIEND: Oh ...
MRS M: I lie in bed thinking about all the problems I need to deal with, and then I start worrying about how tired I'll be if I don't get some sleep. I don't know what to do.
FRIEND: Have you tried a small brandy or something before you go to bed? That always sends me to sleep.
MRS M: No, that wouldn't work. Alcohol just keeps me awake.
FRIEND: Well, what about doing something completely different in the evenings to take your mind off things? Go and see a film, for example – there's a really good comedy on at the Odeon.
MRS M: Yes, you're probably right. A change of scene will do me good. Thanks, I'll try that tonight.

EXERCISE 5 (page 57)

Listen to this conversation between a doctor and her patient.

DR: Hello. Sit down. What seems to be the problem then?
PATIENT: Well, I've been having trouble sleeping – it's been going on for over a fortnight now and it's affecting my work. But I was wondering if you could give me something.
DR: Let's see. Insomnia is a very common problem, and it's usually related to some kind of stress in your life. Are you worried about anything?
PATIENT: No, nothing really – except not being able to sleep.
DR: Hmm ... Do you get enough exercise?
PATIENT: Well, no, I suppose not at the moment. I'm very busy at work, you see, so I work late – and then at weekends I'm too tired. Especially now.
DR: All right. Now I think it's too early to prescribe pills for you. What I advise you to do is to make time every day for a trip to the swimming pool, a game of tennis – or even some exercises at home. Then if the problem continues, come back and we'll think again.
PATIENT: OK, doctor. Thank you.

A healthy body

EXERCISES 1 and 2 (page 58)

You are going to hear the teacher of an exercise class giving instructions to participants while they do the exercises.

Right, everybody. Stand up straight. Now bend forward and down to touch your toes – and up – and down – and up. Arms by your sides. Raise your right knee as high as you can. Hold your leg with both hands and pull your knee back against your body. Keep your backs straight. Now lower your leg and do the same with your left knee – up – pull towards you – and down. Move your feet further apart, bend your elbows, and raise your arms to shoulder level. Squeeze your fists tightly in front of your chest. Now push your elbows back – keep your head up! And relax ... Feet together, and put your hands on your hips. Now bend your knees and stretch your arms out in front of you. Hold that position – now up. Stretch your arms out to the sides at shoulder height, palms up. Rotate your arms in small circles – that's right – and now the other way. Now stand with your hands clasped behind your neck and your legs apart. Bend over to the left, slowly, but as far as you can. And slowly up. And down to the right. And up. OK – if we're all warmed up now, let's begin!

UNIT 8 BUSINESS

The right job?

EXERCISES 3 and 4 (pages 60–1)

You are going to hear part of an interview with a man who is the manager of an estate agency. The manager was asked about the skills he needs to do his job.

EA = Estate agent I = Interviewer

EA: Oh, that's a difficult question. Erm, I think probably the skills that are to do with dealing with people are the most important in my job. Erm, it's terribly important that I win people's trust – after all, I'm trying to sell them houses, or I'm trying to sell their houses for them. Er, they have to trust me. So persuading them is very important. Erm, and then of course I work in, in quite a busy office and I'm the manager of this office, and I have to motivate all the people who work in the office to sell as many houses as possible. So skills of dealing with the people who are employees are as important as dealing with the people who are customers.
I: There must also be a base of *knowledge* that you need to have ...
EA: Well, yes, of course there is a knowledge base, and perhaps you could call these the technical skills of the job, if you like. Of course, anybody who works as an estate agent needs to know something about the legal side of buying and selling houses. Erm, and the, and of advertising – erm what one can say in an advertisement for a house – although in fact lawyers normally deal with the, the detail of the legal side. Erm, and also about the financial side. Estate agents need to know what money can be borrowed by people who wish to buy houses, er, and to put purchasers of houses in contact with, with places where they can borrow money. And of course I have to keep my own accounts for the business. This, this is a skill as well ...
I: There must be a lot of organisational skills that are important too ...
EA: Yes, there are. Um, the life of an estate agent is not an easy one. Erm, the housing market, particularly over the last ten years, has gone up and down in Britain. Um, two years ago, er, I employed 20 people – er, now the office only has eight people working in it. Er, it's clearly important to be able to predict what number of staff you'll need at a particular time of the year. People don't, for example, sell houses very much in the winter – they tend to sell in, in the spring and summer. So it's, it's very important for me to plan how many people are working in the office at any particular time, and to ensure that staff take holidays at times which are suitable for the company, erm, etc.

Applying for a job

EXERCISE 3 (page 63)

Stephen Baker is attending an interview for the job of marketing assistant.

I = Interviewer SB = Stephen Baker

I: Good afternoon, Mr Baker. Do sit down.
SB: Thank you.
I: Now, you're 23 years old and I see you have a couple of years' work experience. What were your duties as administrative assistant?
SB: Oh, everything really. Typing, filing, answering the telephone, making the coffee.
I: Mm ... I see. And why did you decide to leave?
SB: It got boring. I mean, I didn't have any real responsibility – I just had to do what I was told.
I: Mm ... How would you describe your personality, then? Are you ambitious?
SB: Oh, yes. Yes, I don't want to be typing forever. I work hard, I think, and people seem to be pleased with what I do. Then I like meeting people and visiting new places.
I: Do you get on well with your colleagues?
SB: Yes, I've never had any problems. I enjoy talking, you see, and going out for a drink after work.
I: And do you have a reference from your last employer.
SB: Er, no, but I can ask her to send one.
I: Right. Now, are there any questions you'd like to ask about the job?
SB: Yes, one or two. Er, if I got the job, what would my hours be exactly?
I: They would normally be 9 to 6, Monday to Friday, but you could be asked to work later than that. Then there would be some travelling, and in that case you might be asked

to work at weekends as well.
SB: Mm. So what would the salary be?
I: You'd start at £9,000 a year, but we'd review your salary and performance every six months. Well, if there are no more questions, thank you, Mr Baker, for coming. We'll contact you next week.

Dealing with companies

EXERCISE 1 (page 64)

Listen to this telephone conversation between a company secretary and a caller. Notice the polite expressions that each of them uses.

S = Secretary   C = Caller

S: Good afternoon. Firth Computers. Can I help you?
C: Yes, my name's Smith. I'd like to speak to Mr Jones, please.
S: Could I ask the nature of your business with him, please?
C: Oh, he asked me to call him.
S: Right. Just a minute, please ... I'm afraid he's in a meeting at the moment. Would you mind ringing again after 3.30?

EXERCISE 2 (page 64)

This conversation is also between a caller and a company secretary.

S: Daley's. Good morning!
C: Good morning. Could you put me through to Mr Daley, please.
S: Certainly. Hold the line, please, I'm trying to connect you ... I'm sorry, the line's engaged. Would you like to hold?
C: No. I'll try again later. Thank you.
S: Good-bye.

EXERCISE 4 (page 64)

A secretary is speaking on the phone with a man who wishes to make an appointment to see her boss.

S: Hello. Ms Brown's assistant. Can I help you?
C: Yes, I'd like to make an appointment to see Ms Brown, please.
S: May I ask what you'd like to see her about?
C: Well, I've designed this gadget ... It's a kind of tin-opener, actually ... and I'd like to show it to her. I think your customers would love it.
S: I see. Well, would 4 o'clock next Tuesday be convenient?
C: Yes, thank you.
S: And your name, Mr ... ?

UNIT 9 POWER

Power in conversation

EXERCISE 2 (page 66)

A group of people are having a discussion about how people get and show power in conversation – how they dominate others. One way of doing this is by *talking loudly*.

Now listen for other ways.

J: ... and people who continue talking and won't let others come in ... I mean it's very easy just to keep talking, keep talking, keep talking and if anybody tries to interrupt, you talk *more* loudly ... with *more* confidence ... and that's a way of keeping out ...
JE: A lot of politicians do that don't they?
J: Politicians are ... very good examples of that.
A: It's not only carrying on talking though ... I mean it's, it's leaving sentences hanging in the middle is very often a technique, because people make a point and then they say 'and', and they've, they've left the conversation hanging – *they* have the right to continue.

So, we've heard a few examples of ways in which people in general can dominate conversations – but what about men and women? Are there particular differences between the way men and women speak? Listen as the conversation continues.

A: But do you think ... erm ... it's often been said that, that men, in, in mixed gatherings, men dominate groups.
P: Yes. I think that is true. I think, erm, that women more often begin, erm, to give an opinion by saying 'I think that' ... or 'In my opinion', whereas men tend to say 'This is the fact – this is the truth of the situation', and that automatically carries more authority – it sounds as if you know more, whereas ...
T: I think women tend to finish a sentence by saying something like 'Don't you agree?' or 'Do you think that?' ... sort of deferring to someone else's opinion.
P: And women tend to be branded as 'good listeners' because they encourage ... they go 'mm mm' just as you two were doing ... and the man amongst us wasn't.

EXERCISE 4 (page 67)

1 It was terrible ... the rain was pouring down, the wind was blowing, it was so cold I could hardly move my fingers ...
2 She asked me to get something from the shops for her ...
3 He told me he couldn't come ...
4 Nobody understands what she means ...
5 So there he was, standing all alone in the street ...

The power of the way you look

EXERCISES 2 and 3 (page 68)

Here are some more extracts from the conversation you listened to earlier. The topic now is to do with how people's appearance affects the power they have over other people.

P: What people wear can be very powerful as well ... It doesn't necessarily have to be conventional dress, but striking or ... setting, setting them apart in some way.
J: They talk about power dressing don't they, for women wearing suits ... you know ...
P: Sad, isn't it? It has to be a male dress form.

V: Carrying the right props, you know ...
P: 'Props' is an interesting word because it's – that's, that's a term from the theatre, isn't it?
Is, is there something theatrical associated with power?
V: Well you make a point, isn't it, by the way you dress, and the way you stand, and the way you walk ...

So, clothes and other props are important to both men and women. What about men in particular?

A: I think there are other things about men's appearance – I, I think height is a very interesting one ... and hair. But, er, er, it's fascinating in the States, with TV personalities in the States ... erm, the fact that they, you know, all seem to er have hair jobs ... er, wear wigs ... er, the President of the United States – Reagan you know – had to dye his hair until he was 75 and carries on dying it to look young ... so that height and youth appear to be terribly important. And I remember reading some research in the States that ... or the the results of a survey that actually looked at height and ... em, er ... position in companies, and it did seem to be related ...

Well, there we are ... we'd all like to be tall and youthful-looking. But is that enough? Some people actually take courses to help them present themselves well. Politicians, for example ...

J: Oh, politicians take classes ... I know, I know they do ... I mean, not only in ... em, in elocution, so the way they make the sounds, but also in how to present themselves.
V: Margaret Thatcher did, didn't she?
J: Yes, I, I know Margaret Thatcher did, and I know other politicians recently when they started filming what went on in the House of Commons went to classes, er, on how to dress, and how to stand, and how to look at the cameras. That kind of thing.
JE: ... and how to use their arms or hands, probably – I should think hands are quite ...
J: Yes. In order to appear to the people who are watching them ... authoritative, and confident.
V: Body language.
J: Yes. Body language is, is important too.

UNIT 10 HUMOUR

The cartoonist

EXERCISE 8 (page 73)

You are going to hear Mel Calman, a well-known British cartoonist, talking about his work. The interviewer has been asking him about the techniques he uses to make people laugh. Here is one of the things he said.

MEL CALMAN: If you can say something mildly shocking but in such bad taste that it frightens people, er, or – no, sorry – distresses people, er, that can also be funny ... and I have done that sometimes. I mean there was, many years ago there was a spaghetti restaurant which for some reason was put under siege, and there were hostages. I can't even remember what it was – I think it was some form of terrorism or something – many years ago in Knightsbridge, and I think they were all stuck there for about eight or nine days in the basement, and eventually they surrendered to the police. Well, when that was over, I did a joke at the end of that week, when they were all released and it was safe to do a joke, erm, of a man looking at a menu and saying to the waiter, 'Can I have the spaghetti without the siege?' And, you see, there – you know – it's without the salt, without the tomatoes, without the garlic. You take a fairly boring phrase, in fact – you know, a common-place phrase, and give it a little twist, and I'm quite, I'm fond of doing that, and a lot of humour often does do that ...

Jokes

EXERCISES 2, 3 and 4 (page 75)

A man is telling his friends a joke.

A bit like the joke about the man from Texas who had a huge ranch and went to visit his English friend, who had a small farm, and the Texan says to his English friend – er I really can't do an American accent, but he said, er, 'How big is your spread here?' So the Englishman said, 'Well, it goes up to the house over there, you see, and then back across to those trees, then down here to this little stream, and back to where we're standing.' And the Texan said, 'Man,' he said, 'in my spread back in Texas, in my car it takes me a whole day just to drive around it.' And the Englishman said, 'Oh, yes,' he said, 'I had a car like that once.'

EXERCISE 6 (page 75)

The same man is now telling a second joke. This one is set in a supermarket.

There's another kind of joke, isn't there, which is about ridiculous, unexpected responses to situations, like the big man who went into a supermarket and asked the attendant in the supermarket if he could buy half a cabbage. So the little man in the supermarket said, 'Oh, no, frightfully sorry, sir, we don't sell half cabbages, we only sell whole cabbages – you can't possibly buy half a cabbage!' So the big man said, 'Well, why don't you go upstairs and have a word with the manager and see if he'd be willing to sell you half a cabbage?' So the little man said, 'Bm bm bm, OK, so he goes up to the manager's office and he goes into the manager's office and he said, 'There's this man downstairs, great big, tall chap, so stupid – I've never met such a fool in my whole life!' Unaware, of course, to the little man, the big man had followed him into the manager's office. The little man said to the manager, 'This, this huge idiot wants me to sell him half a cabbage!' The little man turned slightly and became aware that the big man was standing behind him. So he said, 'However, there is no problem, because this gentleman has very kindly offered to buy the other half.'

CASSETTE 2

PRONUNCIATION

UNIT 1 WRITING
(pages 80–1)

Look at List A:
What kind of book is it?
fiction   / 'fɪkʃən /
a romantic novel
   / ərəʊ'mæntɪk 'nɒvəl /
a detective story
   / ədɪ'tektɪv 'stɔːri /
a historical novel
   / əhɪ'stɒrɪkl 'nɒvəl /
a play   / ə'pleɪ /
a textbook   / ə'tekstbʊk /
non-fiction   / 'nɒn'fɪkʃən /
science fiction   / 'saɪəns 'fɪkʃən /

a ghost story   / ə'gəʊstɔːri /
a collection of short stories
   / əkə'lekʃənəv 'ʃɔːt 'stɔːriz /
a collection of essays
   / əkə'lekʃənəv 'eseɪz /

Look at list B:
What's the story like?

exciting   / ɪk'saɪtɪŋ /
frightening   / 'fraɪtnɪŋ /
interesting   / 'ɪntrəstɪŋ /
ridiculous   / rɪ'dɪkjuːləs /
terrifying   / 'terɪfaɪ-ɪŋ /
extraordinary   / ɪk'strɔːdənəri /
moving   / 'muːvɪŋ /
humorous   / 'hjuːmərəs /
boring   / 'bɔːrɪŋ /
sad   / sæd /
funny   / 'fʌni /
thrilling   / 'θrɪlɪŋ /
dramatic   / drə'mætɪk /
dull   / dʌl /

Look at List C:
What does a story consist of?

plot   / plɒt /
characters   / 'kærəktəz /
narrative   / 'nærətɪv /
description   / dɪ'skrɪpʃən /
dialogue   / 'daɪəlɒg /
events   / ɪ'vents /
climax   / 'klaɪmæks /
ending   / 'endɪŋ /
background   / 'bækgraʊnd /
murder   / 'mɜːdə /
mystery   / 'mɪstəri /
romance   / rəʊ'mæns /
suspense   / sə'spens /

Look at List D:
How is a book organised?

front cover / 'frʌn 'kʌvə^r /
back cover / 'bæ 'kʌvə^r /
title / 'taɪtl /
blurb / blɜːb /
biographical details
/ 'baɪəgræfɪkəl 'diːteɪlz /
contents page
/ 'kɒntentspeɪdʒ /
index / 'ɪndeks /
bibliography / bɪblɪ'ɒgrəfi /
reviews / rɪ'vjuːz /
chapters / 'tʃæptəz /

PRONUNCIATION Running words together

Exercise 1
Listen:

textbook
ghost story
front cover

Now listen again and repeat:

textbook / 'teksbʊk /
ghost story / 'gəʊstɔːri /
front cover / 'frʌn 'kʌvə^r /

Listen:

You must be Andy.
/ 'juːmʌsbi: 'ændi /
That could be true.
/ 'ðækʊbi 'truː /
Is that picture sold?
/ ɪz 'ðæpɪktʃə 'səʊld? /
He's such a good boy!
/ hi: 'sʌtʃəgʊ 'bɔɪ /

Exercise 2
Listen:

interesting / 'ɪntrəstɪŋ /
frightening / 'fraɪtnɪŋ /
different / 'dɪfrənt /

UNIT 2 PRIVATE LIVES
(pages 82–3)

Look at list A:
How do we want a partner to be?

warm / wɔːm /
affectionate / ə'fekʃənət /
kind / kaɪnd /
open / 'əʊpən /
loving / 'lʌvɪŋ /
strong / strɒŋ /
helpful / 'helpfəl /
honest / 'ɒnɪst /
tidy / 'taɪdi /
sincere / sɪn'sɪə^r /
friendly / 'frendli /
gentle / 'dʒentl /
patient / 'peɪʃnt /
generous / 'dʒenərəs /

Look at list B:
What interests do you have?

theatre / 'θɪətə^r /
fashion / 'fæʃən /
literature / 'lɪtrɪtʃə^r /
architecture / 'ɑːkɪtektʃə^r /
driving / 'draɪvɪŋ /
sports / spɔːts /
computers / kəm'pjuːtəz /
countryside / 'kʌntrɪsaɪd /
cinema / 'sɪnəmə /
painting / 'peɪntɪŋ /
walking / 'wɔːkɪŋ /
building / 'bɪldɪŋ /
pottery / 'pɒtəri /
travel / 'trævəl /
music / 'mjuːzɪk /
flying / 'flaɪ-ɪŋ /

Look at list C:
How can we refer to groups of people?

children / 'tʃɪldrən /
teenagers / 'tiːneɪdʒəz /
middle-aged people
/ 'mɪdleɪdʒd 'piːpəl /
babies / 'beɪbɪz /
toddlers / 'tɒdləz /
adults / 'ædʌlts /
pensioners / 'penʃənəz /
young people / 'jʌŋ 'piːpəl /
retired people / rɪ'taɪəd 'piːpəl /

Look at list D:
How do we refer to individuals?

Mister / 'mɪstə^r /
Mrs / 'mɪsɪz /
Ms / mɪz / or / məz /
Madam / 'mædəm /
Sir / sə^r / sɜː^r /
Dad / dæd /
Mum / mʌm /

PRONUNCIATION Running words together

Exercise 1
Listen:

Eleven people are waiting outside.
There's only one bag in the room.
I can be there at six.

Now listen again and repeat:

Eleven people (ɪ'levən 'piːpəl) are waiting outside.
There's only one bag ('wʌm 'bæg) in the room.
I can be (kəm 'biː) there at six.

Exercise 2
Listen:

I'll see you in class tomorrow.
She can go if she wants to.
You can see him again, can't you?

Now listen again and repeat:

I'll see you in class (ɪŋ 'klɑːs) tomorrow.
She can go (kəŋ 'gəʊ) if she wants to.
You can see him again, can't you? ('kɑːntʃuː)

UNIT 3 FEAR
(pages 84–5)

Look at list A:
What frightens you?

open spaces / 'əʊpən 'speɪsɪz /
old age / 'əʊld 'eɪdʒ /
motorways / 'məʊtəweɪz /
public speaking
/ 'pʌblɪk 'spiːkɪŋ /
crowds / kraʊdz /
heights / haɪts /
rats / ræts /
ghosts / gəʊsts /
moths / mɒθs /
flying / 'flaɪ-ɪŋ /
spiders / 'spaɪdəz /
water / 'wɔːtə^r /

Look at List B:
How do you feel?

frightened / 'fraɪtnd /
terrified / 'terɪfaɪd /
nervous / 'nɜːvəs /
petrified / 'petrɪfaɪd /
hysterical / hɪ'sterɪkəl /
worried / 'wʌrɪd /
uneasy / ʌn'iːzi /
anxious / 'æŋkʃəs /

Look at list C:
What is your response to fear?

run away / 'rʌnə'weɪ /
sweat / swet /
feel sick / 'fiːəl 'sɪk /
scream / skriːm /
cry / kraɪ /

Look at list D:
How can you try to overcome your fears?

talk to a friend
/ 'tɔːktuːə 'frend /
try to relax / 'traɪtərɪ'læks /
ignore them / ɪg'nɔːðəm /
see a doctor / 'siːə 'dɒktə /
be sensible / 'biː 'sensəbəl /

Look at list E:
How can other people help?

reassure / riːə'ʃʊə^r /
calm / kɑːm /
listen / 'lɪsən /,
hug / hʌg /
understand / ʌndə'stænd /
advise / əd'vaɪz /
recommend / rekə'mend /
cuddle / 'kʌdl /
comfort / 'kʌmfət /
support / sə'pɔːt /

PRONUNCIATION Word stress – weak forms

Exercise 1
Listen:

a The bags are in the car.
b She can come tomorrow.
c I've got some dollars.
d He was so naughty!

Exercise 2
Listen:

a The man has been sent to prison.
b There are some large birds in the garden.
c Children have an advantage if they come from happy family backgrounds.

UNIT 4 SPORT
(pages 86–7)

Look at list A:
What kind of sport do you play?

tennis / 'tenɪs /
hockey / 'hɒki /
rugby / 'rʌgbi /
athletics / æθ'letɪks /
ice hockey / 'aɪshɒki /
gymnastics / dʒɪm'næstɪks /
football / 'fʊtbɔːl /
badminton / 'bædmɪntən /
swimming / 'swɪmɪŋ /
squash / skwɒʃ /

Look at list B:
Where are sports played?

pitch / pɪtʃ /
court / kɔːt /
stadium / 'steɪdɪəm /
track / træk /
pool / puːl /
field / fiːəld /
rink / rɪŋk /

Look at list C:
What kind of equipment do you need?

bat / bæt /
shuttlecock / 'ʃʌtlkɒk /
vest / vest /
shorts / ʃɔːts /
pads / pædz /
helmet / 'helmɪt /
racquet / 'rækɪt /
ball / bɔːl /
boots / buːts /
socks / sɒks /
net / net /
cap / kæp /
stick / stɪk /
shoes / ʃuːz /
shirt / ʃɜːt /
puck / pʌk /
trousers / 'traʊzəz /

Look at list D:
What kinds of actions are common in sports?

throwing / 'θrəʊɪŋ /
passing / 'pɑːsɪŋ /
hitting / 'hɪtɪŋ /
serving / 'sɜːvɪŋ /
jumping / 'dʒʌmpɪŋ /
saving / 'seɪvɪŋ /
catching / 'kætʃɪŋ /
tackling / 'tæklɪŋ /
kicking / 'kɪkɪŋ /
running / 'rʌnɪŋ /

PRONUNCIATION Problem words

Exercise 1
Listen:

enough through cough though

Now listen again and repeat:

enough / ɪ'nʌf /
through / θruː /
cough / kɒf /
though / ðəʊ /

Exercise 2
Listen:

tough although rough

Now listen again and repeat:

tough / tʌf /
although / ɔːl'ðəʊ /
rough / rʌf /

UNIT 5 DISCIPLINE
(pages 88–9)

Look at list A:
How can you punish children?

turn off the television
/ 'tɜːnɒfðə 'telɪvɪʒən /
smack them / 'smækðəm /
shout at them / 'ʃaʊtətðəm /
take away their toys
/ 'teɪkəweɪðeə 'tɔɪz /
send them to bed
/ 'sendəmtə 'bed /
tell them off / 'telðəm 'ɒf /

Look at list B:
How can you reward children?

cuddle them / 'kʌdəlðəm /
praise them / 'preɪzðəm /
buy them presents
/ 'baɪðəm 'prezənts /
give them sweets
/ 'gɪvðəm 'swiːts /
give them extra attention
/ 'gɪvðəm 'ekstrəə'tenʃən /

Look at list C:
What happens in a law court?

charge / tʃɑːdʒ /
defend / dɪ'fend /
accuse / ə'kjuːz /
sentence / 'sentəns /
judge / dʒʌdʒ /
prosecute / 'prɒsɪkjuːt /
convict / kən'vɪkt /

Look at list D:
Who's who?

defendant / dɪ'fendənt /
jury / 'dʒʊəri /
judge / dʒʌdʒ /
lawyer / 'lɔːjə^r /
witness / 'wɪtnəs /

Look at list E:
What's the judge's decision?

guilty / 'gɪlti /
innocent / 'ɪnəsənt /
sentence / 'sentəns /
not guilty / 'nɒt 'gɪlti /
verdict / 'vɜːdɪkt /

Look at list F:
What punishment can a criminal receive?

fine / faɪn /
prison sentence
/ 'prɪzən 'sentəns /
community service
/ kə'mjuːnəti 'sɜːvɪs /
probation / prə'beɪʃən /
the death penalty
/ ðə'deθ 'penəlti /
warning / 'wɔːnɪŋ /

Look at list G:
What kinds of crimes are there?

theft / θeft /
vandalism / 'vændəlɪzəm /
assault / ə'sɒlt /
murder / 'mɜːdə^r /
smuggling / 'smʌglɪŋ /
arson / 'ɑːsən /
fraud / frɔːd /
burglary / 'bɜːgləri /

PRONUNCIATION Word stress and parts of speech

Exercise 1
Listen:

convict / kən'vɪkt /
He was convicted of murder.

Listen:

convict / 'kɒnvɪkt /
The convict was taken from the court to prison.

Exercise 2
Listen to the noun, and then the verb:

export / 'ekspɔːt /
export / ɪk'spɔːt /
record / 'rekɔːd /
record / rɪ'kɔːd /
import / 'ɪmpɔːt /
import / ɪm'pɔːt /
escort / 'eskɔːt /
escort / ɪ'skɔːt /
increase / 'ɪŋkriːs /
increase / ɪŋ'kriːs /
insult / 'ɪnsʌlt /
insult / ɪn'sʌlt /
decrease / 'diːkriːs /
decrease / dɪ'kriːs /
transport / 'trænspɔːt /
transport / træn'spɔːt /

contract / 'kɒntrækt /
contráct / kən'trækt /
próduce / 'prɒdjuːs /
prodúce / prə'djuːs /
éxtract / 'ekstrækt /
extráct / ɪk'strækt /
rébel / 'rebəl /
rebél / rɪ'bel /

UNIT 6 PEOPLE ON THE MOVE
(pages 90–1)

Look at list A:
Where can you spend the night?

hotél / həʊ'tel /
guést house / 'gesthaʊs /
yóuth hostel / 'juːθhɒstəl /
night shelter / 'naɪtʃeltə /
cámpsite / 'kæmpsaɪt /
tent / tent /
rénted flát / 'rentɪd 'flæt /
friend's house / 'frendzhaʊs /
the ópen áir / ðiː'əʊpən 'eə /

Look at list B:
How do you feel when you're away from home?

lónely / 'ləʊnli /
hómesick / 'həʊmsɪk /
ísolated / 'aɪsəleɪtɪd /
depréssed / dɪ'prest /
frightened / 'fraɪtənd /
down / daʊn /
míserable / 'mɪzərəbəl /
scared / skeəd /
alóne / ə'ləʊn /

Look at list C:
How do you travel?

bus / bʌs /
train / treɪn /
foot / fʊt /
car / kɑː /
boat / bəʊt /
plane / pleɪn /

Look at list D:
What are the problems of travelling?

cáncellátions / 'kænsə'leɪʃənz /
crowds / kraʊdz /
tráffic jáms / 'træfɪk 'dʒæmz /
deláys / dɪ'leɪz /
hóld-ups / 'həʊld-ʌps /
bréakdowns / 'breɪkdaʊnz /
áccidents / 'æksɪdənts /

Look at list E:
Why do people move?

unemplóyment / ˌʌnɪm'plɔɪmənt /
divórce / dɪ'vɔːs /
chéaper hóusing / 'tʃiːpə 'haʊzɪŋ /
bétter schóols / 'betə 'skuːlz /
unpléasant néighbours / ˌʌn'plezənt 'neɪbəz /
bígger hóuse / 'bɪgə 'haʊs /
change / tʃeɪndʒ /
márriage / 'mærɪdʒ /
 ... fia /
 ... / 'klaɪmət /

TION Word stress
nouns

 ... stel

Exercise 2
Listen:

téapot / 'tiːpɒt /
týpewriter / 'taɪpraɪtə /
nótepaper / 'nəʊtpeɪpə /
cóat hanger / 'kəʊthæŋə /
spórts cár / 'spɔːtskɑː /
grándfather / 'grænfɑːðə /
són-in-láw / 'sʌnɪnlɔː /

Exercise 3
Listen:

a bláck boárd / ə'blæk'bɔːd /
a bláckboard / ə'blækbɔːd /
únder gróund / ˌʌndə'graʊnd /
the Únderground / ðiː'ʌndəgraʊnd /

UNIT 7 HEALTH
(pages 92–3)

Look at list A:
What do doctors do?

exámine / ɪɡ'zæmɪn /
treat / triːt /
cure / kjʊə /
diagnóse / daɪəɡ'nəʊz /
prescríbe / prɪ'skraɪb /

Look at list B:
What's the problem?

spots / spɒts /
pain / peɪn /
swélling / 'swelɪŋ /
déep cút / 'diːp 'kʌt /
inféction / ɪn'fekʃən /
ache / eɪk /

Look at list C:
What's the treatment?

pills / pɪlz /
táblets / 'tæbləts /
injéction / ɪn'dʒekʃən /
súrgery / 'sɜːdʒəri /
cream / kriːm /
médicine / 'medsən /

Look at list D:
Which part of your body needs exercising?

ánkle / 'æŋkəl /
neck / nek /
waist / weɪst /
shóulder / 'ʃəʊldə /
stómach / 'stʌmək /
wrist / rɪst /
thigh / θaɪ /
élbow / 'elbəʊ /

Look at list E:
How can you move parts of your body?

raise / reɪz /
tense / tens /
lówer / 'ləʊə /
rotáte / rəʊ'teɪt /
stráighten / 'streɪtən /
reláx / rɪ'læks /
bend / bend /
turn / tɜːn /
stretch / stretʃ /

Look at list F:
How do you feel in the morning?

sléepy / 'sliːpi /
írritable / 'ɪrɪtəbəl /
wíde awáke / 'waɪdə'weɪk /
exháusted / ɪɡ'zɔːstɪd /
shórt-témpered / 'ʃɔːt'tempəd /
unsóciable / ˌʌn'səʊʃəbəl /
refréshed / rɪ'freʃt /
drówsy / 'draʊzi /
alért / ə'lɜːt /
háppy / 'hæpi /

PRONUNCIATION Silent letters

Listen and repeat:

thumb / θʌm /
lamb / læm /
bomb / bɒm /
tomb / tuːm /
knee / niː /
know / nəʊ /
knife / naɪf /
knot / nɒt /
knickers / 'nɪkəz /
write / raɪt /
wrong / rɒŋ /
wrist / rɪst /
wrínkle / 'rɪŋkəl /
ánswer / 'ɑːnsə /
two / tuː /
hour / aʊə /
hónest / 'ɒnɪst /
hónour / 'ɒnə /
exháusted / ɪɡ'zɔːstɪd /
would / wʊd /
could / kʊd /
should / ʃʊd /

UNIT 8 BUSINESS
(pages 94–5)

Look at list A:
What do businesses provide?

goods / ɡʊdz /
sérvices / 'sɜːvɪsɪz /

Look at list B:
What do company departments do?

ínterview and seléct stáff / 'ɪntəvjuː ənsə'lek'stɑːf /
prepáre búdgets / prɪ'peə 'bʌdʒɪts /
arránge stáff hólidays / ə'reɪndʒ 'stɑːf 'hɒlɪdeɪz /
cóntact cústomers / 'kɒntæ 'kʌstəməz /
colléct débts / kə'lek 'dets /
tráin stáff / 'treɪn 'stɑːf /
prepáre bróchures / prɪ'peə 'brəʊʃəz /
dráw up stáff cóntracts / 'drɔːp 'stɑːf 'kɒntrækts /
prepáre accóunts / prɪ'peə'kaʊnts /
ádvertise góods and sérvices / 'ædvətaɪz 'ɡʊdzən 'sɜːvɪsɪz /
déal with pétty cásh / 'dɪəlwɪð 'peti'kæʃ /
atténd exhibítions / ə'tendeksɪ'bɪʃənz /

Look at list C:
What are your colleagues like?

intélligent / ɪn'telɪdʒənt /
imáginative / ɪ'mædʒɪnətɪv /
tólerant / 'tɒlərənt /
enthusiástic / ɪnθjuːzi'æstɪk /
sénsitive / 'sensətɪv /
pátient / 'peɪʃənt /
púnctual / 'pʌŋktʃʊəl /
lóyal / 'lɔɪəl /
práctical / 'præktɪkəl /
fórmal / 'fɔːməl /

Look at list D:
What do you do on the phone?

make a call
take a call
hear the engaged signal (/ɪŋ'ɡeɪdʒsɪɡnəl /)
pick up the receiver (/rɪ'siːvə /)
put down the receiver
listen for the ringing tone (/'rɪŋɪŋtəʊn /)

connect someone (/kə'neksʌmwʌn /)
put someone through
dial a number
ring someone
hold the line

PRONUNCIATION Word stress — prefixes

Exercise 1
Listen:

unintélligent / ˌʌnɪn'telɪdʒənt /
unimáginative / ˌʌnɪ'mædʒɪnətɪv /
intólerant / ɪn'tɒlərənt /
unpúnctual / ˌʌn'pʌŋktʃʊəl /
dislóyal / dɪs'lɔɪəl /
unenthusiástic / ˌʌnɪnθuːzi'æstɪk /
insénsitive / ɪn'sensətɪv /
impátient / ɪm'peɪʃənt /
imprácticál / ɪm'præktɪkəl /
infórmal / ɪn'fɔːməl /

UNIT 9 POWER
(pages 96–7)

Look at list A:
What do we do when we speak?

insíst / ɪn'sɪst /
disagrée / dɪsə'ɡriː /
prómise / 'prɒmɪs /
advíse / əd'vaɪz /
corréct / kə'rekt /
add / æd /
infórm / ɪn'fɔːm /
requést / rɪ'kwest /
expláin / ɪk'spleɪn /

Look at list B:
What are we communicating?

advíce / əd'vaɪs /
informátion / 'ɪnfə'meɪʃən /
árgument / 'ɑːɡjuːmənt /
explanátion / ˌeksplə'neɪʃən /
prómise / 'prɒmɪs /
requést / rɪ'kwest /

Look at list C:
How do we look?

góod-lóoking / 'ɡʊd'lʊkɪŋ /
overwéight / 'əʊvə'weɪt /
béarded / 'bɪədɪd /
smart / smɑːt /
stúnning / 'stʌnɪŋ /
bálding / 'bɔːldɪŋ /
héalthy / 'helθi /
attráctive / ə'træktɪv /
slim / slɪm /
scrúffy / 'skrʌfi /
cónfident / 'kɒnfɪdənt /
aggréssive / ə'ɡresɪv /
decísive / dɪ'saɪsɪv /
depréssed / dɪ'prest /
intélligent / ɪn'telɪdʒənt /
chárming / 'tʃɑːmɪŋ /
strict / strɪkt /
shy / ʃaɪ /
kind / kaɪnd /
tired / taɪəd /
friendly / 'frendli /
cheerful / 'tʃɪəfʊl /

PRONUNCIATION Word stress — suffixes

Exercise 2
Listen:

explanátion / eksplə'neɪʃən /
informátion / ɪnfə'meɪʃən /
dominátion / dɒmɪ'neɪʃən /
addítion / ə'dɪʃən /

interrúption / ɪntə'rʌpʃən /
corréction / kə'rekʃən /
insístence / ɪn'sɪstəns /
disagréement / dɪsə'ɡriːmənt /

UNIT 10 HUMOUR
(pages 98–9)

Look at list A:
What's in a joke?

húmour / 'hjuːmə /
púnch line / 'pʌntʃlaɪn /
nátional stéreotýpes / 'næʃənəl 'steriətaɪps /
pun / pʌn /
embárrassment / ɪm'bærɪsmənt /
suspénse / səs'pens /
séxism / 'seksɪzəm /
relígion / rɪ'lɪdʒən /
sex / seks /
tóilets / 'tɔɪləts /

Look at list B:
How do we show that we find something funny?

laugh / lɑːf /
chúckle / 'tʃʌkəl /
gíggle / 'ɡɪɡəl /
clap / klæp /
smirk / smɜːk /
grin / ɡrɪn /
smile / smaɪl /
snígger / 'snɪɡə /
títter / 'tɪtə /

Look at list C:
What kinds of stories are there?

amúsing / ə'mjuːzɪŋ /
sad / sæd /
excíting / ɪk'saɪtɪŋ /
térrifying / 'terɪfaɪɪŋ /
embárrassing / ɪm'bærɪsɪŋ /
trágic / 'trædʒɪk /
bóring / 'bɔːrɪŋ /
shócking / 'ʃɒkɪŋ /
hilárious / hɪ'leərɪəs /
ínteresting / 'ɪntrəstɪŋ /

Look at list D:
What makes people laugh?

mímicking / 'mɪmɪkɪŋ /
clówning / 'klaʊnɪŋ /
playing a práctical jóke (/ 'præktɪkəl 'dʒəʊk /)
máking fún (/ 'meɪkɪŋ 'fʌn /) of someone
púlling someone's lég / 'pʊlɪŋsʌmwʌnz 'leɡ /
pláying the fóol / 'pleɪ-ɪŋðə 'fuːl /
impérsonating / ɪm'pɜːsəneɪtɪŋ /
táking someone óff / 'teɪkɪŋsʌmwʌn 'ɒf /
téasing / 'tiːzɪŋ /

PRONUNCIATION -ed endings

Exercise 2
Listen:

amúsed / ə'mjuːzd /
excíted / ɪk'saɪtɪd /
shócked / ʃɒkt /
embárrassed / ɪm'bærɪst /
prómised / 'prɒmɪst /
wáited / 'weɪtɪd /
lánded / 'lændɪd /
begged / beɡd /
tásted / 'teɪstɪd /
amázed / ə'meɪzd /